kabnf

KO

320.011 SHAEL

D1104470

or
er
05-20-2021

DISCARD

Valparaiso - Porter County
Library System

# What We Owe Each Other

MINOUCHE SHAFIK

# What We Owe
# Each Other

*A New Social Contract
for a Better Society*

PRINCETON UNIVERSITY PRESS
PRINCETON AND OXFORD

Copyright © 2021 by Nemat (Minouche) Shafik

Princeton University Press is committed to the protection of copyright and the intellectual property our authors entrust to us. Copyright promotes the progress and integrity of knowledge. Thank you for supporting free speech and the global exchange of ideas by purchasing an authorized edition of this book. If you wish to reproduce or distribute any part of it in any form, please obtain permission.

Requests for permission to reproduce material from this work should be sent to permissions@press.princeton.edu

Published in the United States and Canada by
Princeton University Press
41 William Street, Princeton, New Jersey 08540

press.princeton.edu

First published in the United Kingdom by
The Bodley Head, an imprint of Vintage, in 2021

All Rights Reserved

Library of Congress Control Number 2020952245
ISBN 978-0-691-20445-1
ISBN (e-book) 978-0-691-22027-7

Typeset in 11.5/15 pt Sabon LT Std
by Integra Software Services Pvt. Ltd, Pondicherry

Jacket design by Hillary Leone and Darina Karpov / Cabengo
Jacket image: Shutterstock

Printed on acid-free paper. ∞

Printed in the United States of America

1 3 5 7 9 10 8 6 4 2

*For Adam, Hanna, Hans-Silas, Maissa,*
*Nora, Olivia and Raffael*

# Contents

# Acknowledgements

Not surprisingly, I owe many people a great deal in helping me write this book.

The idea of writing a book was planted by Rupert Lancaster after he attended a lecture I gave at the Leverhulme Foundation in 2018. At LSE, I benefited from being surrounded by people who are interesting and interested, starting with my colleagues in the School's Management Committee and Council. Many colleagues shared ideas and provided generous comments on early drafts, and I am particularly grateful to Oriana Bandiera, Nick Barr, Tim Besley, Tania Burchardt, Dilly Fung, John Hills, Emily Jackson, Julian LeGrand, Steve Machin, Nick Stern, Andrew Summers, Andres Velasco and Alex Voorhoeve. Several friends and former colleagues pointed me to relevant literature, provided helpful comments and much-needed encouragement: Patricia Alonso-Gamo, Sonya Branch, Elizabeth Corley, Diana Gerald, Antonio Estache, Hillary Leone, Gus O'Donnell, Sebastian Mallaby, Truman Packard, Michael Sandel and Alison Wolf. I owe them gratitude for their good ideas; any errors are exclusively mine.

Max Kiefel provided outstanding research assistance, finding interesting material and helpful suggestions even though we only managed to meet in person once because of the pandemic.

James Pullen, my agent at Wylie, helped me navigate the world of publishing and was a constant source of good advice. Will Hammond, my editor at Penguin Random House, encouraged me to avoid academic jargon and helped make the text far more readable. Joe Jackson at Princeton University Press also gave helpful feedback.

I owe so much to my mother Maissa, who drove me to all those libraries and always supported me, come what may. I am grateful to my sister Nazli, niece Leila and my vast extended family, who provide a wonderful example of a social contract that is generous and enables everyone. To my husband Raffael, I owe thanks for making me braver and encouraging me to take on ever bigger challenges. Our children – Adam, Hanna, Hans-Silas, Nora and Olivia – were uppermost in my mind as I wrote the chapter on the intergenerational social contract. For them, and all our children and future grandchildren, I hope we manage to organise a better social contract for all of you to thrive.

# Preface

'Things fall apart; the centre cannot hold ... Surely some revelation is at hand ...'

So wrote W. B. Yeats in the wake of the horrors of World War I as his pregnant wife lay gravely ill from the 1918–19 flu pandemic. The phrase 'things fall apart' was quoted more often in 2016 than at any time in previous years.[1] Yeats' poem captures a sense of foreboding, when change seems inevitable. Recent years have seen the economic aftermath of the 2008 financial crisis, increasingly divisive politics, environmental protests and the coronavirus pandemic. Periods of great instability can result in a radical reordering of our societies. What that reordering looks like depends on the institutions that are in place, which leaders are in power and what ideas are in the ascendance.[2]

Over these recent years, I have seen many of the assumptions and increasingly the institutions and norms that have shaped my world fall apart. I spent 25 years working in international development and witnessed first hand how 'making poverty history' resulted in huge improvements in people's daily lives. Humans really have never had it so good. And yet in so many parts of the world, citizens are disappointed, and this has revealed itself in politics, the media and public discourse.

Rising levels of anger and anxiety are associated with people feeling more insecure and lacking the means or power to shape their future. Support for the system of international cooperation that has existed since the post-war period, and in which I spent much of my career, is also waning as nationalism and protectionism come to the fore.

The global pandemic of 2020 brought all of this into sharp relief. The risks that the poor, those in precarious work and those without access to health care were exposed to were laid bare. The interdependencies between us were revealed as 'essential workers' were largely the lowest paid without whom our societies could not function. We could survive without bankers and lawyers, but grocers, nurses and security guards were invaluable. The pandemic revealed how much we depended on each other for survival but also for behaving in socially responsible ways.

Moments of crisis are also moments of opportunity. Some crises result in decisions that change society for the better – such as the New Deal measures introduced to counter the Great Depression or the rules-based international order that emerged after World War II. Other crises sow the seeds of new problems – such as the inadequate response to World War I or the 2008 financial crisis and the populist backlash it spawned. The impact of the coronavirus crisis remains to be seen. Whether it results in improvements or not depends on what alternative ideas are available and how politics evolves to choose among them.[3] After much reading, listening, thinking and talking, I found that the concept of a social contract, the policies and norms that govern how we live together in a society, was a useful construct for understanding and defining alternative solutions to the challenges we face.

Over the years many of the ideas that shaped thinking about social contracts around the world were forged at the London School of Economics and Political Science (LSE), where I currently serve as the Director. There is a long tradition of thinking about the relationship between the economy and society, starting with the founders of the Fabian Society and the LSE, Beatrice and Sidney Webb. Beatrice spent years collecting data in the poorest parts of London and seeing the impact of deprivation first hand. As a member of the 1909 Royal Commission on the Poor Laws, she authored a dissenting minority report that rejected the harsh system of workhouses and Britain's piece-meal approach to supporting those in poverty. In it, she argued that a new social contract for the UK would 'secure a national minimum of civilised life ... open to all alike, of both sexes and all classes, by which we meant sufficient nourishment and training when young, a living wage when able-bodied, treatment when sick, and a modest but secure livelihood when disabled or aged'.[4] More than one hundred years later, that is still an aspiration in most countries in the world.

Her arguments were reflected in the hugely influential report authored by William Beveridge (LSE director 1919–37) that designed the modern welfare state in the UK, including the National Health Service and a comprehensive approach to minimum incomes, unemployment insurance and pensions. The Beveridge Report (1942) was revolutionary, and more copies were sold than any previous government document as the public queued to buy copies to understand this fundamental reordering of the rights and responsibilities of citizens in the UK. Much of its implementation occurred under Prime Minister Clement Attlee, who had previously been a lecturer at the LSE and won the election in part by backing the Beveridge Report. While the focus of the Webbs and Beveridge was on the UK, their ideas had a huge impact across Europe and in much of the post-colonial world, especially in India, Pakistan, East Asia, Africa and the Middle East.[5]

The LSE was also at the heart of the next reordering of societies, when Friedrich Hayek, a recent émigré from Vienna, professor at the school and Nobel prize winner, published *The Road to Serfdom* (1944). Hayek thought the interventionist state advocated by Beveridge would take society down the path of totalitarianism. He laid the foundations for classical

economic liberalism with his focus on individual liberty and
the efficiency of markets. Hayek left the LSE in 1950 and
went to the University of Chicago, where his ideas influenced
Milton Friedman and provided the basis for what later became
known as the Chicago School, dedicated to liberalism and
laissez-faire economics. Both Margaret Thatcher and Ronald
Reagan credited Hayek with their political philosophies and
their emphasis on individualism and free markets.[6] Hayek was
also hugely influential in central and eastern Europe, where his
books were widely read by dissidents who helped bring about
the collapse of the Soviet Union.

The subsequent Third Way was an attempt to define an
alternative to the interventionist state of the Fabians and the
laissez-faire market liberalism of Hayek. Many ideas on how
to use markets to achieve more egalitarian ends emerged at the
LSE, with Anthony Giddens (another director of the school,
1997–2003) publishing *The Third Way* in 1998.[7] These views
were embraced by social-democratic politicians around the
world, including Bill Clinton in the US, Tony Blair in the
UK, Luiz Inácio Lula da Silva in Brazil, Gerhard Schröder in
Germany, Thabo Mbeki in South Africa and many more. The
Great Recession of 2008 saw the collapse of support for the
Third Way, which lost credibility in the wake of the financial
crisis as centrist leaders were increasingly replaced by populists
around the world.

And so here we are again, in need of a new paradigm.
Profound changes in technology and demography are challenging old structures. The climate crisis, the global pandemic and
its inevitable economic aftermath have revealed the extent to
which our existing social contract is no longer working. This
book is an attempt to understand the underlying causes of these
challenges and, more importantly, provide an alternative view
on what a social contract fit for the twenty-first century might
look like. It is not a blueprint, but I am hoping it is a modest
contribution to fostering debate and providing a direction of
travel for future policy.

I have spread myself thin in this book, trying to cover so many issues from a global perspective, and some readers will be able to identify exceptions to many of the points that I make. I draw heavily on academic research in peer-reviewed journals and meta-analyses – summarised findings of sometimes hundreds of pieces of research. The sources for most of this technical material can be found in the endnotes. I am a strong believer in evidence, the value of expertise and the importance of rigorous debate, but I also express my own judgements about what this literature teaches us about how different countries have developed solutions to what we owe each other in society.

Those judgements are inevitably rooted in my personal experiences of family, education, work and the impact of society and the state. My interest in economics originated from a desire to understand the architecture of opportunity in society. As a child, I would visit my mother's family's village in Egypt and see girls who looked just like me but who couldn't go to school, worked hard in the fields and had few choices about who they would marry or how many children they would have. It seemed so random and unfair that I had opportunities that they did not – I could have easily been them and they been me. Those opportunities changed radically when most of my family's land and property was nationalised by the Egyptian state in the 1960s and we emigrated to the United States, where my father had studied.

For my father, who had a PhD in chemistry and little else, education was the only path to success. 'They can take everything away from you except your education,' was his oft-repeated adage. But the educational opportunities open to us were mixed in the American south during the turmoil and tensions of desegregation. I was bused to more schools than I can remember, some of which had inspired teachers, some in which the main objective was survival. My salvation was the local libraries, where my mother dutifully took me on the weekends. I had memberships in several to maximise the number of books I could take out each week and spent long hours on the sofa at home discovering the world.

After climbing the ladder of educational quality, that curiosity about the architecture of opportunity led me to a career in economics and development that spanned the World Bank, the UK Department for International Development, the International Monetary Fund and the Bank of England. I love universities and spent eighteen years in them, but most of my career has been in the trenches of policymaking. Perhaps what is unusual is having done it in such a broad array of countries – from some of the poorest in the world like South Sudan and Bangladesh to some of the richest, such as the UK or the Eurozone. I have also worked with politicians from across the political spectrum – in the UK, I was a permanent secretary for both a Labour government and the coalition of the Conservatives and Liberal Democrats. In my years at the World Bank and IMF, I worked with hundreds of politicians of every imaginable political stripe. That perspective of having been a practitioner of policy as well as a student of policy permeates this book.

After 25 years working in international economic institutions, I saw how much benefit came from sharing experience across countries. Of course, every country has its distinctiveness, especially on issues such as the balance between the individual and the collective in the social contract. Countries like the US put more emphasis on individual freedom; Asian societies tend to prioritise collective interests above individual preferences. Europe is somewhere in the middle, trying to strike a balance between individual freedom and collective interests. Behind each of those generalisations are many exceptions and examples that can teach us how to tailor solutions for different contexts. Rarely is there one right answer, but a set of options and trade-offs that involve various costs and benefits reflecting different value judgements.

In addition to being global and focused on solutions, I have also tried to make this book personal. For me, the terms of the social contract are not some abstract activity reserved for technocrats and policy wonks. Policy decisions on how an education system is organised or how health care is funded or what happens when you lose your job have huge consequences for everyone. They make the difference between the life I have led and that of those little girls in the village. That is why this book is organised around the stages of life that most of us experience – raising children, going to school, getting sick, finding work and growing old. My hope is that this perspective will make these important issues accessible and encourage us all to have opinions on these vital matters.

# 1

# What Is the Social Contract?

Society is everything. Many of us go through life thinking we are self-made and self-sufficient. Some may credit (or blame) their families for their lot in life, but rarely do we think about the bigger forces that determine our destinies – the country we happen to be born in, the social attitudes prevalent at a particular moment in history, the institutions that govern our economy and politics, and the randomness of just plain luck. These wider factors determine the kind of society in which we live and are the most important determinants of our human experience.

Consider an example of a life in which society plays a very small role. In 2004 I spent time with a family in the Ecuadorian Amazon. Antonia, my host, had twelve children, and her oldest daughter was about to give birth to her first grandchild. They lived on the edge of the rainforest with no road, electricity, running water or sanitation. There was a school, but a considerable distance away, so the children's attendance was patchy. However, Antonia was a community health worker and had access via radio to a doctor in a nearby town who could provide advice to her and others. Apart from this service (arranged by a charity), she and her husband had to be completely self-reliant, gathering food from the forest, educating their children on how to survive in their environment. On the rare occasions when they needed something they could not find or make themselves (like a cooking pot), they panned for flecks of gold in the Amazon, which they could exchange for goods in a market at the end of a long journey by canoe.

This may seem like a very extreme and distant example, but it serves to remind us how accustomed we are to the things that living collectively in a society gives us – infrastructure, accessible education and health care, laws that enable markets in which we can earn incomes and access goods and services. Antonia and her daughter promised to name the baby they were expecting Minouche, which was a great honour. I often wonder what kind of life that other Minouche will be having as a result of being born in a very different society.

The way a society is structured has profound consequences for the lives of those living in it and the architecture of opportunity they face. It determines not just their material conditions but also their well-being, relationships and life prospects. The structure of society is determined by institutions such as its political and legal systems, the economy, the way in which family and community life are organised.[1] All societies choose to have some things left to individuals and others determined collectively. The norms and rules governing how those collective institutions operate is what I will call the social contract, which I believe is the most important determinant of the kinds of lives we lead. Because it is so important and because most people cannot easily leave their societies, the social contract requires the consent of the majority and periodic renegotiation as circumstances change.

We are living at a time when, in many societies, people feel disappointed by the social contract and the life it offers them. This is despite the huge gains in material progress the world has seen over the last 50 years.[2] Surveys find that four out of every five people believe 'the system' is not working for them in the United States, Europe, China, India and various developing countries.[3] In many advanced countries the majority no longer believe their children will be better off than they are. In the developing world, aspirations for education, health care and jobs are often well ahead of a society's ability to deliver them.

And across the world workers worry about losing their liveli-hoods because of a lack of skills or the prospect of automation.

This disaffection takes many different forms. Some in rural areas and small towns argue that disproportionate attention and resources go to cities at their expense. Native populations in some countries feel that immigrants are changing their soci-eties and receiving benefits before they have paid their dues. Some members of once-dominant races resent other ethnicities demanding equal treatment. Some men feel threatened by newly empowered women and policies such as quotas and targets that disadvantage them. A proportion of the young are increasingly vocal about the elderly, who they believe consume a growing share of resources in health care and pensions while leaving them with a legacy of debt and environmental destruction. Some older people feel the young are not sufficiently grateful for past sacrifices made on their behalf.

This book tries to get at the root causes of this disappoint-ment through the lens of the social contract: an approach that recognises the primacy of expectations and mutuality, the effi-ciency and value in collective provision and sharing risks, the importance in adapting to a changed world if we are not to witness a destructive fracturing of the mutual trust on which citizenship and society is based. How much *does* society owe an individual and what does an individual owe in return? And in this time of great change, how might those mutual obligations need to adapt? The answers to these questions would appear to be at the heart of solving many of the political, economic and social challenges facing the world today.

## Expectations and the Social Contract

Who is 'we' in the question 'What do we owe each other?' To whom do we feel mutual obligations? This is a complex ques-tion that has personal, cultural and historical dimensions. I like to think of mutual obligations as concentric circles. At the core, most of us feel the greatest obligations to our immediate family and friends. Parents will make huge sacrifices for their children; friends will go to great lengths to support each other. In the next ring of the circle is the community in which we live. This is often the domain of voluntary groups, religious associations, neighbourhood and local government structures. In the next ring is the nation state, in which we owe each other the duties of citizenship – paying taxes, obeying the laws, voting, engaging in public life. In a regional integration project such as the European Union, there has been an attempt to foster a sense of 'we' in another ring consisting of citizens of the nation states that are members of the union. The final circle is the world, where the obligations may be weaker but become more apparent when there is a humanitarian crisis or a global challenge like climate change, when international solidarity becomes important.

Every day we navigate mutual obligations and take care of others, not just within our families, but within communities and nation states, far in excess of our narrow self-interest. Most obviously we pay taxes that will benefit people in other parts of the country (and sometimes other parts of the world) who we will never meet. We do this because we believe that living in a fair, well managed society helps us to live a better life and we are willing to contribute our share to achieving that for our own interest and because of solidarity with our fellow citizens. Employers in many countries are required to offer benefits to their employees, such as parental leave and pensions, and many add voluntary benefits on top of those. For the provision of fuel and water, transport and sanitation, we rely on publicly provided infrastructure, which we expect to be universally available. We expect decent schools and health care and safety on our streets in return for which we obey the law. All of these are ways in which we balance our individual desires and the need to live collectively with other people. This collective solidarity extends across generations when we make long-term investments and conversely when we consume resources that take possibilities away from future generations.

Throughout history, people have pooled their resources to varying degrees in order to enjoy the benefits and manage the risks that come from living in large groups. These benefits include specialisation of labour, mutual defence and shared infrastructure. As groups get larger – from family to village to major cities and nation states – the mutual obligations become more abstract and are often mediated through institutions and the political process. Rather than 'owe' something to our family or community, our obligations morph into solidarity with fellow citizens or duty to our country. In the past, for example, families educated their children, cared for the sick and unemployed at home; today most rely on schools, medical facilities and (in some countries) unemployment benefits paid by the state. That is why today people are expected to contribute to the common good when they are productive adults and, in exchange, get an education when they are young and support when they are sick, unemployed or old. The exact nature of these expectations varies according to the cultural norms, institutions, policies and laws that define the rights and obligations of individuals relative to those of the wider society, but the existence of such expectations is universal.

While these expectations have existed for as long as human society, they have changed considerably over time. For example, for much of history in virtually every society caring for the young and the old has been the responsibility of women, while the education, health care and employment of the next generation has tended to be a collective responsibility, as it is today. In most countries, there has also been some expectation that wealthier citizens would provide some protection or support to the poor in their communities. Historically, this voluntary approach to charity, often enabled by religious institutions, proved inadequate and had very uneven outcomes. As countries have become richer, citizens have increasingly expected the state to take responsibility for providing services on a more consistent and equitable basis and to raise the required revenues through taxation.[4]

Philosophers have long debated how free individuals might be persuaded to live together in a society and what a reasonable set of expectations should be.[5] It was during the Enlightenment though that this concept – of voluntary mutual dependence in return for otherwise unattainable benefits – became known as the social contract. Different thinkers argued for different kinds of social contract, but all initially framed it in the prevailing terms of the day: the rights of individuals in a monarchy.

Thomas Hobbes argued that self-interested but rational individuals should voluntarily submit to the authority of an absolute sovereign as the only sure way to avoid the brutish state of nature.[6] John Locke's view was that the purpose of the social contract was to preserve the lives, freedoms and well-being of citizens: thus, if the sovereign failed to protect those rights, it was legitimate for citizens to revolt and create a new political society.[7] Jean-Jacques Rousseau was concerned with preserving freedom while recognising that because humans were increasingly interdependent, compromises were required in order to live together in a good society. According to him, the social contract required political institutions – such as a representative parliament – that allowed citizens to make the laws to which they would therefore voluntarily subject themselves, thereby providing the justification for the authority of the state.[8] For all three philosophers, expectations of the individual and of the state were minimal by comparison with our own: the social contract was merely the precondition for living in a society free from exploitation.

But as monarchies increasingly had to cede power to citizens, debate about the social contract shifted to the obligations of citizenship and what we owed each other. In *The Theory of Moral Sentiments* Adam Smith, whose thinking laid the foundations for modern economics, talked about the need for 'circles of sympathy' whereby self-interested individuals also cared about the well-being of others.[9] According to Smith, the social solidarity that empathy fostered had moral, political and economic rationales.[10] The moral rationale is that in every society, individuals have basic needs – such as access to basic health care and safety, enough income to avoid being excluded from society, enough education to find work and act as informed citizens – that it would be morally wrong not to provide. The political rationale for social solidarity is that, for democracies to function, citizens have to share enough common experience to feel they have a common purpose.[11] Finally, the economic rationale is that pooling risks for things like sickness, unemployment and pensions across a large number of citizens is more efficient than individuals trying to insure themselves.

In Smith's vision there are also limits to sympathy, to what the individual can expect, and an unwillingness to share risks when individuals behave 'badly'. And so it is today. Risks that are not the fault of the individual – disability or a job loss resulting from an accident or sudden economic shock – are the ones that most people are willing to share. However, if losses result from smoking or drunk driving or poor performance at work, many believe that individuals should suffer the consequences of their actions. At the same time, others argue that bad behaviour is most often the product of upbringing, deprivation or even mental illness. Moral judgements about individual behaviour and responsibility are often central to questions about how generous the social contract should be.

The most influential twentieth-century philosopher to discuss the social contract as the basis for creating a just society was John Rawls.[12] He argued that we should design our social contract behind a 'veil of ignorance' – meaning without prior knowledge as to what our own status in that society would be. Because we did not know if we would start life privileged or a pauper, we would create a social contract that was just. His principle of equal opportunity states that 'those who are at the same level of talent and ability, and have the same willingness to use them, should have the same prospects of success regardless of their initial place in the social system'.[13] Today, the notion of equality of opportunity lies at the heart of many citizens' expectations the world over, and the perception of its absence is an important source of anxiety and disaffection.

In modern societies there is an expectation that those who try hard will improve their lot. This was not always the case, and in many traditional societies there was an almost fatalistic acceptance of the prevailing hierarchy, with some arguing it was essential for social order. But today most countries include enabling social mobility as part of the social contract because it seems more fair, binds society together and enables collective action. The poor need to have the expectation that they or their children will be better off. The rich need to fear their children may be poorer to foster concern about the less well off and create a sense of common interest.

In practice, countries vary enormously in the architecture of opportunity that they offer their citizens. For example, in Denmark it takes on average about two generations for someone to go from being lower income to middle income; in the UK it is five, and in highly unequal countries like Brazil, South Africa and Colombia it takes more than nine generations. These differences in social mobility (Figure 1) are part of the reason we see most frustration with the social contract in precisely those countries where the prospects of improving your lot over time are low or have fallen in the recent period. There is also much evidence that disadvantage, both within families and geographically, is highly persistent across many generations.[14]

### The Social Contract, the State and the Private Sector

Many people think the social contract is the same as the welfare state, but the concepts are not synonymous. The social contract determines what is to be provided collectively and by whom; the welfare state is one of several possible means of provision. In fact, in every society a huge amount of what falls within the bounds of the social contract continues to be provided by families – for example, through unpaid parental labour educating

**Figure 1. Social mobility: how many generations does it take to go from being low income to middle income in different countries?**

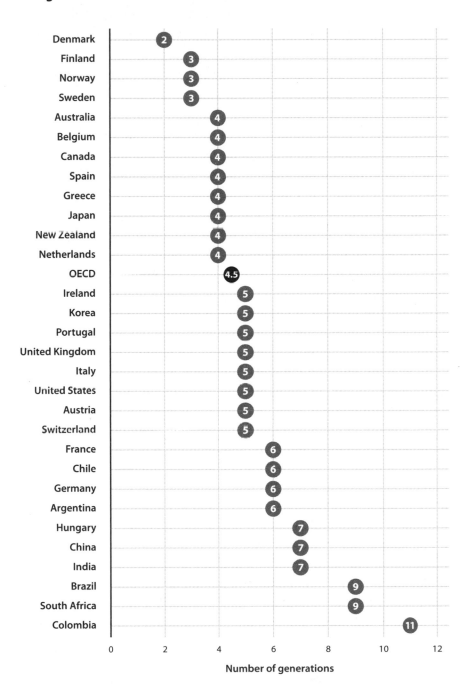

children, pooling resources in times of ill health or unemployment, or by purchasing private insurance. Communities, charitable and voluntary organisations do a great deal to care for the needy and the elderly, respond to humanitarian crises and support people to get back into work. Employers are often required by law to deliver aspects of the social contract by contributing to unemployment benefits and in some countries to mandatory health insurance, with some providing additional services such as childcare facilities, educational benefits and well-being and mental health support.

When I refer to the social contract, therefore, I mean the partnership between individuals, businesses, civil society and the state to contribute to a system in which there are collective benefits. When I refer to the welfare state, I mean the mechanisms for pooling risks and investing in social benefits mediated through the political process and subsequent state action. This can be directly through taxation and public services or indirectly by regulations that require the private sector to provide support. The collective benefits can also include the state serving as the insurer of last resort, for example by preventing people starving or being left homeless or destitute when there is a natural disaster or pandemic.

Before we had nation states, the social contract was based on tribes and local loyalties that provided mutual protection and some sharing of basic needs like food or shelter. This evolved in the feudal period into local rulers who delivered law and order and extracted rents in exchange, with an overarching structure of monarchy on top. It was only in the early-modern period that nation states evolved, not just to secure and extract, but also to invest in collective goods like infrastructure financed by limited taxation. As capitalism developed, the social contract became more complex as families became less self-sufficient with a growing division of labour; systems of regulation emerged and public services such as sanitation and electricity had to be coordinated and financed. Providing such collective goods, including having an educated and healthy workforce, became an increasingly important part of the social contract and grew into what we now call the welfare state.

The conservative Prussian Otto von Bismarck is usually credited with bringing in the first legally mandated requirement for social solidarity when as chancellor he introduced a compulsory insurance scheme for pensions and sickness in Germany in 1889. His motives were to make the economy more efficient and to avert more radical proposals, such as the expropriation of property, of his socialist opponents. In a ground-breaking letter to the German parliament, he wrote, 'Those who are disabled from work by age and invalidity have a well-grounded claim to care from the state.' The retirement age was set at 70, which, given life expectancy at retirement in Germany at the time, meant the state would provide a pension for seven years on average.[15]

In the UK, the first person to call for collective responsibility for health care was Beatrice Webb in her Royal Commission on the Poor Law in 1909, which recommended the creation of a national health service. But William Beveridge (director of LSE 1919–37) is usually credited with the first comprehensive blueprint for a welfare state designed to meet the needs of citizens from 'cradle to grave'. To vanquish the 'five giants' of squalor, ignorance, want, idleness and disease, Beveridge's plan was for everyone to contribute to a social insurance fund and in return receive the same entitlement to benefits such as healthcare or unemployment insurance.[16]

Welfare states evolved very differently elsewhere over the course of the twentieth century. In countries like the United States and Australia there was greater emphasis on individual responsibility, so contributions and low levels of income redistribution by the state were directed only to those who were most needy. In continental Europe, systems were often linked to work and relied on social contributions by employers and employees to pay for unemployment insurance and health care. The Nordic countries tended to have higher levels of state financing of welfare provision and more generous combinations of universal and targeted benefits. A good illustration of these differences is how long collective support in each of these countries lasts for an individual who is unemployed. In the United States unemployment benefits normally last just six months; in countries like France or Germany the limit is about one year; in countries such as Denmark and the Netherlands it is about two years.[17]

Developing countries too have seen a rapid growth in welfare spending as their citizens demand better services and social protection. The number of low- and middle-income countries that have some form of social protection has doubled in the last twenty years – from only 72 to 149 in 2017.[18] The majority (77 per cent) have introduced some form of cash payments to the poorest households, and many (42 per cent) have payments that are conditional on things like sending children to school or immunising them. These payments are often very small but have been shown to have significant impacts on reducing poverty, increasing school attendance, improving nutrition and raising household productivity.[19] The amounts of money can also be adjusted quickly in response to when, for example, a famine or pandemic hits a certain community.[20]

Most developing countries move from relying on families and communities to deliver the social contract to gradually increasing levels of government spending. Although welfare payments in developing countries only benefit about one third of the global poor today, they are growing quickly in response to the rising expectations of citizens, ageing and strong evidence of benefits for school enrolment, health outcomes and economic activity. But the better off in developing countries often rely on expensive private schools and health care and even private security and infrastructure, and therefore feel little obligation to pay taxes. In countries like Nigeria or Lebanon, owning a generator is quite common among the wealthy because the public electricity supply has been so unreliable. Persuading higher-income groups in developing countries to rely on public provision is key for raising revenues to deliver a better social contract.

What accounts for the variations in approach across countries? Some have argued that countries with more homogeneous populations tended to develop more comprehensive welfare states based on greater solidarity than countries with greater racial and ethnic diversity like the United States or Australia.[21] More recent evidence gives a more mixed picture and indicates that other factors matter more, such as the pace of immigration and how ethnic diversity is measured, as well as cultural factors such as attitudes to wealth redistribution and beliefs about the role of luck versus effort in determining income.[22]

One reason why some countries have smaller welfare states may be to do with the common misperception that the purpose of a welfare state is to redistribute money from the rich to the poor. In fact, that is a very small part of the story. The welfare state is three quarters piggy bank (mutual insurance over the life cycle) and only one quarter Robin Hood (transferring resources from the rich to the poor).[23] However, a significant role of the welfare state is to redistribute money *over the course of our own lives*. Children cannot borrow to pay for their education even if their employment prospects are good. People don't know what illnesses they will have when they are old or how long they might live.

Most people contribute to the welfare state in the middle of their lives when they are working and receive benefits from it when they are young (through schooling) and when they are old (through pensions and health care). Figure 2, which displays contributions to the state at different ages, shows this pattern clearly for the UK. In fact, the vast majority of people in the UK put into the welfare state roughly as much as they take out over the course of their lives.[24] This insurance rationale for the welfare states sits alongside the economic argument that investing in citizens is a key part of a country's economic growth strategy, as it helps to ensure the most capable and productive workforce possible.[25]

Different approaches to the terms of the social contract derive from the fundamental question: what should its objective be?

**Figure 2. People pay into the state in middle age and take money out when they are young and old**

Representative age profiles for tax, public services and welfare spending in the UK

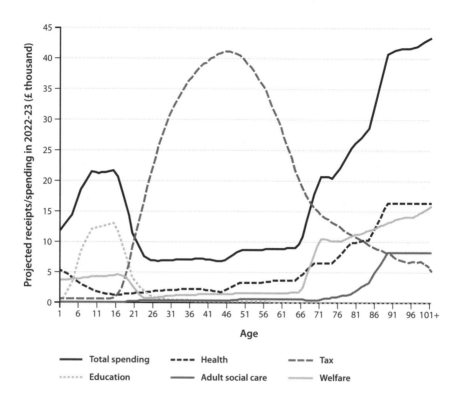

Classical welfare economics developed in the late nineteenth and early twentieth centuries argued it is to maximise the total 'utility', or satisfaction, that individuals in a society achieve. Utility is reflected in market prices – if you are willing to work for a certain wage or pay an amount for a product, that reflects the utility you derive from that activity. More recently, an increasing number of economists have come to define utility more broadly as well-being (not just consumption of goods and services), which includes what makes people happy, such as good health (mental and physical), good relationships and meaningful work. Well-being can be measured through surveys, and several countries, such as Bhutan, Ireland, New Zealand and Scotland, are trying to use this broader measure to inform their social contract.

Critics of the utilitarian tradition, such as Nobel prize-winning economist Amartya Sen, would say the social contract should aim not just to meet people's needs but to improve the capabilities of every citizen to achieve the kind of life they value.[26] Income and market prices are a small part of the story since individuals can vary in the resources they need to achieve literacy, adequate nutrition, shelter or political freedom. This widens the objective of the social contract well beyond income to include more equal outcomes and the capability to have a good life. It also means that where individuals do not have many options – for example are deprived of their entitlement to education or health care – the social contract has failed them. My view, which will underpin the analysis in this book, is that the objective of the social contract should be determined by society and consider a broad range of measures including income and subjective well-being, as well as measures of capability, opportunity and freedom.

Consensus on such questions tends to inform how much of the social contract is provided privately or publicly, which varies enormously across countries. For decades it has broadly defined the left and the right of politics, though those definitions have become blurred in recent years. UK Prime Minister Margaret Thatcher famously said, 'There is no such thing as society. There are individual men and women and there are families. And no government can do anything except through people, and people must look after themselves first. It is our duty to look after ourselves and then, to look after our neighbours.'[27] Implicit in this view is a social contract that relies heavily on individual responsibility – families responsible for caring for their children, encouragement of private schools, a minimalist approach to income support, and heavy reliance on private insurance markets to respond to risks such as accidents, disability and environmental damage such as flooding.

Others have argued for a more maximalist view of the state's role to compensate for the impact of luck on life chances and to achieve greater fairness in economic and social outcomes. Franklin Roosevelt in his second inaugural address argued: 'The test of our progress is not whether we add more to the abundance of those who have much; it is whether we provide enough for those who have too little.'[28] In the wake of the Great Depression, he created an activist state that provided minimum incomes and created jobs through massive public works, making the government the largest employer in the economy. New Deal measures also rebalanced power in favour of trade unions, tenant farmers and migrant workers while imposing stricter regulations on banks to avoid another financial crisis.

There has always been a debate about the role of the private sector in the social contract, but recently it has assumed greater prominence as more business leaders argue that companies should take on wider responsibilities in the wake of economic crises and rising public expectations. The conservative view often associated with Milton Friedman is that the job of business is to make profits, abide by regulations, pay market wages and taxes, and by doing this, the private sector will maximise its contribution to society.[29] However, there has been a long tradition of companies that take a more holistic view of their role, sometimes paying higher-than-market wages or providing wider benefits such as pensions and health care, and sharing their profits with their employees. This tradition is now coming to the fore. Increasingly, businesses are under pressure to focus not just on short-term profits but on the wider interests of society – so-called multi-stakeholder capitalism. Proponents argue that this is not charity but a way to maximise companies' long-term value.[30]

In practice, most countries choose a mix of individual and collective responsibility across different sectors to define their social contracts. Consider traditionally conservative Switzerland. Swiss citizens have relatively low levels of taxation, typical of a small-state approach, but a high proportion of young people go into tertiary education, which is largely free and provided by the state, though about half of those follow a vocational rather than a purely academic track. There is also a complex system of regional redistribution with very high levels of decentralisation and local democracy through referenda. Meanwhile, Singapore, famously organised on free-market rather than big-state principles, also has low levels of taxation and regulation, but over 80 per cent of the population live in public housing socially engineered to achieve racial balance, and all men must do at least two years of compulsory military service as a way to build cohesion in this very multi-ethnic, young country. Meanwhile, nominally communist China until recently had no public health-care provision or unemployment benefits and still does not impose any inheritance tax on the wealthy.

The mix between individual and collective responsibility that countries choose can also vary enormously within any given sector. Consider the approach to financing higher education, which is, in economic terms, both a private good (generating higher income for the individual) and a public good (developing active citizens who are more capable, productive, and commit fewer crimes).[31] How do different countries decide how much to invest in the next generation's productivity and who pays for it? At one end is the United States with a more market-based approach whereby individual students take loans on semi-commercial terms that they are expected to repay over the course of their working lives. In the United Kingdom an intermediate solution has evolved whereby students take out loans but only repay them if their income rises to a certain level. Continental Europe and most emerging markets mainly rely on state funding of higher education, but because it is free and resources are limited, high numbers of students often mean that quality suffers. In China, with its one-child-policy legacy and state-funded education system, six adults (two parents and four grandparents) supplement government spending with significant private investments in exchange for the expectation that they will be cared for in old age. Each of these models reflects a very different view of what one generation owes the next.

## *What Broke the Social Contract? Technology and the Changing Role of Women*

In the past, social contracts were redefined at times of great upheaval – the Great Depression brought us the New Deal in the US; the world wars were the backdrop for the Beveridge Report in the UK; decolonisation was followed by activist governments eager to promote economic and social development. A prolonged period of recession and inflation was the context for the ideological shift behind the Thatcher/Reagan revolution that shaped much of current policy thinking. It is my contention in this book that many of today's challenges – the rise of populism, the backlash against globalisation and technology, the economic aftermath of the financial crisis in 2008 and the coronavirus pandemic, the culture wars around race and women's roles in society and the youth protests about climate change – are bellwethers that a new social contract is needed.

Until the late twentieth century, social contracts were built on the premise that families would have a sole male breadwinner and that women would take care of the young and the old. There was also a general presumption that people would stay married until they died and give birth to children only when married. They would have steady employment with very few employers over a career, and the education and skills accumulated in school would be enough for a lifetime. Most would have only a few years of retirement, and the support needed in old age would be provided by families.

These assumptions still underlie many of the clauses in our current social contracts, and yet they could not be more irrelevant. Today half of women in the world are employed in the labour market, and the upward trend is almost universal. In advanced economies between a third and half of marriages end in divorce; in most developing countries the rates of divorce are lower but generally increasing. A growing proportion of children are born outside marriage. The average worker has more jobs over the course of his or her working life, and technology is likely to accelerate this trend. While many developing countries are still at the early stages of getting more people working in the formal sector (permanent jobs with contractual obligations and regular pay), there are growing signs of informality in labour markets in advanced economies as more are employed in precarious work with few benefits.

At the end of the twentieth century the evolution of technology and the changing role of women were the two major sources of pressure on the existing social contract. Technological innovations in the 1980s and 1990s such as the internet and container shipping dramatically reduced the costs of communication and transport, making it possible to produce goods using components sourced from multiple countries through globally integrated supply chains, which launched the most recent wave of globalisation.[32] Large parts of manufacturing shifted from advanced economies to emerging markets, particularly China. The result was the hollowing-out of middle-class jobs in industrial communities across many advanced economies.[33] Countries have become richer overall but more unequal and insecure. Workers with low skills have suffered while those with more education and skills have seen their incomes rise, including in many developing countries. In countries with less regulated labour markets like the US and UK, where it is easier to dismiss workers, this has translated into stagnant wages for the less skilled. In the more regulated labour markets of continental Europe, it has meant high levels of unemployment for lower-skilled workers as companies are reluctant to create new jobs.

On the other hand, these economic forces saw the fastest reduction in poverty the world has ever seen as millions of people in developing countries, particularly China, secured jobs in manufacturing. Figure 3 depicts what is often called the elephant chart – its shape shows what has happened to the global distribution of income between the fall of the Berlin Wall in 1990 and the Great Recession in 2008. The biggest beneficiaries from technological innovation and globalisation over that period were the top 1 per cent – on the extreme right of the chart. The other major gainers were those between the 10th and 60th decile of global income distribution – the poor and middle class in developing countries. The group that saw the biggest losses in its income was the lower middle class in many advanced economies, who rank between the 70th and 90th decile of global income.

This is one of the key drivers of political discontent in advanced economies as those with once well-paying jobs in sectors like manufacturing, who expected middle-class lives,

**Figure 3. The top 1 per cent and people in developing countries have benefited most from recent economic growth**

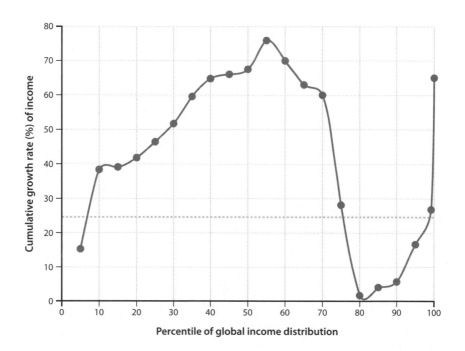

Percentile of global income distribution

find themselves struggling. Some blame globalisation for their difficulties; some blame immigration. In fact, while globalisation accelerates the pace of change, the evidence suggests that advances in technology, which increase productivity and favour the more educated, have been the biggest driver of the fall in wages for low-skill workers in advanced economies. Needless to say, resentment against the top 1 per cent of earners, who have benefited from these trends, has grown.

It need not have been this way. Had policies been in place to help workers adapt to these new circumstances, the negative effects could have been much reduced. For example, in the United States, where the impact of China's integration into the global economy was huge, a policy called the Trade Adjustment Program was put in place to help workers with training, relocation grants and wage insurance. But it was chronically underfunded and high barriers were put into place for accessing it, so that few workers were able to benefit and find new jobs.[34] In the face of the rapid growth of immigration, the UK had a policy to help local government cope called the Migration Impacts Fund, but the money available was too small for the policy to be effective. By contrast, those countries, such as Denmark, that have invested more in what are called active labour market policies, which provide generous support to help all workers adjust to economic shocks, have fared better.

The other major pressure on the social contract has been the massive expansions in girls' education and the number of women working in the labour market rather than in the home. Almost every girl in the world now has access to primary education, and the gender gap in secondary education has closed in most countries. For the first time in history, more women go to university than men. One consequence of these gains in education has been that about half of women now work in the formal labour market, making it increasingly difficult for them to provide traditional care services for free.

Rates of female labour force participation are highest (ranging from 60 to 80 per cent) in some of the richest countries in the world such as Norway and Sweden and in some of the poorest African countries like Mozambique, Ethiopia and Niger.[35] The lowest rates (20–40 per cent) tend to be in south Asia and the Middle East, where traditional attitudes have slowed progress despite rising female education.[36] In south Asia and the Middle East populations are still young, and women devote more time to unpaid care work. But that will surely change over the coming decades as female education changes women's preferences and opportunities.

Women's ability to work outside the home has grown most quickly where the time they have to spend on unpaid domestic work is less (such as when a piped water supply or labour-saving domestic appliances are available) or when men share domestic responsibilities.[37] There is also clear evidence that those countries that spend more on family benefits such as childcare and parental leave enable more women to work outside the home. Those that fail to provide such support tend to see lower levels of female employment.

Nevertheless, the broad trend of more women in the labour market is likely to accelerate and spread globally with major consequences for the social contract. Female employment will grow further as the proportion of people employed in manufacturing (where men are more prevalent) falls, and jobs in services such as health care and education (where there tend to be more jobs for women) grow. As more women than men graduate from higher education, their presence in the workforce will only increase further.

Meanwhile, economic pressure will increasingly force policymakers to find ways to put all that female talent to best use. Recent IMF estimates show that closing gender gaps in labour markets does not just increase economic output but also raises overall productivity because workers are allocated more efficiently to the jobs where they can contribute the most.[38] The potential economic benefits are huge. Higher levels of female employment will also be key to sustaining government budgets, especially pensions. Countries like Japan have realised that getting more women employed and contributing to pension schemes is essential for supporting an ageing population. Chapter 2 will show how changes to the way we raise children can enable better use of female talent.

### *New Pressures on the Social Contract: Ageing, Artificial Intelligence and Climate Change*

While the social contract is already straining under the pressures of technological change and women's changing economic roles, there are other forces on the horizon. Increasing lifespans brought about by advances in health care mean that populations are ageing everywhere, albeit at different paces. In 2018, for the first time in human history, the global population over 64 was greater than the number of children below 5.

Demographic trends have huge implications for the intergenerational social contract. In Japan, which is ageing the most rapidly, every 10 working people support 4 old people and 2 children under the age of 15. In contrast, in youthful Nigeria, every 10 working people support 8 children and only 0.5 of an elderly person. In Europe on average, 10 workers support 3 old people and 2 children. Under current population projections, these dependency ratios will become more acute. For example, in Japan by 2100, only half the population will work, and the other half will be old or young. How will societies support older populations and how will that responsibility be shared between families and the state? How will governments pay for elderly care when the working-age population is shrinking? Bringing women into the workforce is only part of the answer, and Chapter 6 looks at how we can care for the elderly both humanely and sustainably. How we can manage the inexorable rise in demand for health care is addressed in Chapter 4.

In addition to the pressures of ageing, we are now experiencing a wave of technological change driven by artificial intelligence and machine learning. These new technologies favour the highly skilled and those who live in urban areas.

In the past, globalisation resulted in capital moving around the world in search of cheap labour. Clothing manufacturers in Europe or the United States relocated production to lower-wage countries like Bangladesh or Vietnam. In modern knowledge-based economies, capital moves around the world in search of pools of skilled labour in large cities. For example, digital companies in search of highly skilled employees locate in Shanghai or Bangalore or San Francisco, because such people often cluster around major universities and cultural centres. This new dynamic, if not managed properly, risks exacerbating income inequality and regional divergence.

Estimates vary, but automation will probably affect 50 per cent of jobs over the next two decades. Unlike the last wave of technological change, this one will impact not just manufacturing but also service jobs ranging from shop workers to truck drivers to lawyers and accountants.[39] It will also affect developing countries as well as advanced economies since robotics will make it possible for many manufacturing jobs that previously relocated to low-wage countries to be 're-shored' to higher-wage countries again. The coronavirus pandemic may accelerate this trend as companies try to simplify and localise their supply chains, although the ability to work more flexibly from anywhere may result in greater geographical dispersion of jobs.

There is much hype about jobs disappearing, mass unemployment and the need to support those who will be replaced by robots, perhaps with a universal basic income. The most likely scenario is not that jobs will disappear, but that jobs will change. Automation can substitute for labour, but it can also complement labour and create new jobs. Routine and repetitive tasks will be automated, machines will augment human capabilities, and those people who have skills that are complementary to robots will fare the best.[40] Those complementary skills include things like creativity, emotional intelligence and an ability to work with people. The risk is that those with higher level skills will race ahead as they benefit from technology, leaving behind those whose jobs are more routine and repetitive. Chapter 3 (on education) and Chapter 5 (on work) will propose solutions to this growing challenge.

Meanwhile, the environmental protests by young people around the world are indicative of their frustration with a social contract that they feel is cheating them of their right to a stable and inhabitable planet. The Inter-governmental Panel on Climate Change estimates that human activity has already caused one degree Celsius of global warming above pre-industrial levels, with consequences for average temperatures, severe weather events, sea-level rise and species loss.[41] About 80 per cent of forest cover has already been lost globally. Estimated losses of agricultural land range from 6 to 12 million hectares each year.[42] Half of the world's wildlife has been lost in the last 40 years.[43] The United Nations' Food and Agriculture Organization found that unsustainable overfishing has spread to 33 per cent of the world's fisheries.[44]

Is it possible to compensate current and future generations for such environmental loss? Many would argue that the environment has intrinsic value and the economic notion of compensation is not appropriate. Some losses, such as species destruction, are irreversible, and it is therefore impossible to know what future benefits have already been foregone. Moreover, scientists argue that if temperatures rise beyond a certain level, we risk catastrophic flooding, extreme weather events, agricultural and ultimately ecological collapse for which any scale of compensation may be inadequate. Chapter 7 explores the contract between the generations and shows how to achieve greater fairness across generations.

## Whither the Social Contract?

The social contract defines what we can expect from each other in society. The combination of technology, the changing role of women, ageing and concerns about the environment mean that our old economic and social models are under pressure.

The fissures in our social contract were made glaringly apparent during the coronavirus pandemic, when it became clear which groups in society were the most vulnerable. The political turmoil we observe in many countries is only a foretaste of what awaits us if we do not rethink what we owe each other. If we can realign expectations and provide new opportunities and support to cope with change, there is the possibility of a new consensus in which we and our children can thrive in the future.

What would a different social contract better suited to the needs of the twenty-first century look like?

Each of the following chapters will focus on key elements of the social contract from cradle to grave – raising and educating children, dealing with poor health, helping people to adjust to new economic realities, caring for the elderly and balancing the interests of different generations. The examples and lessons will draw on experiences across the globe to show the many ways in which the social contract has been under pressure and can be redefined. There will be a strong focus on solutions and how they can be achieved, but also a recognition that there are no 'right' answers. The social contract must be embedded in and reflect society's values, which all of us must help define.

There are three broad principles that I believe can guide us in designing a new social contract. First, that everyone should be guaranteed the minimum required to live a decent life. This minimum should include basic health care, education, benefits associated with work and a pension that protects against poverty in old age, with the level depending on how much society can afford. Second, everyone should be expected to contribute as much as they can and be given the maximum opportunities to do so with training throughout life, later retirement ages and public support for childcare so women can work. Third, the provision of minimum protections around some risks, such as sickness, unemployment and old age, are better shared by society, rather than asking individuals, families or employers to carry them.

The powerful forces driving the world economy today – globalisation, capitalism, demographic changes, technological innovation, exploitation of the environment – have generated huge material progress, but our social contract has failed to manage the adverse consequences. I will argue that a different social contract could preserve the benefits while creating a better architecture of opportunity for all. In addition, it could break the negative cycle of politics driven by disappointment and anger. Imagining a new social contract will also help with that more fundamental task of changing our expectations and behaviours within our families and communities, and affect what we ask of our employers and our governments. The chapters that follow are intended to enable such a conversation about what we owe each other in future.

# 2

# Children

Deciding whether to have children and if so who takes care of them, especially when they are very young, are deeply personal decisions. Whether we choose to have a parent stay at home, use formal childcare or rely on a grandparent will be determined by a host of factors, from individual preferences, sometimes moral or religious beliefs, to social norms and economic circumstances. However, these seemingly personal decisions have major social consequences. The children of families that fail to care for them adequately often struggle in school and work. They are less likely to be able to fulfil their potential, to become productive citizens and contribute to the common good. And their children are less likely to do well as disadvantage is passed across generations. Because of these wider social consequences, governments almost always try to devise policies that help families raise their children well, which means taking a view (implicit or explicit) about how families should be organised.

Consider the very different experiences of East and West Germany. By the end of the 1980s, East Germany had the highest rate of publicly provided preschool care in the world. Some 70 per cent of infants up to the age of 3 were in formal childcare and almost all children aged 3 to 6 were enrolled.[1] Government policy was focused on getting mothers back to work quickly so parental leave was short and public childcare was extensive and free. The social norm was that this was desirable for both mothers and children. It was also consistent with more egalitarian views about men and women in a socialist economy.

In contrast, West Germany, with a more traditional approach to families, had longer and poorly paid parental leave entitlements, a lack of state-subsidised childcare and joint taxation of couples, which disincentivised mothers from working. The principle of subsidiarity, whereby responsibility for social services was assigned at the most local level in a decentralised federal system, underpinned this approach. Families took precedence over public provision, charities took precedence over the state, and local provision was preferable to central government. As a result, the norm in West Germany was that mothers stayed at home to look after their children. After 30 years of reunification, this principle of subsidiarity and a reluctance to take family responsibilities into the public domain means differences between east and west persist.[2]

Deciding which of these systems is better depends on your perspective and priorities. Some would argue that equity should drive social choices and enable men and women to have equal life chances. Others would prefer to have mothers care for young children because they believe that is in the best interests of the child and of the family.

What is the best way to look after our children? There is no single answer to the question, but whatever solution is adopted will have major consequences for the working lives of women. The two issues are currently inseparable. What is also clear is that to give our children the best start in life, childcare cannot be treated as unpaid work, but must become an essential part of our social infrastructure. This chapter will draw together the evidence and assess how different social contracts affect women's economic roles and the welfare of children.

## An Economy of All the Talents

Today, there are many debates reflecting the tensions around women's changing economic roles. For example, how can increasingly well-educated women overcome discrimination in some sectors and countries? Why do women earn less than men and why have equal-pay laws had so little impact? How can the double burden of work both in and outside the home be eased? In countries with falling birth rates, how can young people be persuaded to have families despite insecure incomes and anxieties about an overpopulated planet? And in Africa, where birth rates are still high, how can women be given access to education and contraception so that they have more choices about their family size? These debates are manifestations of fractures in the social contract, with education and economic needs pulling in one direction while social norms often tug in another.

From the economic perspective, the losses we are incurring by not better supporting women's participation in the labour market are massive. In 1960, 94 per cent of doctors and lawyers in the United States were white men. Fifty years later, that number had fallen to 62 per cent as more women, black men and ethnic minorities were given the opportunity to enter these professions. The benefits from better use of all the talent available across the economy explain between 20 and 40 per cent of the productivity gains in the US between 1960 and 2010.[3] It is worth dwelling on this point – the US economy became far more productive because instead of drawing on a narrow talent pool of white men, it was able to choose from a broader pool of skills and allocate jobs to those that suited them best. The economic gains come both from women entering occupations they have talent for as well as from women replacing less-talented men.[4]

Historically, the misallocation of talent has many causes. Social norms about who does which kinds of jobs – frequently indistinguishable from discrimination by contemporary standards – have been a factor. Despite ranking first in her class at Columbia Law School in 1959, Ruth Bader Ginsberg (who went on to serve on the US Supreme Court) had great difficulty finding a job after she graduated. 'A Jew, a woman and a mother, that was a bit much,' she explained in an interview. 'Three strikes put me out of the game.'[5] Different groups can have varying access to opportunities if parents, educational institutions or employers favour one group over another. While illegal in many places, discrimination on the basis of gender, race, disability, sexual preference or other characteristics is still widespread. For example, many studies find that female names on job applications bring the assumption that the candidate is less qualified, and firms hiring often assume mothers are less committed and competent than fathers.[6]

Today, education opportunities are more evenly distributed and many countries (although not all) have outlawed aspects of gender discrimination. Thanks to mechanisation and automation, the physical requirements of many manual jobs are less important, opening them up to a wider variety of workers. Today it is not uncommon to see women in the military or driving taxis, jobs that were once the exclusive preserve of men. Online job search platforms have revolutionised the matching of workers to the jobs that suit them best. And social norms are changing about which jobs men and women can do. For example, nursing is a profession with growing numbers of men, while women have increased their presence in traditionally male professions like engineering and the law. Moreover, most parents with boys and girls will have observed that their innate talents and interests do not always match gender stereotypes.

Despite all this, women continue to assume most caring responsibilities in the home. As countries get richer, household chores like cleaning, cooking, shopping and household management have increasingly been mechanised by 'engines of liberation' such as washing machines and vacuum cleaners, but caring for the young and the elderly continues to be a very time-intensive business, and the time required does not vary much across countries with different income levels. Even when women are doing more paid work, they still carry a larger burden of unpaid work – often referred to as 'the 'second shift'.[7] On average, women do two more hours of this unpaid work per day than men globally. Using data from 90 countries, the IMF found that the discrepancy is smallest in egalitarian Norway, where women spend 20 per cent more time than men on unpaid work, and

## Figure 4. Women do more hours of unpaid work everywhere

Average number of hours of female unpaid work each day

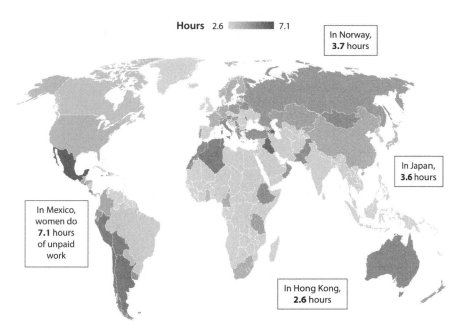

Hours  2.6 ▬▬▬▬ 7.1

In Norway,
**3.7** hours

In Japan,
**3.6** hours

In Mexico,
women do
**7.1** hours
of unpaid
work

In Hong Kong,
**2.6** hours

Ratio of female to male unpaid work

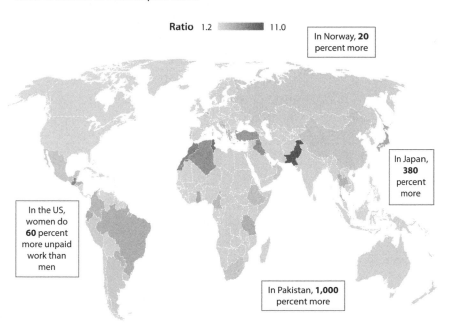

Ratio  1.2 ▬▬▬▬ 11.0

In Norway, **20**
percent more

In Japan,
**380**
percent
more

In the US,
women do
**60** percent
more unpaid
work than
men

In Pakistan, **1,000**
percent more

largest in highly unegalitarian Pakistan, where the time spent on unpaid work is 1000 per cent greater (Figure 4).[8]

In the advanced economies, there are signs that the division of labour at home is shifting. One study found that since 2000 women have been spending half an hour less per day on unpaid work than they did between 1916 and 1989, and that half-hour is now occupied with paid work. In contrast, men are doing less paid work and spend 40 more minutes each day on unpaid work.[9] This rebalancing within couples is most pronounced among women with higher education.

In the developing world, that rebalancing is not yet apparent. Evidence from 66 developing countries shows women spending 3.3 times as much time as men do on unpaid work.[10] In countries where the care load is most unequal, this extra work translates into 10 weeks or more for each year of a woman's life. Older children (almost always girls) often provide childcare as well, but it is estimated that globally about 35 million children under the age of 5 are left unsupervised. When men in the developing world do participate in childcare, there are often considerable discrepancies between their reporting of it and that of their female partners (many female readers are probably smiling at this point). For example, 37 per cent of men in India say they look after children every day, whereas only 17 per cent of Indian women say men provide childcare. In Brazil, the discrepancy is even greater: 39 per cent of men say they participate in childcare daily, whereas only 10 per cent of Brazilian women say this is the case.

So, for all the improvements in women's education and job choices, the mechanisation of work and the shifting of social norms, the biggest obstacle to the optimal allocation of talent remains that, when they have children, women the world over drop out of the labour force or take lower-paid jobs to enable them to balance paid work with caring obligations.[11] The gender pay gap can in large part be explained by the fact that the kinds of jobs that allow women to meet domestic obligations are more flexible, part time or require shorter working hours

– typically work that pays less per hour. And because women work fewer hours, they gain less experience, which delays their career progression and so keeps their pay low.[12] Furthermore, many women who drop out of the labour market when they have children never return, often because long spells of unemployment make this very difficult.

The bottom line is that a truly gender-neutral labour market that allowed talented women to fulfil their potential would increase the productivity of both women and men. The economic gains are potentially huge — closing gender gaps could increase GDP by 35 per cent because women bring additional skills to the workplace.[13] To achieve these economic gains, we need to rethink the way our social contract provides for childcare.

### Families versus the State and the Market

In every country the social contract establishes norms about the division of childcare between men and women and where that care will happen. The former is determined through the allocation of maternity and paternity leave. The latter is determined by the provision of either cash benefits, which encourage care at home, or public subsidies for childcare, which encourage the use of institutionalised settings such as nurseries.

Broadly there are two models. One model reinforces the role of the family by providing individuals with very little or no economic or social support. Southern European and east Asian countries typify this approach. Government policy here focuses on providing leave (usually for mothers) so that they can fulfil caring responsibilities themselves. If state support is provided for childcare, it takes the form of benefit payments, again promoting care by the family. The alternative model enables individuals to fulfil their caring responsibilities independent of family relationships by providing state- or market-based alternatives: free or subsidised nurseries. Northern European countries and countries like France, with its generous provision of state-funded childcare, provide examples of this model.[14]

Not surprisingly, the two models are highly contentious and are rooted in values about how individualistic or family-based our social contract should be. The family model reinforces more traditional roles for men and women. It also encourages inter-dependency and mutual obligations between extended family members and across the generations – grandparents (usually grandmothers) caring for grandchildren with the expectation that they will be cared for in old age. The alternative model enables individuals to organise their lives outside traditional structures – for example as single-parent households – and provides more flexibility on what constitutes a family.

The degree to which grandparents are involved in caring for children, which varies enormously around the world, is therefore a good indication of whether a country is more or less family-based in its approach. In Europe and the United States less than 10 per cent of children are cared for by a grandparent, whereas this ranges from 30 per cent in east Asia to 75 per cent in sub-Saharan Africa.[15] This is partly for demographic reasons. In ageing societies where women have children later, grandparents are often older and unable to help with childcare, whereas in many parts of Africa grandmothers are in their 50s and capable of caring for grandchildren, thus enabling their own children to work.

China has perhaps the highest rate of care by grandparents, with 90 per cent of children in Shanghai, 70 per cent in Beijing and 50 per cent in Guangzhou being looked after by at least one grandparent and with half of these grandparents being the sole care provider.[16] This reflects China's one-child policy, which results in many grandparents per child, limited state provision of childcare, its cultural traditions and low retirement ages, combined with massive rural-to-urban migration, which has left some villages in China populated only by children and their grandparents.[17]

Which is better – care by grandparents or formal childcare? There is no 'right' answer, and families make choices based on their circumstances and preferences. One study found that children looked after by their grandparents appear to have larger vocabularies on average, probably because of the more intense one-to-one interactions with an adult that grandparents provide. However, children looked after by their grandparents performed worse on other cognitive tests such as non-verbal reasoning or mathematical concepts relevant for school readiness. These differences mattered most for children from disadvantaged households.[18]

What is the effect on women's participation in the paid labour force when countries with a more traditional, family-based social contract are compared with those that promote models of childcare outside the home and involving men? And which model is most viable for the future?

### *Childcare in Advanced Economies*

Among the more advanced economies, the average amount spent on support for childcare (whether family-based or provided by the state) is 0.6 per cent of GDP. To put that into perspective, advanced economies spend about 8 times more on education and 21 times more on health.[19] The average duration of parental leave (at least partially paid) is 55 weeks. As noted above, the most generous countries are the Nordics and France; the least generous are the southern European countries, Australia, New Zealand, Switzerland, Mexico and Turkey.

Throughout the more advanced economies that are members of the Organisation for Economic Cooperation and Development (OECD) men get far less generous paid parental leave than women, averaging 8 weeks. In France, fathers are entitled to a relatively generous 28 weeks of paid leave, but in New Zealand, Canada and Switzerland there is no paternity leave at all. This is changing, however. A recent directive by the European Commission requires all member states to offer at least 4 months of parental leave by 2022, only 2 months of which can be transferred from one parent to the other. Germany and Sweden have gone further and offer 14 and 16 months of parental leave respectively, all of which can be shared by parents. Finland now offers 7 months of paternity leave to all men.

The United States, meanwhile, is a major outlier: it is the only advanced economy with no legally mandated paid maternity or paternity leave policy. Since 1993, the Family and Medical Leave Act has guaranteed qualified workers up to 12 weeks of leave per year for medical reasons including the birth of a child, but this is not paid. US public spending on childcare is well below the OECD average at 0.35 per cent of GDP, so American families devote a considerable portion of their private income to childcare, with huge variations across income groups.[20]

These policy choices have huge implications for patterns of work in families. In northern Europe, where there are relatively generous childcare and parental leave arrangements, dual-earner households, in which both parents have paid work, are most common. For example, 55 per cent of couples in Denmark and 59 per cent in Finland are dual earners. In continental Europe, the one-and-a-half breadwinner model is more common with the man in full-time employment and women concentrated in part-time work. France and Belgium follow a mixed model in which women are provided with long and well-paid parental leave, particularly when children are young, but are also supported to engage in full-time work when they can.[21] Economically liberal welfare states such as the UK offer various private-market solutions – such as childcare vouchers – and focus public support for nurseries on where there are market failures or acute needs, such as for families that are very poor or face other challenges.[22] This has the consequence of putting most women in the position of being secondary earners. In southern Europe, where the social contract favours family support, the male breadwinner model is most common.[23] The same is true in large parts of the developing world.

## Childcare in the Developing World

In the developing world childcare is still primarily focused on family support. This tendency is exacerbated by the fact that many women work in the informal sector and do not have any legal right to maternity leave. The International Labour Organisation estimates that 830 million working women still lack access to maternity leave in the developing world.[24] In most countries in Asia, Africa and the Middle East, statutory maternity leave is 12–13 weeks at 100 per cent of prior salary, but the number of women in the formal labour market is so low that very few actually benefit from this policy.

Paternity leave is starting to appear in a few developing Asian countries, but slowly and at low levels – the Philippines provides 7 days; Bangladesh, Cambodia and Vietnam 10 days; China and India none at all. Paternity leave is rare in Africa and the Middle East. Parental leave which can be shared between partners is even more unusual in the developing world (the only examples are in Burkina Faso, Chad, Guinea, Nepal, Mongolia) and paid parental leave virtually non-existent. However, there is already evidence that those developing countries that do offer paternity leave are seeing benefits in terms of higher levels of female employment.[25]

Against this backdrop, however, there are many examples of increasing public support for childcare in the developing world, resulting not only in more women being able to work outside the home but in the creation of jobs in the childcare industry for other women. In Mexico, the Estancias programme provides childcare for a minimum of 8 hours a day, 5 days a week, with good staff ratios, nutritious food and an education programme. Public funding of up to 90 per cent of the cost has meant that most children who attend are from the poorest families. Women sending their children to the centres have increased their daily hours of work by an average of 6 hours. The programme also provides employment for up to 40,000 women. Similar programmes in India have cared for over a million children; in South Africa they have provided employment for over 20,000 women.[26]

## Childcare and Women Working

Extensive research has shown that as the price of childcare falls, more mothers enter the labour market.[27] And countries that invest more in supporting mothers to go back to work reap

economic gains in terms of higher female labour force participation (Figure 5). Accessible, affordable, high-quality childcare
helps mothers achieve a work–life balance, and take-up is greatest when some public subsidy is provided. Many other factors
matter too – women's education, average wages, social norms,
childcare regulations – but countries with the most generous
social contracts have sustained higher levels of female employment and fertility levels that keep the population stable.

Among these countries, however, there is still significant
variation. In most advanced economies the earnings of men
and women follow a similar path and then diverge sharply
after the birth of their first child. Women experience a sharp
drop in their incomes while men are essentially unaffected.

**Figure 5. Countries that spend more on families enable women to stay in paid work**

Female employment and public spending on family benefits in OECD countries, 2015

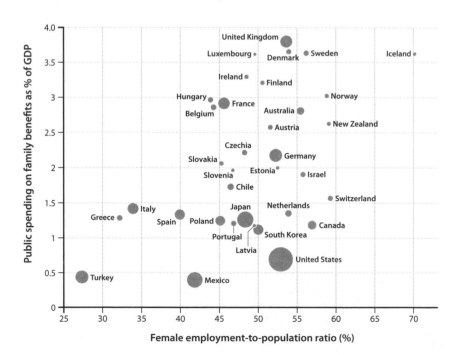

The size of this 'child penalty' (the drop in incomes 5–10 years after having a first child) varies enormously, from 21–26 per cent in Sweden and Denmark to 31–44 per cent in Germany and Austria, to 51–61 per cent in the UK and the US.[28] In the short run, these differences are associated with policies around parental leave and access to childcare, but are only part of the story. In the longer run, cultural norms around the respective roles of men and women and the prevalence in some countries of more conservative attitudes to whether mothers should stay at home seem to play a more important role.[29]

Several countries struggling with declining populations such as Japan, Korea and Taiwan have increased financial support to families in the hope of halting the drop in fertility.[30] Japan and Korea, which face the sharpest falls in fertility in the world, now offer the most generous paid paternity leave – one full year – yet less than 3 per cent of men take advantage of this. Why? A recent study in Korea with the wonderful title of 'I Want to but I Won't' found that even though many married working men aged 20–49 wanted to take advantage of paternity leave, they were stopped by their perception that other men thought this was not normal. Even though they all individually held the same view, their inaccurate assumption about others' opinions prevented them from taking time off when they had a child.[31] Similarly, even though paternity leave is available in the UK, 40 per cent of fathers take no leave at all; less than 10 per cent take more than 2 weeks.

These efforts have failed because they reinforce family-based care without a shift in men's willingness to carry a greater share of the unpaid work. Providing more public support for childcare is not enough if male attitudes do not change. But designed in the right way, policies can help to encourage behaviour change. Iceland gives families choices that seem to have successfully rebalanced unpaid work between men and women. Parents are given 9 months of paid parental leave – 3 months for the mother, 3 for the father and 3 to share between them. If the father does not take his share of the leave, it is lost. Since the policy was introduced in the year 2000, almost all fathers in Iceland now take paternity leave, and surveys show they play a much more active role in children's lives as a result.[32]

Countries like Italy, Spain and Ireland, traditionally associated with large Catholic families, are now facing a real risk of declining populations. Why? Childcare is not well funded by the state, policies continue to favour family-based care, and men do little unpaid work. The problem is compounded by high rates of unemployment and job insecurity, which delay the ability of young people to form their own households and have children. The consequence has been that women in these countries now have some of the lowest birth rates in the world.

## Impact of Childcare Arrangements on Children

One reason for slow progress on providing childcare is the traditional belief that if a woman goes out to work, this adversely affects her children. Typically, this rests on the notion that only a mother can provide the care for a child that it needs to develop healthily. But what does the evidence tell us about the impact of a mother working on her children's development? And what about the impact of fathers? A vast amount of research has been conducted on this subject.

Psychologists agree that the first months of a child's life are crucial for brain and emotional development.[33] Delaying a mother's return to work allows breastfeeding to continue for longer and for more parent–child interactions during this critical phase. Research has also found some association between mothers' early return to work and poorer academic achievement in early childhood.[34] One summary of various empirical studies concluded that the evidence shows that children benefit if mothers are allowed to postpone their return to work until after the first year after birth.[35] Of course these findings do not take into account the impact on the mother of losing skills and economic independence, nor do they measure the impact on children relative to an ideal of high-quality institutional childcare. We also do not have enough data or research to judge whether fathers staying home in the early months of a child's life has an equivalent benefit.

However, once children are a bit older, they benefit from the additional influence of caregivers, their peers and school. Mothers going back to work after children reach 2–3 years old is associated with better academic and behavioural outcomes for those children.[36] A meta-analysis of 69 studies found that mothers' employment is rarely associated with adverse outcomes for children; in fact, teacher ratings of achievement seem to indicate that children benefit from their mothers being employed. If anything, mothers going back to work seems to result in better academic and behavioural outcomes for their children than if they stayed at home.[37] That improvement is greater when the quality of the available childcare is higher.[38] Clearly timing matters – having a parent at home in the first year of a child's life can have positive effects, whereas parental employment in years 2 or 3 generally has positive effects on children's educational achievement.

In the recent past several countries increased maternity leave in the hope of improving the welfare of children. For example, Germany increased maternity leave from 18 to 36 months in 1992, which resulted in a large drop in the number of working mothers.[39] The objective of this change was to foster child development, but when the educational and labour-market outcomes of children born before and after this reform are compared, they show no evidence of improvement. In fact, the reform may have slightly lowered children's educational attainment, and the fall in family incomes was probably also detrimental. Similar results were found in Canada and Denmark, although one study found that countries with longer maternity leave in Europe had lower infant and child death rates.[40] In the United States, the introduction of paid maternity leave led to small improvements in birth weight, fewer premature births and lower infant mortality.[41]

Having mothers go back to work is especially beneficial for children from poorer families. Children from families that are at risk financially, especially those with single parents or on welfare benefits, tend to do better when their parents work.[42] Maternal employment brings greater financial security and reduces family stress, which compensates for a mother's absence. In contrast, children from better-off families benefit less because the added income is less critical for their well-being.

There are also very different consequences for girls and boys. Recent research followed 105,000 children to adulthood across 29 countries in North and South America, Australia, Europe, Asia and the Middle East.[43] The daughters of women who worked outside the home are more likely to be employed, hold more senior positions, work more hours and earn more than women whose mothers were not employed. Sons raised by mothers who worked outside the home spend more time caring for family members, while the daughters spend less time doing unpaid housework. These differences are attributed to the fact that working mothers convey to their children more egalitarian attitudes to balancing paid and unpaid work in the household.

In addition to the benefits for children and to the economy of women returning to work, there is growing evidence that fathers' engagement with infants is highly beneficial too. Children that grow up with fathers who are present and engaged have better emotional and behavioural development. As incomes rise, fathers tend to spend more time with their children, and the nature of their engagement can often be different and complementary to that of mothers. Observational studies have shown that fathers' interactions can be more stimulating and vigorous and promote risk-taking and exploration, which is beneficial to children's cognitive development.[44] For example, 3-month-old infants who have engaged fathers perform better on cognitive tests at age 2.[45] Paternal involvement in caretaking tasks in the first month of a child's life has also been associated with improved mental development one year later.[46]

## Families of the Future

Employing the talents of women in the labour market is economically beneficial and improves the welfare of children after the first year of life. More involvement by fathers in their early years also shows clear benefits for children. A social contract that rebalances the caring responsibilities between men and women and converts unpaid work by women into paid work would make our societies both richer and fairer. Our children will do better academically and psychologically if they are raised by engaged parents early in their lives and have access to high-quality childcare thereafter. This is especially important for children born into poorer families and will improve social mobility.

There are many models that involve allocating more public resources to the provision of affordable and high-quality childcare. Whether that support encourages family-based care or care outside the home is a choice that is best left to individuals and families. Having the costs of that parental leave and childcare financed by the state, rather than by employers, would further level the playing field for men and women in the workplace. The key is that public policies need to support men and women equally so that they have the freedom to choose, and the allocation of talent in the economy is optimal.

Ideally, governments would provide a menu of options for families – maternity and paternity leave, or better yet, parental leave that can be shared – and public funding for institutionalised childcare as well as for home care. These choices are deeply personal and depend hugely on individual circumstances. The critical change that must occur is that caring for the next generation can no longer be ignored, taken for granted or discounted as unpaid work. It needs to become an essential part of public-service infrastructure, like health or education services. It also needs to be flexible to recognise the ways that the organisation of both work and families is changing. This will improve the lives of both men and women, support children more effectively and create jobs, often for women.

But while the provision of childcare is key, there are many other policies that can help us move to a more equal labour market. More-flexible work with benefits that accompany people when they change jobs and can be adjusted when they work part time would help both men and women balance caring responsibilities with changing patterns of work (more on this in Chapter 5). Taxing people as individuals is better than a system that encourages couples to file taxes jointly. When couples file jointly, the second earner (typically the woman) is taxed at the same rate as her partner, which usually means paying more than she would as an individual, thereby discouraging female labour-force participation.[47] Meanwhile, school calendars with long summer holidays create challenges for working parents and make little sense in societies in which so few people are employed in agriculture and child labour is illegal. Moving towards a social contract that supports dual-earner families in all of these dimensions is vital.

Policies alone are not enough, though; the social contract needs to change within the home too. As we have seen in Japan and Korea, even the most generous paternity leave policy in the world will only work if social attitudes adjust. The Nordic countries provide an interesting contrast – of a social contract that has evolved over decades to one characterised by high levels of female employment, generous public support and men sharing a greater proportion of unpaid work. That model has been able to sustain high levels of income and levels of fertility that maintain the population. In contrast, despite increasingly generous policies, Korea now has the lowest fertility rate in the world at 0.9 per cent (it needs to be 2.1 per cent to keep the population level stable), because social attitudes have not changed.

Can we afford to undertake such a massive change to our social contract? I would argue that we cannot afford not to. Family structures are evolving quickly: couples are marrying later, and women are bearing children when they are older; there are more single-parent households; populations are ageing, and birth rates are falling everywhere except Africa. Our social contract needs to catch up with the needs of modern families and modern economies. Enabling more women to use their talents in the workplace will increase output, productivity and tax revenues far in excess of the costs of providing better public support for childcare. Engaging fathers in childcare more will also improve the welfare of children, enabling us to raise a more productive younger generation whose higher incomes will contribute tax revenues towards the pensions and health-care needs of a growing older generation. Rather than trying to manage intergenerational commitments within families, which has resulted in the highly unequal outcomes that we have seen throughout history, we need to share those risks with each other.

# 3

# Education

In 2005 I visited a village in southern Ethiopia, home to the dramatic scenery of the Great Rift Valley but also to some of the poorest people in one of the poorest countries in the world. The parents I met there were very, very thin, having clearly suffered long periods of hunger in the recent past, but when I met them, they were very happy. The reason was that, with the help of the UK government's aid programme, a new school had been built for the benefit of their children. There was only one thing wrong – the Ethiopian government could only afford to pay for one teacher, which meant that there was just one class – of about 80 pupils. They proudly told me that the parents' association had pooled its meagre resources to hire an additional teacher so that their children could get a better education.

The determination of parents to give their children the best possible start in life is universal. In richer countries it translates into mothers and fathers competing fiercely to get their children into the best schools or paying for private tutors to give them a better chance of success in exams. In poorer countries it often means families making huge material sacrifices to enable their children to attend school. In all cases the value of education reflects both the benefits to the individual and the gains to society as a whole of having an educated population.

Every society includes education as a central part of its social contract. Almost all societies focus their investment in education on young people from around age 6 to the early 20s, but we now know that children's educational attainment is significantly affected before the age of 6 – by varying levels of nutrition, mental stimulation and parental engagement. Meanwhile, in a world where working lives are growing longer and more varied, investments in education for adults will be needed if workers are to keep their skills relevant as economies evolve. What does this mean for the social contract around education?

## What makes education so valuable?

Education can achieve many objectives – ensuring children's physical, cognitive and emotional development; shaping us into citizens who share common values; helping individuals to discover their talents and the way they can contribute to the world. In terms of the social contract, education also fulfils the vital economic role of preparing the workforce of the future by equipping us with the skills we need to find employment, be productive and thereby contribute to society.

The economic benefits of education can be seen over the last 50 years, during which time countries the world over have made huge progress in primary and secondary provision. Although about 60 million children are still out of school, mainly in Africa and south Asia, universal, free primary education has been made available almost everywhere.[1] Moreover, 4 out of every 5 children in the world are now enrolled in lower secondary school – what is called middle school in many countries.

In fact, many developing countries have caught up by outpacing the historical performance of today's advanced economies. For example, by 2010 the average worker in Bangladesh had completed more years of schooling than the typical worker in France had in 1975. It took the United States 40 years to raise girls' enrolment from 57 per cent to 88 per cent; Morocco managed it in just 11 years.[2] As a result, by 2008 the average low-income country was enrolling children into primary school at nearly the same rate as the typical high-income country.

Tertiary education, which includes universities, colleges, technical training institutes and vocational schools, is a slightly different story. It has expanded more slowly, with about 200 million students enrolled globally, and there is huge variation between countries: some 10–20 per cent of adults in middle-income countries like Brazil, China and Mexico are enrolled in tertiary education, whereas in higher-income countries, enrolment rates range from 30 per cent in Austria to 42 per cent in the UK, 44 per cent in the US and 54 per cent in Canada.[3]

Overall, though, this global investment in education has paid off handsomely. In economic terms, we can calculate a rate of return on education by dividing the benefits it produces – measured in the form of higher wages, minus the costs of providing the education – by the number of years of education received, which results in an annual percentage yield, similar to a return on a savings account or a shareholding. Drawing on 1120 years of data from 139 countries, economists have calculated that each year of additional education has generated an average private return – that is, to the individual receiving the education – of about 10 per cent.[4] This is significantly more than the 8 per cent average annual return of the US stock market since 1957, when the S&P 500 index was created.[5]

Moreover, these returns are underestimates because they only take account of higher expected earnings for individuals and do not measure wider social benefits. The scale of those social benefits can be huge. For example, in the UK, every £1 invested in university education generates £7 for the individual (private return) but £25 for the state (social return) in the form of higher tax receipts, lower welfare spending and fewer crimes.[6]

The returns to both the individual and to society vary by level of education. For example, the highest returns tend to be found at the primary levels of education, simply because it costs less to provide than secondary or university education. Table 1 provides estimates for private and social returns of different levels of education in low-, middle- and high-income countries.

**Table 1. Returns to education are high, especially to primary school and in poorer countries**

Rates of return on different levels of education by country income level

| Per capita income level | Private | | | Social | | |
|---|---|---|---|---|---|---|
| | Primary | Secondary | Higher | Primary | Secondary | Higher |
| Low | 25.4 | 18.7 | 26.8 | 22.1 | 18.1 | 13.2 |
| Middle | 24.5 | 17.7 | 20.2 | 17.1 | 12.8 | 11.4 |
| High | 28.4 | 13.2 | 12.8 | 15.8 | 10.3 | 9.7 |
| Average | 25.4 | 15.1 | 15.8 | 17.5 | 11.8 | 10.5 |

Overall, the returns are also highest in poorer countries. Again, this is not surprising as it is in these countries that the skills provided by education are relatively scarce. But might this increase in earnings reflect something else? Might it simply be that employers use schooling as a screening device to select workers, so that the fact of having been to school leads to higher earnings rather than the education acquired there? Research shows this is not the case – firms do not retain educated workers simply because of their degrees, but because they are more productive as a result of their education.[7]

What is more surprising is that in countries where more workers have higher levels of education, the rate of return on that investment does not decline very much. This is because technological innovation has created more jobs that favour those with more education, meaning that the higher wages that university graduates tend to receive have continued to rise in most countries. This trend has meant that those with more education tend to earn even more as technology advances, contributing to rising inequality in many countries.[8] If we do not do more to equalise opportunities for education, this trend – technology driving greater inequality – will only get worse.[9]

But this is merely the tip of the iceberg. There are two massive challenges on the horizon – one technological, one demographic – which will require us not just to make education more widely available but to change the fundamental shape of the systems we use to provide it. In addition to the question about *what* we teach, we also need to think about *when* we teach.

## The Need for Problem-Solving and Flexibility

Much discussion of how education needs to change focuses on what we should be teaching and how we should be teaching it. Traditional education systems often place major emphasis on rote memorisation. Teachers transmit information and students do their best to retain it and reproduce it in various tests. But today most educationalists recognise that this is a waste of time: we are in a world where 3.5 billion people have access to smartphones with search engines at their fingertips and almost infinite access to information. More important now is the ability to sift through information, make critical judgements about its validity and come to a view about its implications. Education should focus on equipping children with these abilities.

In advanced economies technology is also leading to a bifurcation of labour markets: on the one hand we see increased demand for those with 'high' skills (like scientists or data analysts) and 'low' skills (like care workers), while the jobs in the middle (such as factory or clerical posts) are disappearing. In developing countries the pattern is more complex – everywhere there is growing demand for higher skills, but the demand for low and medium skills varies depending on the competing forces of automation and globalisation.[10] What is true in all countries, advanced or developing, however, is that in the short to medium term cognitive skills, such as being able to come up with a new solution to a problem, are being highly rewarded by the labour market. In countries like Denmark,

France, Germany, the Slovak Republic, Spain and Switzerland being good at complex problem-solving is associated with an income that is 10–20 per cent higher.[11]

What is also undeniable is that ageing will require the next generation to work much longer and change jobs many times over a lifetime. An adult today might be able to get through a working life of 40 years based on what they learned in their teenage years and their twenties. This is highly unlikely when working lives stretch to 60 years. A child born today in an advanced economy is more likely than not to live to 100 years.[12] That amounts to 873,000 hours of existence. If it takes about 10,000 hours to master a new skill, then it becomes feasible to do so several times in an age of longevity.[13]

And people will need to. We are already seeing evidence of workers changing jobs more often in many countries. In advanced economies average job stability as measured by the length of time spent in a job has fallen.[14] This has affected workers with low skills (without an upper-secondary qualification) the most adversely. There is also evidence of rising underemployment – people employed part time who would prefer to be in full-time work. This is most common in the service sectors such as hotels, food and restaurants, where workers are employed on hourly contracts to accommodate variation in demand. Underemployment has most negatively impacted workers with low skills, young people and women.

So, not only will a longer work life require frequent reskilling, it will also mean a very different career structure. I often tell students to think about their careers not like climbing a ladder, but like climbing a tree. Often you have to move sideways before going to the next level, and detours can reveal interesting new vistas. Education increasingly needs to enable people to climb trees, explore new opportunities and follow their curiosity. They also need to come down from the tree, not by jumping abruptly from the top to the ground into full retirement, but by climbing down gently via varied, partial roles as they get older.

Given these various factors – the burgeoning demand for cog-nitive skills on the one hand, and the impending reality on the other that jobs will change and that job stability is decreasing – what we need is a system of education that is more *flexible*. It needs to equip children not just with knowledge and skills but with the ability to *acquire* knowledge and skills. And it needs to provide more opportunities for second chances and the scope to retool at various stages in a working life. The key to providing this kind of education, it turns out, is timing.

Of course, the best education has always been about learning how to learn. In the slightly old-fashioned words of William Cory, master of Eton college (1845–1872), 'At school you are engaged not so much in acquiring knowledge as in making mental efforts under criticism.'[15] These mental efforts are what equip you to acquire knowledge for the rest of your life. For teachers, 'under criticism' means shifting 'from being the sage on the stage to the guide on the side', as the saying goes in current educational parlance. The advantage of this approach is that it instils in students the possibility of constant renewal as learning opportunities occur throughout life.

But what few appreciate is that this ability to learn is estab-lished very early in life. The architecture of the brain is formed before the age of 5, the most important stage for the devel-opment of the cognitive and socio-behavioural skills that are becoming ever more important. If this window of opportunity is missed, it has negative consequences for the ability to learn in adulthood. And because learning is cumulative, stronger foundations established early in life enable more to be built on top, which amplifies the benefits of early-years education – as well, of course, as the disadvantages of its absence. This is why the early years also provide the best opportunity for equalising the chances of children from less-advantaged backgrounds.

In Figure 6 we can see that a selection of societies from across the world currently puts the bulk of their investment in education at the primary and secondary levels – about five times more than the other levels. Tertiary education receives

# Figure 6. Countries spend most on primary and secondary education

Education spending by level as a share of GDP

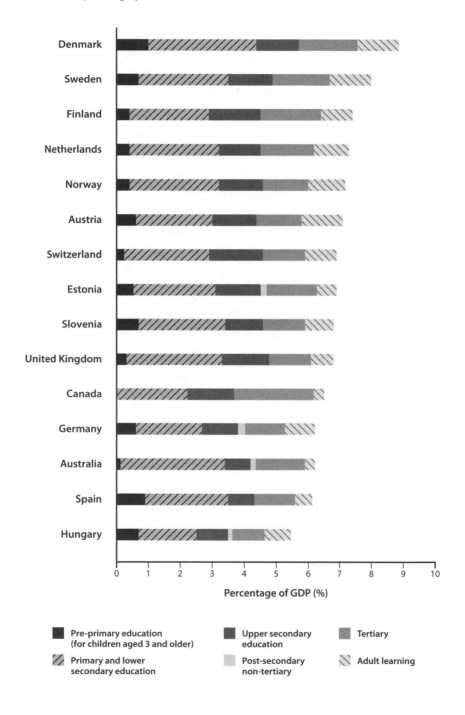

Percentage of GDP (%)

- ■ Pre-primary education (for children aged 3 and older)
- ▨ Primary and lower secondary education
- ■ Upper secondary education
- ■ Post-secondary non-tertiary
- ■ Tertiary
- ▨ Adult learning

significant funding in many countries but benefits a smaller share of the population. The picture is clear: pre-primary and adult learning (the bottoms and tops of the histograms), the times in life at which education is and will be more needed in future, receive by far the lowest levels of funding. This is what needs to change.

### Early Years are the Most Important Years

Recent research shows how important the first 1000 days of life are for a child's cognitive development and their ability to learn. It is during this period – before the age of 3 – when brain development is highly influenced by nutrition, mental stimulation and social and emotional development, that the foundations for learning are laid. The importance of this time has been shown in numerous studies that look at children who have been deprived of opportunities from birth – for example, those raised in orphanages relative to those raised by families.[16]

Children who fall behind in their physical, cognitive, linguistic or social and emotional development are more likely to fall behind in school, repeat grades and drop out, suffer from health problems throughout their lives, engage in high-risk behaviour and earn lower wages as adults. Early interventions in child development have been shown to have a sustained impact on health, education and economic success.[17] Yet their adoption around the world has been uneven, perhaps because in many societies they are not seen as part of the social contract but as the responsibility of families. (As we shall see later, this also needs to change.)

The benefits of early intervention are most apparent in the developing world, where 30 per cent of children under 5 are physically stunted, meaning they are short for their age, usually because of chronic malnutrition.[18] These children are more likely to achieve less academically and exhibit poorer cognitive ability.[19] In other words, many children arrive at school already disadvantaged by impaired brain development and poor skills, meaning they cannot benefit fully from the education they receive, even if they attend a good school. And because the brain becomes less malleable over time, it is harder for these children to catch up, which means initial learning differences tend to widen over time. Poor early-childhood development has lifelong consequences for children and for a country's economic and social development.

An important series of articles on child development in one of the world's most highly regarded medical journals, the *Lancet*, makes the case for early-childhood interventions.[20] The studies argue that more than 200 million children under the age of 5 do not reach their developmental potential, mainly as a result of stunting, iodine and iron deficiency and inadequate cognitive stimulation. These are sometimes exacerbated by maternal depression, exposure to violence, environmental contamination and malaria.

But these disadvantages can be addressed. What is needed are quality programmes, targeting the most disadvantaged, that provide direct learning experiences to children and families which help them understand health, nutrition and education. For example, countries like Ecuador, Mexico and Nicaragua have reduced stunting and improved children's cognitive development by giving very poor families cash benefits alongside prenatal care and support for their children. In these types of programmes, caregivers benefit from coaching on positive discipline, the use of stimulating activities such as storytelling or singing, and managing the stresses of parenting. This support can be delivered through home visits, community meetings and health check-ups, and has been shown to have significant benefits to physical and cognitive development and child health. The rate of return on these interventions depends on many factors, including the focus, duration of exposure and quality of the programmes being implemented, but the benefits of every $1 spent range from $6 to $17.[21] From the perspective of the child, it is the difference between a good start in life or not.

And these benefits can last a lifetime. In another pioneering study, toddlers living in poverty in Jamaica received weekly visits lasting an hour each from community health workers over a 2-year period. During these visits the mothers were encouraged to interact and play with their children to develop their cognitive and personality skills.[22] When the children were interviewed 20 years later, they were earning 42 per cent more than a control group of children who had not benefited from the weekly visits. A relatively simple intervention very early in childhood can have a major effect on future income and can compensate for disadvantages early in life.

Major benefits from early-years education have also been found in advanced economies.[23] A study in the United States evaluated the impact of a preschool programme that provided up to 6 years of support to disadvantaged families in inner-city Chicago. When assessed 25 years later, children who had participated in the programme had better educational outcomes, incomes, socio-economic status and access to health insurance relative to children who had not participated. They also had lower rates of criminal behaviour and substance abuse. The benefits were greatest for males and the children of parents who had not finished secondary school.[24]

And yet, despite all the evidence of huge benefits, most countries underinvest in young children. Only half of all children aged 3–6 have access to pre-primary education around the world, falling to a fifth in low-income countries.[25] North America and western Europe spent a mere 8.8 per cent of their education budgets on pre-primary education in 2012; in sub-Saharan Africa the share allocated was only 0.3 per cent.[26] In Latin America governments spend three times more on children aged 6–11 than those under the age of 6. When governments do invest, they tend to focus on building preschools, but these do not benefit children under preschool age, which is where cognitive development needs are greatest. Advanced economies tend to have higher rates of enrolment in preschools, but spending varies enormously with countries like Iceland and Sweden investing more than 1.5 per cent of GDP, while about a third of that is spent in places like the US, Japan and Turkey.[27]

Why is underinvestment in early-years education the norm? One reason is that many are still unaware of or do not appreciate the high pay-offs of early interventions and why these benefits may become even more important in future. At the same time, the problem is rendered effectively invisible to politicians by the widespread assumption that families, not governments, are responsible for early years. Limited budgets are often an issue too, and established providers of primary and secondary education have legitimate claims on resources. And finally, high-quality early-years education cuts across health, nutrition and education, so it is unclear which government department or budget is responsible for it.

It is important to acknowledge that poor-quality early-years education can be worse than none at all. In Kenya one programme for 3–6-year-olds was so academically oriented they even forced the children to sit exams. Poorly trained caregivers in Peru meant that an early-years programme was good at childcare and nutrition but didn't improve language or motor development.[28] Providing high-quality care to children under 3 can be expensive because of the need for high ratios of staff to children. In these cases, and when resources are limited, it can be more cost-effective to support parenting skills at home. However, in countries from Ethiopia to the United States high-quality programmes that typically start with targeting parents during the first 1000 days of their child's life and are then followed by day-care centres and preschool programmes for children aged 3–6 have substantially improved the development of the linguistic, cognitive, motor and socio-emotional skills that provide the foundation for education and employment later in life.

The bottom line is: investment in children's early years is one of the most cost-effective ways of producing an educated labour force capable of acquiring new skills. It also produces citizens who are less likely to require support from social assistance programmes or commit crimes and more likely to contribute to society, including by paying taxes through higher incomes. And because the costs of early intervention are a fraction of what would be otherwise required later for remedial education and welfare payments, it is also arguably the best way to equalise opportunities for children born into disadvantaged backgrounds.

### Learning for a Long Life

Every year I award thousands of degrees to students during graduation ceremonies at the London School of Economics and Political Science. Occasionally, some of the students are older than me. I am especially proud of these graduates because they are at the forefront of redefining our social contract. By embracing education later in life, they are opening up new possibilities for themselves both professionally and personally in a world of increasingly long and changeable careers.

People have talked about lifelong learning for decades, but the experience in most countries has been mixed. Today, though, in an era when careers will span 50–60 years and rapidly changing technology will change the nature of the work that needs doing, learning in adulthood is no longer a nice-to-have but an essential part of the social contract. Having been blocked from certain careers by the many bottlenecks and hurdles of traditional education, such as exams and streaming children into different tracks at a very young age, many want a second chance.[29] In addition, some adults turn to education to pursue their interests and for its life-enhancing qualities. To satisfy these needs, educational systems will have to become more permeable, flexible and adapted to the needs of adult learners, and they will need new ways to finance education throughout life. So what is the best way to provide this?

Adult learning differs in important ways from the education of the young.[30] In fact, educational specialists have a different word for it – andragogy – which means 'leading adults', in contrast to pedagogy, which translates as 'leading children'.[31] For a start, adult brains are less efficient at learning new things than children's brains are (think how easily a 5-year-old learns a new language compared to a 50-year-old). Adults also have many other challenges to deal with, including work, family, childcare as well as the lost income from taking time off to study. However, adults also bring with them experience, which can enhance (as well as encumber) their learning and that of those learning with them.

With children, a hierarchal relationship between teacher and student is generally the norm, and the curriculum is highly structured to build skills in a sequential fashion. Adults, by contrast, work best in a collaborative environment where they are equal partners in the process, and learn better through active participation and problem-solving. Even more so than young people, they must be intrinsically motivated to learn and will tend to focus on what is relevant to their goals.

Furthermore, whereas the education of young people is typically provided by schools or colleges, there is a much wider range of institutions where adults can learn and develop their skills. In most countries, in fact, it is employers who provide the bulk of adult training, followed by institutions such as further-education or community colleges, technical and vocational schools, private training providers, universities and trade unions. More adults are also turning to online providers, both formal and informal, and many educational institutions now offer training via the internet.

This is no bad thing. Training provided by employers is often the most effective because it is usually very well tailored to the needs of the labour market. Employers wish to recruit and retain the best workers and have an interest in training their employees to meet the needs of the business and increase productivity. Companies also make sure that the benefits typically exceed the costs of their investment in training. However, training also makes workers more attractive to competitors, so employers may underinvest for fear of losing talent they have trained to rivals. For example, in areas where skills are in short supply, like computing and information technology, workers with recent training may be tempted to jump ship.

The training provided by educational institutions, on the other hand, such as further education and community colleges, vocational training programmes and various commercial providers, is far less consistent, and some can be very poor. There are many examples around the world of low-quality training providers with grand names like Global Technology Institute that charge unwitting students high fees for poor programmes. The challenge for adult learners is to assess the quality of what they're being offered and its relevance to their careers. This is another reason why programmes most closely linked to employers tend to be the most effective.

Nevertheless, the explosion of learning opportunities enabled by technology has helped make training more accessible and cost-effective around the world. Massive online courses, instructional videos on YouTube, TED talks and online university programmes have made knowledge available on a global scale. Interestingly, the largest markets for distance learning are in countries such as India, China and Brazil, where students can access world-class education on affordable terms.[32] Such online learning options now have millions of users, though completion rates for most large-scale courses are below 10 per cent.[33] Online programmes with a common start date, peer group and a greater sense of community have been more successful at getting students to stay the course and achieve certification of their knowledge. This is because, however effective online education may be at transmitting information, if people do not have the ability to absorb and make the knowledge their own, as well as mechanisms for engaging practically with the content and certifying their achievement, it is less useful and enduring.

Overall, though, adult learning works. Rigorous studies that evaluate the impact of adult learning on employment prospects have demonstrated benefits. A recent study synthesised the findings of 207 evaluations of 857 programmes to reskill workers – referred to as 'active labour market programmes'.[34] A major finding was that the benefit of a programme tended to be small in the short term (1–2 years), but highly significant in improving employment in the long term (2 or more years after completion). Chapter 5 will say more about how training can help workers reskill to cope with unemployment, technological disruptions in the labour market and the need to change jobs over a long career.

One major challenge is getting people to participate. Paradoxically, those who engage in adult learning tend to be younger, more educated and better off financially, so those who need it the least. This largely reflects a positive previous experience of education, hence their willingness and ability to afford re-engaging later in life. It is older, less-educated workers who stand to benefit the most if they can be persuaded to participate, but it is they who are more likely to lack the necessary confidence and/or the means to do so. Perversely, those who receive the least adult training are those who are unskilled; employers focus their resources on higher-skilled employees. Only 2 in every 5 adults have access to education and training opportunities each year in advanced economies, and those with low skills are three times less likely to participate.[35] Workers in low-skill jobs are the least likely to have access to training from their employer, especially if they work in a small or medium-sized firm.

This is especially problematic for workers with outdated skills or in jobs that are potentially automatable, such as hospitality workers and data-entry clerks, sales reps and secretaries, drivers and those who work in manufacturing and warehousing. There is a high risk that their skills will become obsolete and yet they are least likely to participate in training.[36] Identifying and supporting these workers to acquire new skills should ideally happen before they become unemployed. Some countries and companies are good at this (more on this in Chapter 5), but most are not.

We have discussed the need for a rebalancing of our education system towards early-years and lifelong learning, and we have seen that there are many effective ways of delivering what is needed. One major question remains, though.

## *Who Should Pay?*

In almost all countries it is widely accepted that primary and secondary education should be available to all for free, but as we have already noted early-years education is traditionally thought to be the responsibility of families. Given recent research on its wider social benefits, the gains in equality of opportunity it provides and the relatively low cost of provision, there is surely a strong case for it to receive more public support. Making early-years education a key element of the social contract, at least for the poorest families, makes both economic and social sense.

The financing of tertiary and adult education is far more complex, however. The state benefits from a more productive workforce that pays higher taxes and costs less in social benefits, health care and policing. But the costs of tertiary and adult education can be high and the benefits that accrue to the individual are more apparent than those for society. Moreover, the fact that individuals who participate in adult learning can expect to earn higher wages as a result suggests that they should share in the costs of that education. On the other hand, employers also benefit from their workers being more highly trained, so perhaps the burden should fall on them. But as we have noted above, employers are unlikely to invest in training if they fear the result will be their workers leaving the company for greener pastures. These complexities all point to the need for a formula by which the relatively higher spending needed for adult learning is somehow shared between individuals, employers and society.[37]

However, these same complexities – the fact that the provision and funding of adult learning is already highly fragmented between individuals, employers, unions, private training providers and the state – make an assessment of how much funding is required and how it is currently distributed very difficult. The best available data for adults over the age of 25, excluding those in higher education, in selected advanced economies is in Figure 7.

## Figure 7. Adult learning is funded from multiple sources

Distribution of funding for adult learning by source of finance

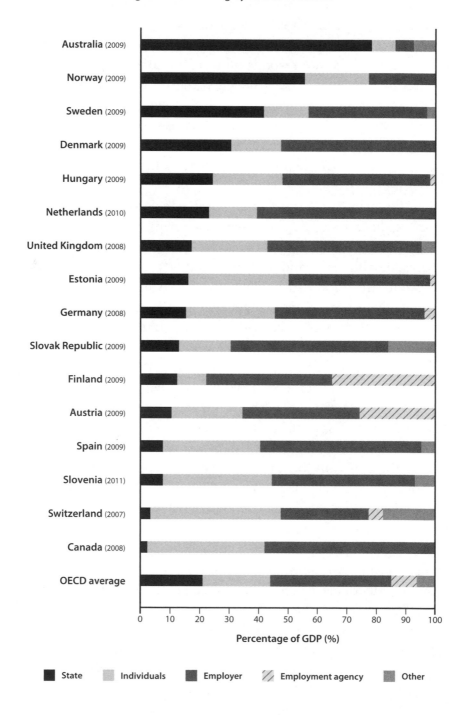

Percentage of GDP (%)

State | Individuals | Employer | Employment agency | Other

On average just 0.9 per cent of these countries' GDP is spent on adult learning, compared to 2.6 per cent for primary, 1.3 per cent for upper-secondary and 1.6 per cent for tertiary education. Within adult learning, public funding varies substantially across countries – from 2 per cent in Canada to 78 per cent in Australia – but in most places the state pays the least (22.1 per cent on average), followed by individuals (24.7 per cent), with the largest share borne by employers (44.7 per cent). Overall spending and government support for adult learning are likely to be far lower in developing countries, where efforts are focused on achieving universal primary and secondary education and fewer employers invest in training.

While countries use a variety of mechanisms to promote adult learning, these essentially revolve around providing subsidies to firms and/or individuals. Many provide tax incentives to encourage firms to train their workers.[38] Several countries (Germany, Austria, Singapore, the Nordics) are introducing tax credits, analogous to research and development tax credits, whereby the costs of training are seen as an investment in human capital which reduces the firm's tax bill. Some countries (such as the US and the UK) provide loans to individuals on concessional terms or have no age limits on eligibility for student loans. Many countries also tax employers via levies (0.1–2.5 per cent of payroll) to finance training programmes paid for by the state but provided by employers. To encourage trained workers to stay, employers often specify that those leaving before a certain amount of time has passed have to repay the costs of the training they have received. Singapore is now compensating employers with 90 per cent of the costs of retraining workers over the age of 40 and paying some of the wages of employees undergoing reskilling.

Persuading companies to improve the skills of their workers ultimately makes the most sense as research on vocational training consistently finds that employer-based training is the most effective, but employers only have incentives to train workers up to a point. To encourage them to train employees to the level that might benefit society the most, they need as many additional incentives as possible, especially in labour markets where workers change jobs more frequently, such as technology or nursing. The case for incentives is especially strong for workers from disadvantaged groups and those working in small and medium-sized enterprises which lack the scale to deliver their own training.[39]

What is critical is that the incentives are focused directly on the specific needs of adult learners and prospective employers. So, for example, providing funding based solely on the number of individuals trained, which is a widespread practice, does not actually achieve what is required. In contrast, I recall visiting a successful vocational training programme for construction workers in Nepal where the private training provider got paid a third of the fee when students enrolled, another third when they got a job and the final third when they had been in the job over a year. Estonia, meanwhile, allocates funds in response to performance, weighing factors such as the dropout rate, the quality of the training and how well aligned the training is with the needs of the business sector. In the United States, over 100 training providers and universities offer income-sharing agreements whereby students get trained for free and promise to pay over a percentage of their future income to cover the costs.[40]

A few countries, such as the UK and Singapore, have experimented with programmes whereby every citizen is given a voucher which they can use for the sole purpose of adult learning. For example, Singapore's FutureLearn programme gives each Singaporean $500 annually to be used for training which they can cumulate over time. In both the UK and Singapore, however, the programmes have faced problems with fraud. Corrupt or fake providers have cashed in public vouchers from unwitting students while providing little or no training. Singapore is persevering and regulating training providers more intensely. But the overall sums of money involved in these experiments is fairly modest, which limits the extent to which new skills (rather than new hobbies) can actually be acquired.

## A Fairer System

Current systems of educational funding are highly unequal because they provide the most public support to those who remain in the system the longest. Consider the situation in France, for example: on average, a 20-year-old in 2018 received about €120,000 of public investment in education from pre-school to university.[41] But someone who left education at the age of 16 only benefited from €65,000–70,000 of investment, while someone who went to the top universities received €200,000–300,000 in public subsidy. Such disparity in investment in the next generation often compounds existing inequalities of opportunity. So what would a fairer system look like?

One solution could be to give every 18-year-old an entitlement for lifelong learning. In the UK this could amount to about £40,000, in the US roughly $50,000. This might be a grant or a loan that could be used for university or vocational training at regulated and certified institutions. Society would invest in young people by giving them the means to acquire qualifications to meet their needs over a lifetime. If it were provided as a loan, governments could justify offering it at their own cost of borrowing on the basis that it was an investment in human capital that would increase future tax revenues.[42] Rather than graduating with a burden of debt, every young person would start life with an entitlement empowering them to invest in their own employability.

The fact is that in future most people will have to acquire more education at different stages in their lives to enable them to thrive in a longer career. The providers of that education will be more varied – universities, further-education and vocational institutions, online providers, commercial training providers and various combinations of these – and ideally closely linked to employers. Providers will have to adapt to this new world by providing educational credits that can be added up across institutions and over time. This will allow individuals to build formal qualifications in a flexible way, combining different providers over time. More of this education will need to be part time, more will need to be partly online and partly in the classroom, and the hours at which it is provided will need to be flexible to suit the needs of adult learners. Certification of learning will also need to evolve to include online certificates, 'nano' degrees, 'mini-masters' and a variety of vocational qualifications.

To enable this change, everyone (individuals, employers and training providers) needs to be better informed about current and future labour market trends – in other words, about what the future actually holds for them if they do not retrain. As well as expanding support for early-years education, governments need to put in place incentives and endowments that increase spending from the current inadequate levels. Individuals will need to be supported through these career transitions with career advice, information about where jobs will be in the future and which training providers can best prepare them. And employers will need to recognise that in a fast-changing workplace adaptability is more important than experience. They should be more interested in what workers can do in the future rather than what they have done in the past. These kinds of educational opportunities, which prepare citizens for their new reality, must lie at the heart of a new social contract.

# 4

# Health

Being healthy is the most important determinant of our well-being. Physical and mental health (subjective well-being as it is called in the academic research) rank at the top of every major study of happiness across the world. Ultimately, this is why every society aspires to provide health care for its population. And because the costs of providing health care are reduced when a large population pools its resources, and because a healthy labour force is also good for the economy, the social contract in every society includes health care in some form or another.

While in many countries there is public support for spending on health care, the social contract in health is under pressure everywhere. The twin forces behind this are ageing and technology. People are living longer and require more care as they get older. Meanwhile, technological innovations in the form of new drugs, medical devices and treatments offer longer and better lives, but often cost a great deal. Most people now expect to be active and independent well into old age. How to meet these rising expectations while maintaining universal and equitable access to care for those with the greatest health needs is one of the biggest policy challenges of our time.

The major questions the social contract in every health system faces are the following. How much health care can societies afford to provide to everyone? Is there a minimum that should be guaranteed and, if so, how do we decide what that is? How should the costs of that provision be shared between the individual, families, employers and the state? And should decisions about health be left to individuals or should society have some say where there are wider public interests at stake?

## Defining a Minimum for Universal Health Care

Almost every country aspires to provide its citizens with a basic level of affordable, good-quality health care, but in practice the scope of that provision varies enormously depending on what the state can, or chooses to, afford. The World Health Organization has set out what it considers a universally available essential health package should consist of: prenatal care, immunisations against and treatment of communicable diseases such as pneumonia and tuberculosis, bed nets against malaria, treatment of cardiovascular illness and access to hospitals, medical staff and medicines.[1] This definition has been adopted in most developing countries. At the other end of the spectrum, the National Health Service in the UK is committed to providing health care to all citizens free at the point of delivery from 'cradle to grave'.

The World Health Organization recommends governments spend about 5 per cent of GDP to achieve this minimum universal coverage,[2] and most countries are raising spending on health, except in low-income countries where populations are growing fast and there remains a dependency on aid to meet minimum health requirements. Spending per person varies enormously – from $2937 on average in high-income countries to only $41 in low-income countries.[3]

A large share of the spending on health goes on staff, and everywhere there are shortages. The International Labour Organisation estimates that 10.3 million additional health-care workers are required to close the current global shortfall, of which 7.1 million are needed in Asia and 2.8 million in Africa.[4] Many highly skilled health workers from developing countries emigrate to advanced economies, where demand for their services is growing and pay and career paths are more attractive. International agreements to try to manage the cross-border flow of health workers so as not to damage services in poor countries have not been successful.[5] Training more health workers globally and finding ways to increase their productivity through the use of technology are essential.

## How Should Health Care Be Provided?

In all countries some portion of health care is privately funded either directly or through the provision of insurance. Where insurance is not available or widely used, major health costs are often pooled across families and communities. However, it is common for all governments to intervene more heavily in health care than in other areas of the social contract, either through direct provision or through regulation.[6]

There are a number of reasons for this. One is that a purely free-market approach is in many respects unworkable. Most patients simply do not have the knowledge to make informed decisions about their needs and therefore rely heavily on better-informed medical professionals to advise them. And yet it is not unusual for those medical professionals to gain financially from their advice (in private systems) or to be completely insulated from the costs of their advice (in public systems or insurance-based systems).

Another is that medical insurance is fraught with challenges, most obviously that it is in the insurers' interests to exclude those who are sick to reduce their own costs. To incentivise those with insurance to be prudent, insurers use co-payments to control costs, reduce reckless behaviour and encourage greater individual responsibility.[7]

There is a third important reason that governments intervene in health care: many diseases are contagious. It is therefore clearly in the wider public interest to treat individuals – through vaccination, the sharing of information and the provision of sanitation and clean water – to prevent widespread infection.

Of course, the objective of these kinds of intervention is not (solely) to improve the health of individual patients, it is also to maximise the health of society as a whole. Indeed, in the public-health context, the interests or preferences of individuals may even be sacrificed for the wider benefit.

The coronavirus pandemic has brought the question of when it is legitimate for society to constrain the behaviour of individuals for the sake of public health to the fore. In many countries, for example in Asia, there was widespread acceptance of significant curtailments in citizens' freedom to travel, to see family and friends, and of mandatory surveillance and wearing of masks. In other places, especially the United States and some parts of Europe, people resisted such restrictions or (in many developing countries) couldn't afford to comply.[8] These reactions reflect how differently people view the social contract and the trade-offs between individual freedom versus public health.

In those countries that had experience of higher levels of general civic engagement (higher participation in elections, more trust in institutions and greater newspaper readership) there was higher compliance with mandatory social distancing measures and better health outcomes. A simulation for Italy found that if the entire country had had the same level of civic engagement as the most engaged quartile, the death rate from Covid-19 would have been ten times lower – even after controlling for variations in incomes, demography and health-care capacity.[9] In fact, analysis based on Google data on travel, restaurant reservations and consumption patterns found that people in many countries practised social distancing voluntarily and well before lockdowns were imposed.[10]

The state need not be the provider of universal basic health care; in practice countries use a variety of approaches, and even within a single country often have various ways of financing provision for different groups in society. There is no single, best way to organise the delivery of health care, and it is possible to achieve good health outcomes (and bad ones) under various structures.[11] Most advanced economies have publicly funded systems that provide shared insurance for health care or require people to have private insurance (which is highly regulated) and provide subsidies for the poor. In some countries, such as the UK, the state is the major supplier, but in much of continental Europe the state acts primarily as a funder of public and private services. Meanwhile in many emerging markets, such as China and India, a model is emerging whereby the poor are publicly funded and the better-off are offered insurance. Alternatively, employers can co-fund care with their employees, with the state filling in for those who are not employed, such as in the United States.

Most developing countries are still building their universal health systems.[12] Many are choosing a two-tier model whereby the poor and those in the informal sector are covered through a public system managed by the government and paid for through general taxation, sometimes supplemented by contributions from households. Those employed in the formal sector, meanwhile, contribute through a payroll tax to an insurance-based system, while the better-off have the option of buying insurance on the private market. It is in the poorest countries – where state capacity is limited – that people depend the most on private markets for health care. In some countries charitable organisations also play a major role, often in partnership with governments and the private sector.[13]

An example of an attempt to achieve universal basic health care in a large developing country can be found in India. In 2018 it launched a national health programme (called Ayushman Bharat) comprising two separate components. The first part aims to set up approximately 150,000 public health and wellness centres that will provide comprehensive primary care with basic services such as immunisation and treatment for contagious diseases. The second component is a national health insurance scheme that will provide cover of 500,000 rupees (approximately $7000) per family per year for secondary- and tertiary-care conditions such as heart disease or cancer. The scheme targets more than 500 million poor and vulnerable

people across the country, making it the largest completely
government funded scheme in the world.

China has also launched a public insurance-based scheme.
Interestingly, this is complemented by a thriving private market that in many cases derives from an older, more traditional
approach: in the past, villagers in China would pool their
resources when someone was critically ill. Ant Group (an affili-
ate of the Alibaba Group) has adapted this tradition for the
digital age by creating an online market for mutual insurance.
Most of the participants are of low income, and the scheme
pays out a lump sum of about $45,000 for the treatment of
100 critical illnesses with the costs shared equally by all other
participants.[14]

## Health Spending Is Only Going Up

The amount countries spend on health varies enormously
according to what they can afford, from an average of $200 per
person per year in India and $300 in China to European levels
of $3000–6000 (Figure 8). OECD countries spend about $4000
on health per person on average. As noted already, most of this
is spent by governments, with the private share tending to be
higher in low- and middle-income countries. Of course, spending most is not the same as spending wisely. The US spends
far more than any other country in the world (about $11,000
per person and 17 per cent of its GDP) but achieves poor outcomes in terms of access to care. US life expectancy is actually
one year less than the average of other advanced economies.
Many advanced economies have seen life expectancies plateau
in recent years, but the US is the only country where life expectancies, especially those of men, are actually declining.[15]

But while health spending varies widely between countries,
the evidence suggests that one characteristic is true across the
board: it is going to increase everywhere. Between 2000 and
2015, health spending in the OECD countries grew by 3 per
cent, and it is expected to continue to grow by 2.7 per cent

## Figure 8. Health spending per person varies greatly across countries

Health expenditure per person, 2018 (or nearest year)

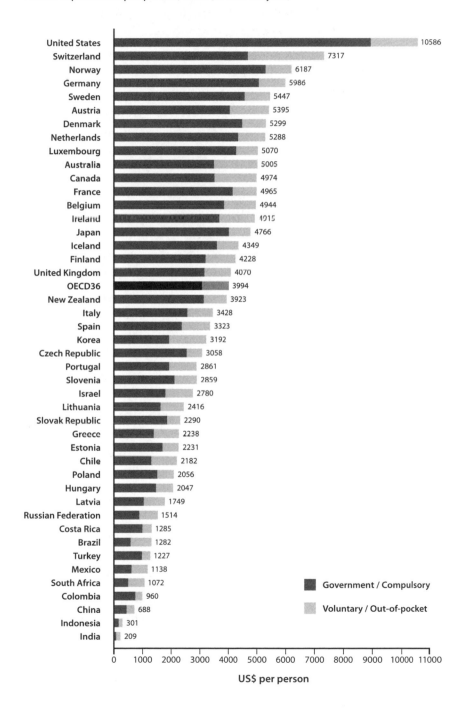

|  |  |
|---|---|
| United States | 10586 |
| Switzerland | 7317 |
| Norway | 6187 |
| Germany | 5986 |
| Sweden | 5447 |
| Austria | 5395 |
| Denmark | 5299 |
| Netherlands | 5288 |
| Luxembourg | 5070 |
| Australia | 5005 |
| Canada | 4974 |
| France | 4965 |
| Belgium | 4944 |
| Ireland | 4915 |
| Japan | 4766 |
| Iceland | 4349 |
| Finland | 4228 |
| United Kingdom | 4070 |
| OECD36 | 3994 |
| New Zealand | 3923 |
| Italy | 3428 |
| Spain | 3323 |
| Korea | 3192 |
| Czech Republic | 3058 |
| Portugal | 2861 |
| Slovenia | 2859 |
| Israel | 2780 |
| Lithuania | 2416 |
| Slovak Republic | 2290 |
| Greece | 2238 |
| Estonia | 2231 |
| Chile | 2182 |
| Poland | 2056 |
| Hungary | 2047 |
| Latvia | 1749 |
| Russian Federation | 1514 |
| Costa Rica | 1285 |
| Brazil | 1282 |
| Turkey | 1227 |
| Mexico | 1138 |
| South Africa | 1072 |
| Colombia | 960 |
| China | 688 |
| Indonesia | 301 |
| India | 209 |

Government / Compulsory

Voluntary / Out-of-pocket

US$ per person

from 2015 to 2030.[16] Moreover, health spending in most countries is growing faster than the population and faster than the economy. This means that health consumes a growing share of government budgets over time – now averaging 15 per cent of public spending in the OECD. Public support for this tends to be high, but some advanced economies have little room to raise taxes further – in countries such as France and Denmark the state already absorbs about half of GDP. Most developing countries have more room to manoeuvre, particularly given the evidence that more stable public funding is associated with better performance on achieving universal health care.[17] We will return to the question of how these increases can be afforded, but first we must understand the causes.

Most people assume that the ageing of populations is the main cause of rising costs and that these increases are therefore inevitable. It is indeed true that health systems tend to spend more on the old than on the young (Figure 9). This demographic change matters especially for middle-income countries, where populations are ageing rapidly and the burden of disease is shifting from infectious diseases (like malaria or tuberculosis) to chronic diseases (like heart attacks and cancers) that are more expensive to treat. Ageing also moderately increases the costs of acute care (since treating an old person who has had an accident costs more), but has a huge impact on the costs of long-term care.[18] And yet, with the exception of the highly inefficient US system, most countries spend only about 4–5 times as much on the average 80-year-old as on the average 20-year-old (as Figure 9 below shows), which is significantly less than you might expect.[19] So ageing alone cannot account for the rapid growth in health spending.

In richer countries, two other factors, mentioned at the start of the chapter, are critical: one is that expectations of higher quality (and thus more expensive) care are rising. Some of the biggest increases in health spending are projected in countries like Turkey, Korea and the Slovak Republic, where public expectations are growing most. But the bigger culprit

**Figure 9. Health spending rises with age**

Per capita health care spending by age group in eight high-income countries

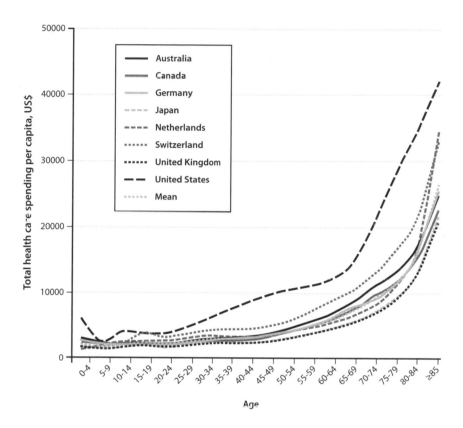

for rising health spending is technology: new medical technologies, such as drugs or devices that improve or extend life, tend to be more expensive.[20] This is in part because developing new drugs and clinical trials are expensive, but also because competition is often weak in the industries that produce new medical technologies.

There is an expression: 'Demography is destiny.' This means that age patterns are impossible to change quickly and so their effects are inevitable. But there is nothing inevitable about technology driving health-care costs up. Societies can make choices about what treatments they choose to fund, how drug and technology prices are negotiated, how health services are delivered and whether lower-cost interventions might be used. It is therefore possible to contain the costs of health care.[21] For example, many countries have expanded the roles that community health workers, pharmacists and nurses play in delivering care, thereby lessening the need for more expensive doctors, without any adverse effect on health outcomes. Using generic drugs is another mechanism for managing costs.[22] How providers are compensated for treatments also has a huge impact – whether for each intervention, for treatment of a disease, by individual treated or through a payment for keeping a person healthy.[23]

But containing costs takes us only so far. The more challenging question is how health technologies are rationed – which interventions are provided as part of the social contract and which must be paid for by the individual if they can afford them.

## How Should Health Systems Ration Demand?

Every health-care system in the world struggles every day with the question of how best to ration its resources. Demand for health care is always growing as incomes rise. How much can be spent publicly is constrained by how much one can tax the population. In systems dominated by the private sector individuals decide how much they want to spend (either out of pocket or through the type of insurance they buy) and so resources are allocated by market mechanisms. Put another way, they are rationed by income and how much people can afford. Unsurprisingly, the wealthy in private systems get better care than the poor. In publicly funded systems, which give greater weight to equity, it is the social contract that has to decide what gets paid for by society and how it is delivered. It must also decide whether everyone is entitled to the same services, or whether health care should be allocated on some other basis – to those in greatest need, for example, or where it is most cost-effective.

The mechanisms used by health systems for rationing care are various.[24] Some use co-payments – making patients pay something towards their treatment so they are encouraged to take costs into account – although this tends to most adversely affect the poor. Some use queueing as a way to prioritise who gets treated first. By making people wait several weeks for an appointment or many months for a procedure, those who can afford it are encouraged to turn to private options. For example, in the UK median waiting times for admitted treatment increased from 7.6 weeks in 2008 to 10.1 weeks in 2019. In Sweden, despite a law requiring a maximum waiting time of 90 days, more than 20 per cent of patients wait longer than that. In both countries demand for private health insurance has grown as public queues have grown longer.[25] Rationing by queueing focuses resources on those with lower incomes, although the poor are also adversely affected by delays.

In the end, decisions must be made about which technologies will be paid for collectively as part of the social contract and which will not. To do so, about two thirds of advanced economies and a growing number of developing countries use independent experts to assess how effective a treatment is relative to its costs.[26] There are usually two steps: first, a medical assessment of whether a treatment is effective; second, an evaluation of whether it is in the public interest to pay for the intervention. Such 'health technology assessments' are used to create positive lists of what will be paid for (such as specific drugs or overall categories of intervention such as primary care services) and negative lists of what will not be covered. Health technology assessments are the practical manifestation of the social contract in health.

What is excluded from the social contract is especially revealing. High-cost medicines with low therapeutic value rarely make the grade. Nor do interventions such as surgery for weight loss, where the risk of inappropriate use is high. Likewise, alternative medicines, spa treatments and interventions provided by non-physicians, such as psychological treatment, are excluded in many countries. Dental care is often excluded, as are treatments that are cosmetic, such as orthodontics or breast surgery. Some countries restrict access to fertility treatments to heterosexual couples. Many countries do not pay for treatments that most people can afford, such as over-the-counter medicines or glasses. Asking individuals to carry these costs presumes they can judge their efficacy and can afford the costs.[27]

Deciding which interventions to include is more complicated. How are the benefits and costs assessed? Countries use different criteria to assess the benefits of a treatment, such as whether it reduces risk of death or degree of illness, or whether it promotes longevity or quality of life. Weighed alongside this are economic evaluations of its immediate cost and, for example, the potential savings it affords in the form of reduced sickness leave or higher productivity. Because these assessments can involve life-and-death decisions and a great deal of money, they can be very controversial and subject to extensive lobbying by commercial interests and by patients. It is therefore important that decisions are taken by independent experts, are subject to scrutiny and transparency, and that conflicts of interest are carefully managed.

Invariably, decision makers must choose between a range of possible interventions. In order to decide between, say, paying for a new drug or paying instead for a procedure enabled by a new medical technology, it is necessary to have a common metric to compare their relative efficacy. One of the most widely used is the incremental cost per quality-adjusted life year (or QALY), which means essentially a year in good health. By this measure, a new medical device that adds five QALYs is more valuable than a new drug that costs the same amount of money but might increase the quality of life for just six months. The use of cost per QALY (or some variation thereof) enables health systems to prioritise and spend public money most cost-effectively, although some argue that QALYs are unfair, since people's health may vary according to their circumstances.[28]

So, how much should society pay for another year of good health? Many countries avoid answering this question because a specific number is sure to be controversial, and they worry that producers of new health technologies will use it to guide their pricing strategy. The World Health Organization, however, has suggested that per capita income is a good proxy to assess affordability of each additional year of life.[29] A health intervention that costs one to three times a country's average income per person can be considered cost-effective, while one that costs the same or less than the average income per person can be considered very cost-effective. Health interventions that cost more than three times the average income per person should not be considered cost effective, and on that basis can be excluded from the social contract.[30]

While the WHO's recommendations are very useful as a guide for policy, very few countries are as explicit about where they place this important threshold. But some do. For example, in Hungary and Korea the state will fund a health intervention that delivers an additional year in good health at a cost of 2–3 times income per capita. A major advantage of linking one's threshold to income per capita is that as countries grow richer, they have a clear criterion for deciding which additional health interventions become affordable. Other countries set a simple financial threshold for each additional year of quality life delivered by an intervention – €18,000 in Poland, €26,500 in the Slovak Republic and £20,000–30,000 in the UK.

Being explicit in this way is transparent and fair, and it achieves the most good with the resources available. By the same token, the risk of not being explicit is that those who allocate resources are less easily held to account and more susceptible to outside influences. Even in the UK, where the National Institute for Health and Care Excellence, which makes these decisions, has an explicitly stated threshold, political pressure can still result in misallocation of resources. For example, lobbying by cancer patients resulted in the government establishing the Cancer Drugs Fund to pay for expensive treatments that did not meet the NHS's criteria for cost-effectiveness. The treatments paid for by the fund added about 5600 additional years to the lives of cancer patients; had that money been spent on other interventions that met the National Health Service's criteria, 21,645 additional years of healthy life would have been gained.[31]

Another difficult question is how health spending should be rationed across generations. Some argue that we are all entitled to a 'normal' span of good health (around 70 years), which is why people often feel differently about the death of a young person than that of someone who has lived to old age. This notion of a 'fair innings' has been used by some to justify giving higher priority to the treatment of the young, who are on this basis more deserving, and lower priority to the elderly, despite the fact that good health in old age necessitates more care.[32]

One way to avoid comparing the value of different people's lives in this utilitarian manner is to think about rationing as something we must do over the span of an individual's lifetime rather than a competition for resources between individuals at any single point in time. If each of us was given a fixed amount by society to spend on health care over our lives, most of us would probably spend more on improving our health and well-being earlier on, in order to increase our quality of life and longevity, rather than save it up in order to be able to spend our allocation on expensive treatments that add a few months in old age. The notion of lifetime rationing arrives at a similar conclusion but without suggesting that the young are more deserving than the old because it 'operates within a life rather than between lives'.[33]

If this still makes you feel uncomfortable, consider the very different ways that acute care has been rationed in the UK compared to the Medicare system, which is the government medical insurance programme for the elderly in the US.[34] The 1980s was a time of limited resources for the NHS, so physicians in the UK coped, not by reducing the quality of care, but by using the principles of lifetime rationing and cost-effectiveness to limit quantity through waiting lists.[35] In the UK it is accepted that some treatments that may be beneficial are too expensive for their provision to be justifiable, and so the NHS does not provide them, even if the patient is willing and able to pay – although there is nothing to prevent them from getting private care. In the US, by contrast, those covered by Medicare are thought to have paid for their entitlement through past contributions, so rationing is unacceptable and cost-effectiveness is immaterial. And so while Medicare continues to provide generous coverage to the elderly, there is increasing rationing for those who rely on Medicaid – the state programme for the poor which mainly benefits low-income adults and children but also pays for the long-term care of those elderly who cannot afford the costs. As a result, Medicaid spends about five times more on every old person in long-term care than it spends on every poor child.[36]

## A More Digital Future for Health

So far, we have focused on the way that technology is raising the costs of care. But what about innovations that might reduce costs?

The coronavirus pandemic forced a rapid shift towards digital care – things like online consultations with doctors and the use of mobile phone apps for contact tracing and monitoring of patients – in countries that had the infrastructure. Many of these digital tools were already under development, but the pandemic accelerated their adoption. For many richer countries, these and emerging digital solutions offer a clear opportunity to manage the rising costs of their health systems. For developing countries that are still at the early stages of building their health systems, meanwhile, these tools could be transformative.

Many developing countries will never be able to achieve universal health care based on the prevailing model in which medical interventions take place in dedicated facilities overseen by highly trained doctors. Digital technologies open up the possibility of completely new models of care, such as patients having access to high-quality information and controlling their own medical records, artificial intelligence to aid diagnosis and robotic delivery of many procedures.[37]

It is now possible to measure vital signs like temperature, blood pressure and oxygen saturation at home at very low cost, obviating the need to visit a clinic. This is especially important for the treatment of chronic health problems such as diabetes, for which home-based care is more effective and less costly than regular visits to a health facility. Increasingly, less complex ailments that are now treated as outpatient care will be managed in the home, remotely, using smartphones, and it will be possible to receive treatment from a doctor or health-care professional located anywhere in the world. (One effect of this may be to reduce the pressure on health-care workers migrating in pursuit of greater earnings).

Wearable devices, meanwhile, will make it possible to monitor patients remotely, with the data gathered by such devices becoming a vital tool for both patients and health-care professionals. Electronic records compatible across digital platforms will enable more-personalised treatments. India is already exploiting this opportunity, based on the biometric universal identity programme used to deliver its health insurance scheme. Imagine a world in which every health worker is equipped with a device that provides access to their patients' health records, that responds to the inputting of key symptoms data with recommended diagnoses and treatments and that can immediately order any relevant medicines. In isolated parts of Rwanda and Tanzania, drones are already being used to deliver vaccines and blood.

One of the major costs to health systems is that between 30 and 50 per cent of patients prescribed medications for long-term conditions do not adhere to their treatment. Fixing this could result in less medication being wasted, fewer hospital admissions, plus faster recovery and improved quality of life and productivity for patients.[38] Here too technology may be able to help. Text and mobile phone applications can be used to remind patients to take their medicines, exercise and do physiotherapy. Another promising intervention is an electronic medication bottle which registers the dates and times when it is opened and reminds patients to take their medicines at the right time.

But the social contract will need to change if this new world of digital medicine is to work. Probably the most important question we will have to answer is who owns and controls patients' data and how its privacy and confidentiality can be assured. This is an unavoidable issue because many of the wider benefits of digitalisation – for research and monitoring public health – rely specifically on pooling and sharing data. There have already been cases of violations of privacy in the pursuit of developing better treatments.[39] Many people are thinking about how to develop a set of principles that ensure each individual has control of their own data while allowing the wider public benefits to be realised.[40] There is also a growing awareness of the need to address bias in the algorithms that are fed by this data: currently most of the research that underpins their design has been conducted on white men, rendering them potentially ill-suited to the diagnosis and treatment of women and people from different ethnic groups.

It is likely that countries will arrive at different decisions on the balance between individual privacy and collective benefit. During the coronavirus pandemic citizens in many Asian countries willingly accepted their governments having access to personal data for the purpose of contact tracing, whereas in Europe there was a preference for decentralised systems that specifically prevented governments from having a central source of information. In democratic countries there is an emerging consensus that citizens should control their own data and their permission be required for it to be used for any wider purpose. But there is wide variation in practice and the situation is still evolving. It may be necessary to have an approach whereby some data (such as having an illness that is stigmatised) is more protected than other data that clearly serves a public purpose (such as having an infectious disease).

Despite the challenges, digital provision offers a real opportunity to deliver better health care at lower costs, and at the very least liberate doctors from some of the more routine aspects of care such as taking patients' blood pressure or temperature. This will allow them to focus on the higher-quality human interactions with patients that ensure adherence to treatment plans and ultimately better outcomes. This combination of 'high tech' and 'high touch' may be the way to reconcile cost and quality in the future of health care, but however successful and efficient the provision may be, the best outcomes will come not from the treatment of illness, but from its prevention. This takes us to the heart of the social contract.

### *Individual and Social Responsibilities – Where Is the Balance?*

The saying 'An ounce of prevention is worth a pound of cure' is usually attributed to Benjamin Franklin. It is strongly supported by the evidence. In advanced economies the average return on investment in preventative health-care interventions is 14.3 per cent.[41] When public health measures are national or backed by legislation, the return on investment rises to 27.2 per cent. We also know that the majority of the improvements in infant mortality and life expectancy are determined by factors like environment, nutrition, income and lifestyle, and are only fractionally affected by the health system. There can be no doubt that directing public resources towards the improvement of nutrition, the promotion of healthy behaviours and early screening for illnesses are some of the best investments a society can make.[42]

As infectious diseases decline because of effective public health interventions, non-communicable diseases such as cardiovascular illness, cancer, respiratory conditions and diabetes have emerged as the leading cause of death worldwide.[43] Many of these are associated with smoking, alcohol and obesity. They do not necessarily affect overall health expenditure since those who smoke or are obese tend to die earlier.[44] Nonetheless, these and other unhealthy behaviours impose massive direct costs on the health-care system and have devastating consequences for the lives of individuals.

The economic costs of smoking were estimated at over $1.4 trillion globally (equivalent to 1.8 per cent of GDP in 2012), consisting of $1 trillion lost in productivity and $422 billion in treatment costs.[45] Alcohol consumption imposed economic costs of about $600 billion (equivalent to 1 per cent of GDP in 2009) on middle- and high-income countries. In the UK obesity costs the National Health Service £5.1 billion every year, with the wider costs to society estimated at over £25 billion. Smoking costs the NHS £2.5 billion, and the cost to society is over £11 billion. Alcohol consumption costs UK society about £52 billion, with around £3 billion falling on the NHS.[46]

This all raises an important question. If we care about good health, should more resources and interventions be focused on improving people's circumstances, preventing illnesses and changing individual behaviour? If people drink and smoke, fail to exercise, eat a poor diet, do not take their medications or skip appointments, thereby imposing costs on others through the higher taxes required to pay for their health care, does society not have a right to influence their behaviour? Does it even have a responsibility to intervene? Should health systems, for example, find ways to make individuals carry some responsibility for the costs of these lifestyle diseases?

Making individuals who engage in risky behaviours cover the costs of their health care is problematic. For a start, deciding which behaviours qualify as sufficiently risky is difficult. Eating junk food? Sunbathing? Riding a motorcycle? In the case of riding a motorcycle or, say, skydiving, it may make sense to require people to take out insurance to help defray the health costs of risky behaviours.[47] But those who engage in behaviours that lead to drug addiction or alcoholism often do so as a result of circumstances beyond their control or as a result of genetic predispositions or environmental factors.

Nonetheless, in countries where health costs are shared, the social contract generally does place an obligation on individuals to take some responsibility for their own health. The promotion of healthier lifestyles, both within and beyond the health sector, is considered a legitimate area for society to intervene in individual behaviour.

Not everyone agrees with such 'paternalism'.[48] Some argue, in the tradition of John Stuart Mill, that true liberty means freedom from all restraint as long as there is no harm to anyone else.[49] Others, such as Rawls and Sen, argue that freedom is about being able to decide for yourself rather than having decisions made for you, but that this kind of autonomy includes the freedom to accept reasonable constraints on one's own behaviour that make everyone better off.[50] On that basis, a free individual would agree to interventions such as taxing unhealthy products (like cigarettes), laws requiring healthy behaviours (wearing seat belts, helmets or masks), incentives for good health (lower insurance costs for those who exercise regularly) and social marketing campaigns to promote healthy behaviours, because these measures benefit society as a whole. The state may have to demonstrate that people have inadequate information (for example by labelling unhealthy products) or there may be a wider public interest (such as reducing crime or traffic accidents) to justify public intervention.[51]

In my view, there is a hierarchy of what society can ask of individuals. In the case of infectious diseases or a pandemic, there is a clear public interest and therefore justification for strong state actions that might override individual preferences. The imposition of lockdowns, travel restrictions and the wearing of masks in response to Covid-19 are clear examples of this. At the next level are behaviours that are not contagious (such as smoking or being obese) but have an impact on the rest of society because they result in higher spending on health or welfare support. I find it difficult to argue that someone addicted to cigarettes or bombarded with junk food advertising or living in a community without access to fresh food or recreational facilities is 'free'. At a minimum, society has the right to support behaviours that will improve healthy outcomes for the population as a whole. This is sometimes referred to as altering the choice architecture – the incentives people face – because society owes everyone a fair chance at having a healthy life.

There are various ways the state can do this. Taxation, for example, has proven very effective. In developing countries, on average, tax changes that result in a 10 per cent increase in prices reduce tobacco consumption by 5 per cent,[52] alcohol consumption by 6 per cent,[53] and sugary beverage consumption by 12 per cent.[54] One study found that in the US a tax of 1 cent per ounce on sugary beverages could save $23 billion in health-care costs over ten years.[55] In the UK and Mexico similar benefits have been estimated if taxes were used to reduce obesity and diabetes.[56] If all countries increased their excise taxes to raise the prices of tobacco, alcohol and sugary beverages by 50 per cent, over 50 million premature deaths could be averted worldwide over the next 50 years while raising over $20 trillion in additional revenues.[57] It is also possible to pay people to make healthier decisions – for example, in Latin America, cash transfer schemes are sometimes conditional on vaccination of children.

Other kinds of interventions aimed at encouraging behavioural change can also work well, although it is always hardest to have an impact in deprived communities. One programme whose purpose is to help people better manage chronic diseases has been delivered to over a million people in 30 countries. Participants meet in small-group workshops to learn about managing pain and depression, exercise, appropriate use of medications, nutrition, evaluating new treatments and communication with those who care for them. A rigorous evaluation found that those who participated had less-frequent hospital stays and fewer nights in hospital relative to those who did not participate, and the cost savings were substantial.[58] Quitlines, which use regular phone calls with counsellors to help people stop smoking, have proven effective in many countries and among different populations at very low cost. School-based programmes that encourage exercise and behavioural support to reduce calorie intake have also been shown to be cost-effective in improving quality-adjusted life years.[59]

Many countries have used 'nudges' to encourage people to make better choices, although the evidence that these interventions last is mixed.[60] These are often inconspicuous and seemingly small interventions in one's environment or in the way options are presented that are designed to harness people's unconscious preferences and patterns of behaviour. Probably the most effective nudges are default options whereby an individual is asked whether they wish to opt out of a desired behaviour or choice rather than opt in to it.[61] The human tendency to inertia means that individuals tend to stick with the default option, whatever it might be. Thus, organ donation tends to be four times higher in countries where schemes operate that presume consent unless people choose otherwise. Default options have also been effective at increasing the take-up of flu vaccinations and HIV tests, and enrolment in savings or pension schemes. Such interventions tend to be more effective when they require a one-off behaviour change (such as a vaccination) and less so when permanent behaviour change is required (an alteration in diet or exercise regime). Often nudges work best when complemented by changes in the law (like banning smoking in buildings) and public information campaigns (such as labelling cigarette packets).

But while encouraging healthier individual behaviour is important, a great deal of research reveals that a suite of other, social factors are even more important. Unhealthy lifestyles are closely associated with growing up and living in poverty.[62] In every country in the world the rich live longer and healthier lives than the poor. This reflects the fact that they have better opportunities to achieve good health. These opportunities arise from: the quality of a child's experiences during the early years, education and the building of personal and community resilience, good-quality employment and working conditions, having sufficient income to lead a healthy life, living in a healthy environment, and public health measures around issues like smoking and obesity.[63] Effective interventions in these six areas will massively reduce the cost of better health for all. And yet none of these factors relate to the quality of the health-care system; instead, they are determined by the other aspects of the social contract described in this book.

This chapter has shown how a new social contract in health might be shaped. At its core is a guaranteed minimum of primary care and public health benefits for all. As countries' incomes rise, they will be able to offer a growing menu of improved health technologies. The cost of such improvements can be managed through attention to cost-effectiveness and fairness in combination with digital technologies aimed at more individualised and home-based care. And individual behavioural change can be encouraged through fiscal policy and nudges that encourage healthy lifestyles. But underpinning all of this is the social contract as a whole. Only this can ensure that everyone has the opportunity to have a healthy life.

# 5

# Work

After the fall of the Berlin Wall, I visited a former tank factory in Slovakia that had been part of the highly integrated Soviet military production system. The factory was the only game in town, not just providing jobs to the community, but also funding the local kindergarten, sports facilities and community centre. The engineers who worked there had developed an ingenious plan to cope with the collapse of the communist economy – they had switched from producing tanks to forklifts. The workers greeted me and my World Bank colleagues at the factory entrance with the most extraordinary ballet performed by their newly manufactured forklifts, elegantly lifting their arms and doing pirouettes accompanied by classical music. It was a rare case of the successful conversion of a dying industry into a new one.[1]

In every society able-bodied men and increasingly women work to support themselves and their families and to pay taxes for the common good. This is the most important way in which we engage with the social contract and contribute to our communities and society. But work is also an important part of self-determination, giving people a sense of purpose and of self-worth. And by contributing to society in our working years, we ensure that the next generation is able to benefit from social spending just as we did, and that we will be able to benefit from it again when we are old. As noted in Chapter

1, the welfare state is often less about transferring money from the rich to the poor (the Robin Hood function) and more about helping people even out consumption over their own lives and, crucially, providing them with insurance when things go wrong (the piggy bank function).

The collapse of the Soviet Union and the fall of the Berlin Wall were momentous events, affecting the lives of millions and forcing whole industries and communities to adapt. But economic dislocations often occur, some sudden and dramatic, others more gradual and harder to discern, invariably causing periods of unemployment. When this happens, the social contract determines how society supports people until they get back to work to contribute again.

In the coming years, economic dislocations are likely to continue – not just because of the Covid-19 pandemic and its aftermath but because of rapid technological change associated with the digital revolution and automation. Anxiety about these dislocations is already spilling over into the politics of many countries. Meanwhile, across rich and poor countries alike, we are seeing an increasingly diverse workforce alongside a fall in job security.

This has been especially devastating for those who work in industries that are geographically isolated, such as mining, or who live in large-scale company towns dominated by a single manufacturing plant like the one I visited in Slovakia. Modern economic geography draws talent and investment to major cities, creating tensions between the urban hubs and those in the communities that have been left behind.[2] Those who live in such communities often feel they have been deprived of the chance to thrive. What happened in large parts of eastern Europe after the collapse of the Soviet Union has also happened in places like the 'rust belt' in the United States, the north-east of England, and regions of the developing world dependent on extractive industries.

This chapter will show how the social contract around work needs to change if we are to cope with economic shocks and technological changes both efficiently and humanely. This means thinking differently about the sharing of risks between individuals, families, employers and society as a whole.

## *What Has Happened to Work?*

The traditional model of work in advanced economies is that most adults take part in full-time employment and make mandatory contributions to society via some form of payroll tax. In exchange, they receive unemployment insurance, a pension when they are old and, in some countries, health insurance. In low-income countries, meanwhile, the majority of the population works in the informal economy without access to legal contracts, unemployment benefits or other forms of social insurance.[3] Instead, they must rely on their family and community in times of economic distress. But who is working has changed dramatically in recent years, and this in turn has affected the nature of these arrangements.

Traditionally, the workforce was mainly men between 18 and 60 years of age. Today, women have entered the workforce in large numbers across the world. Fewer young people are in employment as more of them remain in education for longer in the hope of higher wages later in life; many people now do not join the workforce until well into their twenties. More old people are working, as retirement ages rise in many countries and as many need to save more to cover their needs in old age. Today's global workforce is older and more diverse in terms of gender and work patterns.

A more diverse workforce has resulted in a growing proportion of workers operating under more flexible work arrangements. Indeed, this has been the primary driver in the growth of jobs in recent decades.[4] Jobs are increasingly characterised by temporary contracts, part-time arrangements and so-called gig work, serving multiple employers enabled by a technology platform. Benefits like social insurance are often not provided, leaving the risks of dislocation to be borne exclusively by the worker rather than shared with a single employer. Workers increasingly bear the responsibility for how many hours they will work, keeping their skills relevant, supporting themselves if they get sick, and securing their income for when they are old.

Interestingly, the pattern is the same everywhere. We tend to associate the informal economy of casual work without benefits with developing countries where only a tiny fraction of the labour force is employed in the formal sector such as in government or large corporations. Yet growing informality is now a feature in both rich and poor countries, as permanent employment in advanced economies is replaced with more part-time work, self-employment and zero-hours contracts – where employees have to be available but are not guaranteed any hours or income.

Job stability, measured as the length of time a worker has spent in their current job, has fallen across advanced economies.[5] The sharpest falls in job security have been for lower-educated workers without an upper-secondary qualification (more than nine years of education). Underemployment, where workers would prefer to work more hours, has also increased, especially for young people, women and those without any higher education. Young people without higher education have fared particularly poorly, often underemployed or in very low-paid work. Young people with higher education have fared better, but on average across the OECD are still more likely to be in low-paid than high-paid jobs relative to the past.

This phenomenon has been enabled by a reduction in labour market regulations since the 1980s and 90s. Across the advanced economies, the drive for efficiency has given employers more flexibility in hiring and firing and in what benefits they are required to provide. Even in Europe, usually considered to have the most highly regulated labour markets, about one third of employees have what are called alternative contracts, under which they earn less and are usually not entitled to benefits such as bonuses, profit sharing, overtime pay, training and career development opportunities.[6]

Ironically, these alternative contracts have come into being largely as a result of employers' efforts to circumvent the strictures of a highly regulated formal sector. The result is a two-tier labour market – one highly regulated and formal, the other less so. In recent years, government policy in many countries has been designed to accommodate and encourage flexible working. For example, the Hartz reforms in Germany, launched in 2002, increased the number of temporary workers to about 5 per cent of employees, representing about one million people.[7] Most of these temporary jobs lasted less than three months and tended to be in low-paying sectors such as retail, hospitality and construction. Zero-hours contracts now cover about 3 per cent of the working population in the UK, 2.6 per cent in the United States, 4 per cent in Finland and 6.4 per cent in the Netherlands.[8]

In the United States, the growth of outsourcing has spawned the phenomenon of workplace fissuring, whereby workers are not employed by the company that benefits from their labour. In economics, the theory of the firm tells us that the reason companies exist is that it is not possible to contract out everything, so it makes sense to put activities inside one organisation. Many companies started by outsourcing non-core activities such as cleaning, catering, security, accounting and payroll, often to agency workers. But, increasingly, many core jobs are being outsourced, with computer programmers, product designers, lawyers, accountants and architects working on a piecework basis. The share of US workers on alternative contracts rose from about 11 per cent in 1995 to 16 per cent in 2015.[9] This has evolved even further as technology platforms like Uber and Deliveroo have made it possible for individual workers to sell their labour to a firm and not be considered an employee at all, although this is being challenged in many places.

The self-employed and gig workers are perhaps at the most flexible end of the employment spectrum. Gig work is characterised by low wages and low hours and represents a small (but often growing) proportion of the workforce – 5 per cent in Italy, 7 per cent in the UK and 14 per cent in the US.[10] The majority of gig workers can choose when and where they want to work. Surveys show that 80 per cent of these workers use gig work to supplement their income when it falls or top it up when they need to. Only a minority (16 per cent in one survey) · rely on gig work as their sole source of income.

This trend towards more flexible labour markets has paralleled the fall in the proportion of the workforce represented by unions. Recent decades have been characterised by a steady decline in union power across the world as membership halved from an estimated 36 per cent of workers in 1990 to 18 per cent in 2016.[11] This decline has been driven by many factors, including the decline of industry relative to services, the growth of flexible working and the changing behaviour of young people. Today, union membership varies enormously from well over 60 per cent in Nordic countries like Denmark, Sweden or Finland, to below 10 per cent in most developing countries.[12] Employment protection, defined as legislation that protects workers from individual and collective dismissal, has also tended to weaken.

While labour market reforms in many advanced economies have been aimed at liberalising and deregulating, in many developing countries the tendency has been in the opposite direction, with an expansion in labour market regulations for the small proportion of workers in the formal sector. These regulations are meant to make up for the absence of adequate social protection systems and often concern notification requirements for contract termination, regulation of fixed-term contracts and requirements for severance pay.[13] In effect, they reduce flexibility to offset the lack of security, while providing protection for only a minority of the labour force – a poor set of policy choices that tends to create the same kind of two-tier labour market as in Europe, where workers in the formal sector are protected, and those outside (often the young and the poor) are unprotected.

## What Has More Flexible Work Meant for Workers?

More flexible working arrangements are an important reason why many jobs are created. Firms are willing to hire because they know they will have the ability to fire if demand falls. Employers in sectors like agriculture or tourism who face cyclical demand can expand their workforce when they need to and reduce it when they do not. Flexibility enables more efficiency and probably resulted in companies rehiring workers more quickly after the global financial crisis in 2008. For some workers, such as women, greater flexibility has meant they are able to balance work commitments with other dimensions of their lives.

But flexibility also means less security as more of the risks are put onto workers. The recent coronavirus pandemic revealed the perils of this situation, with workers in precarious jobs, the self-employed and those on temporary contracts around the world most likely to lose their livelihoods. Precariousness has significant consequences for workers' physical and mental health. Faced with uncertain incomes, many modern workers struggle with anxiety about paying bills and cannot plan their lives. Workers who are laid off are more likely to develop a new illness, have lower life expectancies, earn less later in life and trust other people less.[14] Firms too suffer negative consequences from lay-offs, including reputational damage, lower stock prices, higher staff turnover and worse performance and job satisfaction from the employees that remain.[15] All of this is bad for productivity and the ability to create new jobs in future.

These trends have affected general living standards too. On the one hand, the new types of employment have meant that prices have fallen in those sectors where jobs are flexible and competition is strong such as clothing, communications, furnishing, restaurants and airlines, to the extent that the average person can work six fewer weeks a year and still consume the same amount of these goods as they did in 2000.[16] On the other hand, the cost of basics such as housing, education and health care, sectors where competition is constrained, have risen much faster than other consumer prices and are absorbing a growing share of household income.

Housing is the biggest expense for most households, and workers have to pay more for it where the best jobs are. Yet in many places social or public housing is in decline, and private-sector investment in real estate is constrained by zoning, regulation and inadequate infrastructure provision. The average person works four extra weeks to consume the same amount of housing, education or health care as they did two decades ago. While we can buy electronic goods, data and fast fashion more cheaply than ever, the things that matter most to people – like having a home and taking care of their health – are more expensive. In some countries, such as the UK, higher prices for the basics have absorbed all the gains in income achieved in the last two decades. These trends go some way towards explaining why, despite income gains in many countries, many households feel they are worse off.

A good example of these trade-offs in living standards is the low-cost airline industry. Budget airlines have made foreign holidays accessible to millions of people. The low fares have been achieved in part because jobs in aviation which used to be permanent and full time have been replaced by agency work, self-employment and zero-hours contracts. In Europe 20 per cent of cabin crew and 18 per cent of pilots did not have a permanent contract with a single employer before the pandemic. Ninety-seven per cent of cabin crew on more flexible contracts worked for a low-cost carrier.[17] Those who fly on these airlines clearly benefit; those who work for them have jobs they might otherwise not have had, but are probably worse off than they would have been with a more traditional employment contract had it been available.

In summary, today's workers face a world in which they have less job stability and more individual risk around unemployment, sickness and old age. If they are educated, highly skilled and live in a major city, they are likely to do well. If they are not, their prospects are less good and more uncertain. But overlaying this situation is another factor that will dramatically affect the future of work: automation.

## What Will Happen to Work in Future?

Ever since the Luddites attacked machines in the newly automated textile factories of nineteenth-century England, every wave of technological innovation has been accompanied by fears of job loss. Of course, technology often does substitute for labour (that is where many of the productivity gains come from), but it also complements labour by creating new opportunities.

Today's automation and machine learning will tend to replace some workers – those doing tasks that are repetitive and routine – but they will also enhance the productivity of others: those performing roles that involve problem-solving, creativity and engaging with people. A doctor may rely on a machine to conduct a diagnosis for breast cancer, but that will free up more time to consult with patients about treatment plans and probably achieve better health outcomes as a result. Table 2 provides examples of roles that are likely to remain the same, those that may become redundant and new roles that will create job opportunities in future. Interestingly, the jobs likely to become redundant include not only lower-skill roles, such as data entry clerks and drivers, but traditionally higher-skill roles such as lawyers and financial analysts.[18]

Fears that robots will replace most human workers and that we need to find a way to transfer income to a future mass of unemployed are probably premature. During a previous wave of concern about technological unemployment in the 1960s, Nobel laureate Herbert Simon wrote, 'Insofar as they are economic problems at all, the world's problems in this generation and the next are problems of scarcity, not of intolerable abundance. The bogeyman of automation consumes worrying capacity that should be saved for real problems – like population, poverty, the bomb, and our own neuroses.'[19]

# Table 2. Jobs that are stable, emerging and becoming redundant

## Stable Roles

Managing Directors and Chief Executives
General and Operations Managers*
Software and Applications Developers and
  Analysts*
Data Analysts and Scientists*
Sales and Marketing Professionals*
Sales Representatives, Wholesale and
  Manufacturing, Technical and Scientific
  Products
Human Resources Specialists
Financial and Investment Advisers
Database and Network Professionals
Supply Chain and Logistics Specialists

Risk Management Specialists
Information Security Analysts*
Management and Organization Analysts
Electrotechnology Engineers
Organizational Development Specialists*
Chemical Processing Plant Operators
University and Higher Education Teachers
Compliance Officers
Energy and Petroleum Engineers
Robotics Specialists and Engineers
Petroleum and Natural Gas Refining Plant
  Operators

## New Roles

Data Analysts and Scientists*
AI and Machine Learning Specialists
General and Operations Managers*
Big Data Specialists
Digital Transformation Specialists
Sales and Marketing Professionals*
New technology Specialists
Organizational Development Specialists*
Software and Applications Developers and
  Analysts*
Information Technology Services
Process Automation Specialists

Innovation Professionals
Information Security Analysts*
Ecommerce and Social Media Specialists
User Experience and Human-Machine
  Interaction Designers
Training and Development Specialists
Robotics Specialists and Engineers
People and Culture Specialists
Client Information and Customer Service
  Workers*
Service and Solutions Designers
Digital Marketing and Strategy Specialists

## Redundant Roles

Data Entry Clerks
Accounting, Bookkeeping and Payroll Clerks
Administrative and Executive Secretaries
Assembly and Factory Workers
Client Information and Customer Service
  Workers*
Business Services and Administration
  Managers
Accountants and Auditors
Material-Recording and Stock-Keeping Clerks
General and Operations Managers*
Postal Service Clerks
Financial Analysts

Cashiers and Ticket Clerks
Mechanics and Machinery Repairers
Telemarketers
Electronics and Telecommunications
  Installers and Repairers
Bank Tellers and Related Clerks
Car, Van and Motorcycle Drivers
Sales and Purchasing Agents and Brokers
Door-To-Door Sales Workers, News and
  Street Vendors, and Related Workers
Statistical, Finance and Insurance Clerks
Lawyers

* Appear across multiple 'Roles'. This reflects the fact that they might be seeing stable or declining demand
across one industry but be in demand in another.

Instead, the really important questions are the following. How can we retain the benefits of flexibility while reducing risk and insecurity for workers? How do we provide income security and benefits to workers under alternative work arrangements? How can we create more high-quality jobs? How do we enable workers to learn and adjust as jobs change, as inevitably they will, in response to automation and machine learning?

## How Should the Social Contract Change?

Most countries' systems of labour regulation and social protection are not well suited to the kinds of work that are increasingly prevalent in today's labour market, nor for the faster pace of job destruction and creation we are facing. Overall, the balance has tilted too far in the direction of providing flexibility and not enough security and support.

The exact balance of flexibility and protection that countries currently provide varies enormously, as can be seen in Figure 10. Some, including most of Europe, provide low flexibility and high protection; others, such as the United States, provide high flexibility and low protection; most of Asia, Africa the Middle East and Latin America, meanwhile, provide low protection and low flexibility in the formal sector and high flexibility to those in the informal sector. Only a few countries, such as Denmark, New Zealand, Japan and Australia, occupy the sweet spot, providing high flexibility and high protection. These countries strike the balance between giving employers flexibility to adjust their labour force to economic shocks, but also make sure that workers are supported to be able to move to other jobs while maintaining a reasonable standard of living.

In the Nordic countries workers move easily between jobs.[20] In fact, workers in Sweden, Denmark and Finland change jobs more often than anywhere else in Europe. This gives employers the flexibility to change their workforces in order to adapt to market conditions in the knowledge that their workers will find other jobs easily. They can have that confidence because their

## Figure 10. Countries strike very different balances between flexibility for employers and security for workers

Index of labour market flexibility relative to social protection by country

'Flexibility' is defined as the inverse of rigidity of hours, restrictions on hiring, financial costs of dismissals and procedural requirements for dismissals. 'Protection' is defined as public spending on health, education, income support and employment services as a share of GDP using the latest available data for each country. For a fuller set of countries, see original.

governments spend more on education and labour retraining than most other countries – over ten times more as a share of national income than countries such as the United States and the United Kingdom.

A new social contract that successfully balances flexibility and security will need to have several dimensions, since the dislocations people may face will vary. First, a key feature underpinning any system will be ensuring that everyone is guaranteed a minimum income to sustain a decent life – shelter, food and medical care. Second, it will also need to provide security to those working in non-traditional, part-time and flexible arrangements. Third, when workers face economic dislocation, support will need to be tailored to the nature of the shock being faced: in some cases workers may be able to find jobs within the same industry, role or region, while in others a more comprehensive response that involves helping workers retrain and acquire new skills will be needed. Let's consider each of these aspects – a floor on incomes, more security regardless of the type of work and greater focus on retraining and finding new work – in turn.

## Putting a Floor on Incomes

In traditional societies, those who fall on hard times have to rely on their families and communities for financial support, which may or may not be available. As societies get richer, they find more reliable and consistent ways to protect people from the most catastrophic consequences of unemployment or financial setbacks, including by putting a floor on income. Countries have found many ways of providing this floor.

Almost every country in the world has minimum wages, set either by legislation or as a product of collective bargaining agreements.[21] They have become particularly important in countries where the wages of many workers have stagnated. But while minimum wages put a floor on income and protect workers from exploitation by employers, they are not income guarantees; rather they are designed to ensure that workers are fairly compensated for their efforts. Indeed, it is important that minimum wages are not set too high, because those workers who are not productive enough to justify the minimum level may end up unemployed. For those workers, a negative income tax (or an earned income tax credit) is a better mechanism for providing a decent standard of living while preserving their incentive to work.

In addition to minimum wages, most advanced countries have unemployment insurance to support those who lose their jobs. This pays as little as 30 per cent of previous wages (in Kazakhstan and Poland) to as much as 90 per cent (in Mauritius and Israel). Meanwhile, the duration of benefits ranges from 1.2 months' support in Kazakhstan to indefinite support in Belgium. In general, payments in advanced economies are more generous and include requirements to be available for work and to report regularly to the authorities. For example, Denmark's system of 'workfare' provides very generous unemployment benefits (about 90 per cent of previous wage) but also mandates training and ultimately mandatory job placement after training is complete. However, as most insurance schemes only support those with formal employment contracts, three quarters of the world's workers, mostly in the developing world, are not covered since they are employed in the informal sector.

An alternative way to put a floor on incomes is to provide cash transfers to the poorest households. Programmes started in Mexico and Brazil provide regular cash transfers to poor families on condition that they have enrolled their children in school or participated in public vaccination programmes. In Africa cash transfers have tended to be unconditional and designed to supplement very low incomes. More than 130 developing countries have now introduced some form of cash transfer to provide a safety net to the poorest households, whether or not they are employed. This has been made possible by the spread of mobile phones, which enable governments to identify the poorest households and transfer funds directly to their bank accounts with minimal administrative costs. In my years at the World Bank, the Department for International Development and at the IMF, I have seen dozens of these programmes implemented and rigorously evaluated. The overwhelming evidence is that they have efficiently and effectively prevented destitution, increased nutrition, supported children's education and improved the health of the poorest families in the world.[22]

Countries have found different ways to ensure that these benefits go to those who need them most, while maintaining incentives to work. India's Guaranteed Employment Scheme provides 100 days of work at the minimum wage to any citizen, usually in low-skill jobs in fields such as construction. The rationale here is that because the work on offer is arduous, only those most in need will sign up. Ideally, any guaranteed minimum income should taper off as someone's income or wealth rises in order to avoid the so-called eligibility cliff, whereby people find themselves worse off when moving from benefits into low-paid employment, thus removing the incentive to work.

Recently, there has been much debate about the provision of a universal basic income (UBI). This increasingly popular concept abandons the idea of targeting and making minimum income payments conditional on participation in work, enrolling children in education or health programmes. Instead, every adult receives the same cash payment unconditionally. Advocates argue that UBI not only empowers workers but is the best safety net against economic shocks and will therefore become increasingly necessary in a world where more people are displaced by automation.[23]

There have been many experiments with UBI.[24] One of the best designed took place in Finland and gave 2000 people aged 25–58 an unconditional €560 per month, which they were entitled to keep even if they found a job. After two years, the evidence showed no impact on employment – participants were neither more nor less likely to find a job than someone on unemployment insurance – although UBI recipients did score slightly higher on well-being than those who received conventional unemployment insurance. But because UBI failed to achieve the government's objective – to help people find work by giving them support to learn new skills or start a new business (rather than make them happier) – they ended the programme in 2018. Most experiments in advanced economies show similarly mixed results.[25]

My view is that most countries can offer a social contract that does much better than UBI. One of the main problems with UBI is that the costs are prohibitive – reaching 20–30 per cent of GDP if UBI is set at a generous level – requiring unsustainably high levels of taxation.[26] There will be a few cases where UBI may be the best option – such as in very poor countries with no institutional capacity to target benefits or where UBI is a replacement for a worse policy like energy subsidies (as it was in Iran when in 2011 fuel subsidies were replaced with a cash transfer to every household).[27] But for the vast majority of countries, if the goal is to reduce poverty, then targeted benefits are a better option. Ideally, these should be combined with support to ensure that everyone capable of working is able to do so and thus make a contribution to society. The empowerment of workers can be achieved through better minimum wages, benefits, unions and retraining programmes.

Some argue that rather than putting a floor on incomes, it is better to even out life chances by giving people a more equal amount of wealth. For example, Thomas Piketty argues that wealth should be taxed heavily each year to enable every 25-year-old to receive a capital grant of €120,000.[28] The only country to attempt such a scheme, albeit on a very modest scale, was the UK, which between 2002 and 2011 granted £250 to every child as part of the Labour government's Child Trust Fund programme. Children in poor families got an additional £250 and could top up the amount and eventually use it at the age of eighteen. Unsurprisingly, the impact of the scheme has been relatively modest, given the amounts involved.

There is an argument that the transfer of assets – whether in the form of cash or some other piece of property, such as land or machinery, that can help generate income – in addition to improving equality has a more lasting impact than a transfer of income, which just keeps people afloat. An asset-transfer programme in Bangladesh, mainly involving giving poor women livestock or something else that generated income, was able to permanently shift the poorest households out of poverty.[29] Crucially, the asset transfer was accompanied by substantial advice and support for the women, which was key to its success. Rather than giving someone a fish, it is better to give them a fishing rod, but teaching them how to fish with it is every bit as important as the rod itself.

In summary, some combination of minimum wages and minimum income guarantees is possible in all countries. In developing countries cash transfer schemes have proven an effective way to support the poorest households. In advanced economies mechanisms that top up the wages of the low skilled (through earned income tax credits for example) to achieve a decent standard of living have also worked well. The idea of capital transfers is more untested and deserves further study. My own view is that an endowment dedicated to education and reskilling as discussed in Chapter 3 would be a more acceptable and, in the long run, more effective way of investing in future generations and achieving equity. As the great economist and LSE Nobel laureate Arthur Lewis said, 'The fundamental cure for poverty is not money, but knowledge.'[30]

## Providing Security to Flexible Workers

The coronavirus pandemic revealed the perils of precarious work in a time of crisis. Suddenly, huge proportions of the population had no income, and governments in advanced economies had to step in to support the self-employed and flexible workers alongside funding to help more traditional employers retain their employees. Those most adversely affected tended to be the young, those with low skills and ethnic minorities.[31] In the developing world those workers whose jobs were disrupted by the virus simply lost their livelihoods.

As noted already, employers prefer flexible arrangements because these reduce the amounts they pay for social insurance, severance, pensions and health care. In the Netherlands, for example, the cost to an employer of a dependent employee can be 60 per cent higher than for an otherwise similar independent contractor. And flexible workers are especially vulnerable not only to economic dislocation but also in old age, since they make no or very low contributions to pension schemes in most countries. In countries like the US, where health insurance is often linked to employment, flexible workers can be excluded from good quality health coverage, while those with full-time contracts are locked into their jobs by fear of losing them.

There are essentially two options for tackling this problem: we can either make employers pay social insurance for flexible workers proportionate to how much they work, or we can move the burden of social insurance away from employers altogether and pay for it instead through general taxation so that its protections are provided to everyone regardless of the nature of their employment. By taking a more consistent approach to taxing labour across types of employment, both options would be good for competition, innovation and fiscal sustainability, as well as provide greater security to flexible workers. And if in addition to this we make social protections earned in this way portable between jobs, sectors and different types of employment, we will be better able to cope with the major changes that will come with automation. Many countries are experimenting with how to do this.

The Netherlands, for example, has legislated to prevent discrimination against part-time workers and requires that those who employ them provide access to social security and other entitlements in proportion to hours worked. As a result, 77 per cent of women and 27 per cent of men work part time in the Netherlands – the highest rate in the world.[32] Similarly,

Denmark has mandated that flexible workers are entitled to the same benefits as more traditional employees.

It is also possible to level the playing field for the self-employed. In most countries self-employed workers do not contribute as much as employed individuals to social insurance schemes. Consider the UK, where employers pay 13.8 per cent in National Insurance contributions for an employee while paying nothing for a self-employed worker. Attempts to reform this have been thwarted, but a system that taxed the employment of freelancers at an equivalent level to salaried workers would reduce the bias towards flexible forms of working and widen the pool of funds contributing to social insurance.[33]

A growing number of governments are introducing measures to force employers to provide more security to flexible workers. For example, the state of California tried unsuccessfully to introduce legislation that requires digital platform service companies such as Uber and Lyft to treat contract workers as employees. Oregon, New York City, San Francisco, Seattle and Philadelphia have passed laws requiring businesses to offer workers guaranteed hours and prior notice of schedules in an attempt to ensure more predictable and dependable incomes. There are also partial and voluntary options. New York State created the Black Car Fund, a non-profit insurer that provides an income to limousine drivers in New York if they are injured.[34] The fund adds a surcharge of 2.5 per cent to passengers' fares and also reduces risk by providing training in safe driving to its members.

Some argue that many workers are happy to trade security for the advantages of working when they want. They point particularly to those younger gig workers who do online work to supplement their incomes. But there is also evidence that flexible workers in the US and the UK would prefer more traditional working arrangements: most would be willing to give up 50 per cent of their hourly wage in exchange for a permanent contract, and 35 per cent of their hourly wage for a one-year arrangement rather than a one-month contract.[35] A survey of gig workers in the UK, Italy and the US found that about 80 per cent supported the idea of creating 'shared security accounts' with their employers to stabilise their incomes. After that, their priorities for work-related benefits were pensions in Italy and the UK and health insurance in the US.[36]

McDonald's recently offered their 115,000 workers in the UK the opportunity to shift from their zero-hours contracts to a fixed contract with a minimum number of guaranteed hours per week.[37] Many employees on zero-hours contracts are unable to get mortgages or mobile phone contracts because they cannot show they have a regular income. Despite this, and in contrast to the previous study, 80 per cent of their workers preferred to remain on flexible contracts. That may tell us more about the particularities of the McDonald's workforce than the preferences of workers in general, but perhaps the most interesting finding was that, having given their workers the opportunity to choose between flexible and more secure contracts, McDonald's noted an improvement in both employee and customer satisfaction.

Many leading companies are moving away from a narrow focus on maximising shareholder value to a broader focus on the purpose of the firm and serving a variety of stakeholders, including offering more security and benefits to employees.[38] Some economists have argued for the importance of creating 'good jobs' or encouraging 'high road employers' – those that can afford to pay above-market wages and benefits because they invest in training and improving the quality of jobs they offer.[39] The fact that many employers manage to do this and remain competitive shows that it is possible. But while such initiatives should be praised and encouraged, my view is that moral suasion is not enough – we will need legislation or regulation to achieve the universal adoption of good practices in corporate social responsibility, benefits and training to create a level playing field among all firms.

Unions have an important role to play in pressing for greater security for flexible workers, who are an important potential new constituency for them, and there are some examples of flexible unionisation happening. In Italy a charter was agreed between the association of delivery workers, the trade unions and the council in Bologna, setting minimum standards for pay, hours and insurance for home food delivery services such as Deliveroo and Uber Eats. When some of the platforms refused to sign the charter, the mayor organised a boycott, which proved effective.[40] In India the Self-Employed Women's Association has been supporting more than 2 million women to achieve their civil, social and economic rights by working as both a trade union and a cooperative. The same digital technologies that have led to a rise in flexible work can also be used by flexible workers to organise themselves in response to it.

## *Helping Workers Adapt*

Supporting workers with minimum levels of income and benefits whatever form their employment takes is an essential piece of a new social contract. In return, those who lose their jobs have an obligation, if they are physically and mentally able to do so, to retrain if necessary and return to work as soon as possible. How should society support those who are unemployed to return to productive work? What happens when large numbers of workers lose their jobs because their skills have become obsolete? Is it possible to retrain low-skill workers or those in declining regions to find new opportunities?

There have been hundreds of academic studies on the effectiveness of worker retraining programmes in both advanced and developing countries.[41] The record is mixed, but the lessons on what works are clear. Interventions focused on job placement – such as help with searching for a new job and monitoring the behaviour of job seekers – are effective at getting people, especially lower-skill workers, back to work in the short term and are not costly to run. Training programmes designed to satisfy the specific needs of employers combined with work experience have bigger impacts and are more effective than classroom training unconnected to the private sector. Although training of this sort can be costly, the benefits are significant when measured over several years, especially for the long-term unemployed. It also helps if training leads to some form of accreditation or formal qualification. For lower-skill workers, programmes that provide administrative support to participants also tend to result in better employment outcomes.[42]

We also know what does not work. Simply sending workers for classroom training at colleges or vocational training institutes is usually a poor investment. Subsidies that encourage firms to hire displaced workers can increase employment but also result in waste since employers often recruit people they would have hired anyway. Schemes involving the public sector creating artificial jobs for the unemployed invariably do not work. Training workers who are already at risk of displacement works less well than training them in anticipation of technological change.[43]

A good example of a well planned and comprehensive approach to supporting workers at risk of collective dismissal is the Swedish Job Security Councils, which provide advice, training, financial assistance and support with starting new businesses to individual workers before jobs are lost.[44] Working collaboratively with unions and employers, the councils target workers at risk of unemployment for technological or economic reasons. Employees are given dedicated coaches, who start working with them six to eight months before dismissal takes place. The package of support is funded by a levy on employers of 0.3 per cent of payroll. The councils' success rate is high: 74 per cent of workers go on to find a new job or further training and 70 per cent of those who find work manage to maintain or increase their salary.[45]

Ideally, countries should think strategically about where future jobs will emerge and prepare young people and current workers for that future. In the 1950s and 60s manpower planning (as it was then called) got a terrible reputation as Soviet-style central planners tried to estimate with precision how many welders, bakers, teachers and nurses the economy

would need. Not surprisingly, their predictions proved inaccurate as they were unable to anticipate technological changes that
would emerge and disrupt jobs. Nonetheless, it is possible at
least to identify the kinds of skills that will be needed in future,
if not specific jobs, given the likely evolution of technology.

Denmark, for example, has shaped its strategy for education
and employee training using just such an analysis. It spends
more than any other country in the world (about 1.5 per cent
of GDP) on active labour market policies – programmes aimed
at helping workers renew their skills and stay employed. The
Danish Workfare and Disruption Council describes its objective as follows: 'We must make everyone the winners of the
future. We must not become divided into those who benefit
from change and those who are left behind because of it.'[46]
This translates into a comprehensive and forward-looking programme from primary education to vocational training with
a strong focus on supporting those less likely to be employed
– the disabled, recent immigrants and the low skilled. While
the system is generous, it is also firm: unemployment benefits
expire after one year, and active participation in training or an
apprenticeship is mandatory for up to three years thereafter.
The unemployed are actively monitored and supported by a
caseworker and the vast majority are back in work within a year,
well before they become disconnected from the job market.[47]
As a result, Denmark has consistently had one of the lowest
unemployment rates in the world and the highest proportion
of its population in work.

There is also growing evidence that engaging workers early
in the process of technological adaptation is not just good for
them but also for the productivity and efficiency of the business as a whole.[48] For example, a study of 304 nursing homes
in New York State that introduced electronic medical record
systems found that those workplaces where employees were
encouraged to collaborate in the implementation of new technology with suggestions, participation in decision-making and
problem-solving enjoyed far greater productivity as a result.[49]

The most successful nursing homes notified employees well in advance of technological changes and gave them the opportunity to train and shape work practices to maximise the benefits around these technologies – or to retrain for a new position if the technology substituted for their previous work.

Again, such an approach is not just in the interests of workers but can also benefit employers. When companies fire workers and replace them with new ones, they incur severance, recruiting and induction costs. Even taking into account the costs of retraining, including the lost output while it took place, an assessment in the US found that it was more profitable for employers to reskill 25 per cent of their own workers whose jobs would be disrupted by technology over the next decade rather than hire new workers.[50] If the costs of retraining could be shared industry-wide, it made financial sense for firms to reskill half their labour force, and when one takes into account the wider public benefits of maintaining continuous employment – ongoing tax payments and reduced welfare costs – it made sense to reskill 77 per cent of displaced workers.

This chapter has shown that a different social contract around work is both needed and possible. In poor countries a minimum income can be provided to the poorest, and that can increase over time as societies become wealthier. In advanced economies minimum incomes are already possible and can be designed to incentivise a return to productive work. More flexible work can be balanced with greater security by providing benefits to all, regardless of the nature of their employment contract. Knowing that if you cannot work, the risk will be shared will do a great deal to reduce insecurity. Finally, investing more in helping people renew their skills throughout their lives enables them to get back to work quickly and continue to contribute to society for longer.

# 6

# Old Age

All of us will (hopefully) grow old. As we do, most will face two
major challenges – how to sustain ourselves financially when
we can no longer work, and how we will be looked after when
we can no longer live independently. Most societies expect to
have to provide a minimum level of support so that those who
are unable to work or care for themselves can still live a decent
life when they are old. As in all aspects of the social contract,
the key question is how the risks around old age are shared
between individuals, families, society and the market. But what
makes planning for old age so much more difficult than other
aspects of the social contract is that no one knows how long
they will live or how healthy they will be. My paternal grandfather was a prudent scientist but never imagined he would live to
the age of 94; my more extravagant maternal grandfather died
suddenly at the age of 72 having just ordered a new wardrobe
after selling the orange crop on the family farm.

Historically, most men who made it over the age of 60
continued to work; the notion of retirement is a twentieth-
century phenomenon. Traditionally, the old would be cared
for by the women in their family home. But longer lifespans,
rising expectations that we will spend a significant part of our
later years not working and the fact that women are increasingly employed outside the home have made the challenges of
old age more acute. It is commonly said that respect for the

elderly increases as you move east, but even in countries like Japan and Korea multigenerational households are becoming less common and the elderly tend to live on their own. As with many parts of the social contract, it is increasingly being left to us as individuals to carry the risks around old age.

How much retirement and care in old age does a society owe an individual? How long should one expect to work to be entitled to a pension? Should society provide a minimum income to avoid the old becoming destitute? How can care of the elderly and the end of life be organised in a manner that is both humane and financially sustainable? Most countries are ageing faster than they are answering these questions. The risk is that the old will soon lack the means or the ability to care for themselves in future.

## Ageing and the Changing Labour Market

The gains in life expectancy over the last century have been a great achievement, but they have also created a significant challenge: those of working age need to support a growing number of old people. Japan has the highest ratio of over 65s to working-age population (20–64 years), and that ratio is set to double across the advanced economies over the next 50 years, by which point every worker will be supporting at least one old person. Most middle-income countries currently have much younger populations, but they are ageing fast at a much earlier stage of development and thus have fewer resources to cope. Low-income countries in Africa and south Asia tend to have young populations, and here the challenge is creating enough jobs and the mechanisms to ensure adequate retirement income later in life.

Societies make decisions about the amount of retirement an individual is entitled to through the political process by setting the age at which people are eligible for pensions. When Bismarck created the first compulsory pension insurance scheme in Germany in 1889, the retirement age was set at 70. Given life expectancy at the time, that meant the state needed to provide a pension for an average of seven years. In 1916 the German retirement age was lowered to 65, which today means the state pays out for about 20 years. It is a similar pattern in most countries: retirement ages have been slower to rise than life expectancy, meaning retirement is getting longer. In most middle- and high-income countries, workers today can expect to spend about a third of their life in retirement (Figure 11). Some of the largest increases in the number of years spent not working have been in Austria, Belgium, Chile, Germany, Luxembourg, Poland, Slovenia and Spain.

The basic problem is that years in retirement relative to years in work have grown too much, so the amount workers have put into pensions during their working lives is not enough to pay for the number of years of support they will need in old age. This is most obvious in pay-as-you-go systems, where the pensions of former workers are paid for by current workers. As the old population grows and the working population shrinks, the financial burden for the working population becomes greater. By 2060 all the G20 countries will have shrinking populations, and the number of people over 65 who need to be supported by the working-age population will have at least doubled. To pay for this, most countries will either have to raise taxes substantially or massively increase their debt burdens.[1]

The problem here is not that people are living too long, it is that they are not saving enough and retiring too soon. At the same time, ageing societies have fewer children, so they need to invest more in the younger generation so that they are productive enough to be able to afford to take care of a larger population of elderly people. In both dimensions, more saving and investment are essential.

The challenge is all the greater because pension systems have not kept up with changes in employment patterns and particularly the growing importance of flexible working, as outlined in the previous chapter. In many countries the self-employed

## Figure 11. Workers are spending more of their life in retirement

Length of the retirement period as a share of adult lifetime

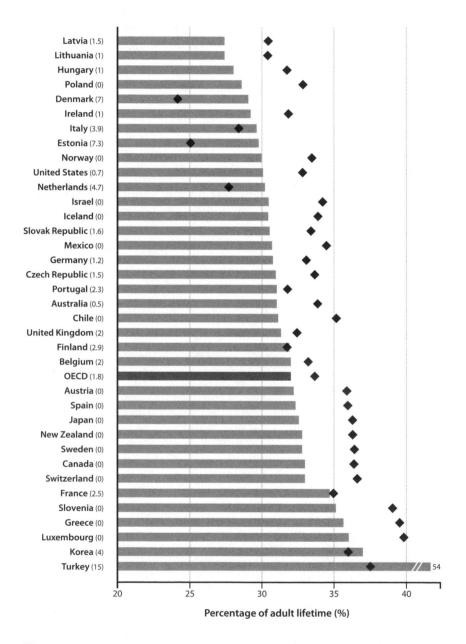

Percentage of adult lifetime (%)

■ Cohort retiring on average about today ◆ Cohort entering the labour market about today

Note: Figure in brackets refers to increase in retirement age to get a full pension.

can opt out of pension schemes or pay lower contributions, thereby lowering their future benefits. Some pension systems penalise workers who change jobs frequently. Those who don't stick with a single employer are often left to take out personal pensions and tend to under-save for retirement, putting themselves at risk in old age. In particular, women suffer from the lack of pensions that can adjust to flexible and part-time work. The bottom line is that pension reform is essential.

## The Challenge of Reforming Pensions

As noted above, most advanced countries are coping with the financial pressures of ageing by shifting the risks onto individuals. In a traditional pension, known as a defined benefit scheme, the employer commits to providing an employee with a fixed pension amount (the defined benefit) depending on their salary and years of employment. The employer bears the risk that the employee's invested contributions might not cover the cost of the pension. These pensions are now being replaced with defined contribution schemes. Here, the employer contributes a certain amount towards investments the worker uses to finance their retirement (the defined contribution), but the employer bears none of the risk of how well these investments perform and whether they are adequate to fund the worker's old age. Few people have the financial skills to manage such risks, and yet defined contribution pensions are becoming more common everywhere.[2]

In the developing world, meanwhile, pensions only exist in the formal sector, which in many countries is a very small part of the economy. The cost of caring for older people tends to fall primarily on families and to a lesser extent on voluntary organisations. The challenge is that the population in developing countries is ageing much faster than the spread of pension systems. Unless more of the workforce is brought into the pension system, the burden on families and on government-financed safety-net pensions will become excessive. Developing countries must therefore prioritise the promotion of formal work, the expansion of mandatory pension coverage and the setting of realistic expectations about retirement ages.

Despite recent reforms, the sustainability of pensions is under pressure in most countries, especially in a world of low interest rates, where returns on pension investments are low. There are three possible solutions: increasing retirement ages, increasing contributions or reducing pension promises. In recent years countries have tried all of these options.[3] One way of increasing contributions is to import labour of working age by allowing greater immigration, but this raises other political and social challenges.

In other words, pension reform requires renegotiating a social contract that is no longer viable. This means encouraging individuals to save more for old age and to work longer; making it easier and more automatic for flexible workers to participate in pensions; and providing ways for individuals to pool their risks more effectively. Finally, as a safety net, it means guaranteeing a minimum pension for all, to avoid destitution in old age for the most vulnerable, especially low earners and those people, mainly women, whose careers have been interrupted. An ideal pension system would provide a minimum public pension for all and enable a variety of insurance-based options with which workers could supplement their incomes in old age.

The problem is that pension reform is deeply controversial; people are generally very reluctant to give up something they believe they have earned and are entitled to. It is also highly political for the simple reason that the old vote more than the young. In OECD countries, for example, the turnout in 2012/13 of voters aged over 55 was 86 per cent, while only 70 per cent of young adults voted. The old also tend to be very effective at political lobbying. It is no accident that as the age of the median voter has risen in advanced countries, public spending on pensions has grown by 0.5 per cent of GDP.[4]

In most countries reforms happen in moments of crisis when fiscal pressures build up. Even then, gaining political consensus for pension reform usually involves 'grandfathering' – previous commitments are honoured, and changes only apply to future generations with long transition periods. Countries with younger populations in Africa, the Middle East and south Asia would be well advised to act early before vested interests lock in unsustainable promises.

## Working Longer

The good news (at least from the point of view of pension provision) is that people are already working longer, and they expect to work longer in future. In the OECD, for example, the rate of employment of those aged 55–64 increased massively from 47.7 per cent in 2000 to 61.4 per cent in 2018, while it changed very little for those aged 25–54.[5] The duration of working lives has increased most in countries like Germany, Italy, France and Australia and among more educated workers. Retirement ages are rising everywhere (Figure 12) and are increasing to the late 60s and in some cases above 70 in high-income countries. For most middle-income countries, retirement ages just under the age of 60 are more common, as they have been slower to adjust to gains in life expectancy.

However, even these increases in working lives are not enough to cover the costs of the additional years in retirement. The most obvious way to close this gap is to link retirement ages directly to life expectancy, ensuring that the number of working years is always the right proportion to the number of years in retirement. Many countries have done this, including Denmark, Estonia, Finland, Greece, Italy, the Netherlands and Portugal. In Portugal's case, the retirement age rises by two thirds of the increase in life expectancy. This formula allows people to enjoy the gains of longer lives while still improving the financial sustainability of the pension system. Whatever the formula adopted, by making the relationship proportionate and thus the adjustment automatic when life expectancy increases, we can obviate the need for frequent political rows

**Figure 12. Retirement ages are rising everywhere (just not fast enough)**

Normal retirement age of men entering the labour market at age 22, with full career

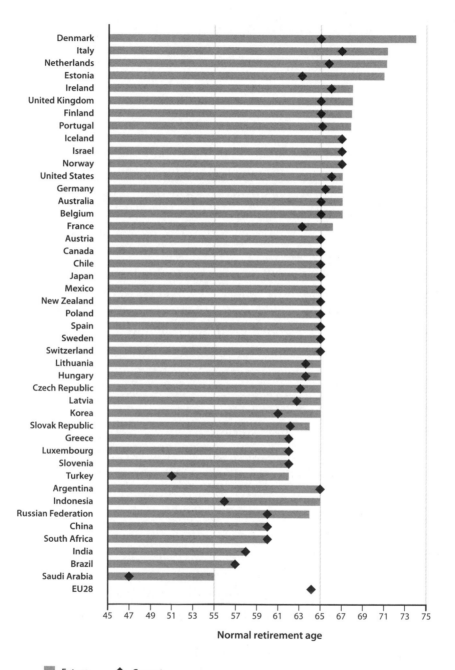

about raising retirement ages and give people time to adjust their expectations.

However, this approach has been controversial, and some countries have backtracked because of political opposition. The Slovak Republic has abolished the link with life expectancy and simply raised the retirement age to 64. Italy has suspended the link for some workers until 2026. Spain has also suspended the link to life expectancy, and the Netherlands has temporarily frozen its implementation. Similar reversals have happened in Canada, the Czech Republic and Poland.[6]

Resistance to raising pension ages usually stems from concerns about fairness. One argument against is that the additional years of life may be unhealthy ones and it is therefore unreasonable to expect people to work when they are not fit. In fact, the evidence seems to show that this is not the case – these years of life tend to be healthy, suggesting that people do have the capacity to work longer. Another argument is that those who are poorer tend to die younger, and those who do more physically demanding jobs may not be able to work longer; therefore, increasing retirement ages for these groups is regressive. While these are valid points, estimates show that those groups who lose out do so by only a small amount.[7] Nonetheless, it is possible, if complicated, to take socio-economic differences in life expectancy into account so that greater benefits could be offered to people with higher health risks.[8]

Fairness is also an important issue in the context of women's pensions. In many countries women have lower retirement ages than men, even though they tend to live longer. Combined with the fact that they also tend to have shorter careers and receive lower wages than men, this results in lower pensions. In Europe, for example, women's average pensions are 25 per cent lower than men's. That is why the elderly poor are disproportionately women. There is a trend towards unifying retirement ages for men and women over the long term; alongside policies that equalise opportunities for women in the world of work, this will help to close the pension gap.[9]

## Getting Everyone into the Pension System

The bigger the pool of people contributing to a pension system, the more the risks are shared, the more efficient and sustainable it will be. So to guarantee a minimum state-funded safety-net pension for all, everyone needs to contribute. As with the minimum wage and health entitlements described in previous chapters, the level of this minimum pension will vary enormously between countries, depending on what they can afford. But at the very least it should be enough to avoid destitution in old age, and to maintain its value over time in a way that is fair the state pension should be indexed to a mix of prices, wages or average incomes. Voluntary pensions, which tend to be more common among the better-off, would then be added to the public minimum pension and taxed at a rate close to the rate of normal savings, although some tax incentive to save for retirement is probably worthwhile.

But problems remain: lower-income workers have limited capacity to save, often do not have the requisite financial skills, and do not benefit from the tax incentives available to higher-income pension savers. How can they be brought into the pension system? Some countries, like New Zealand, have provided incentives for workers to sign up to pension schemes by matching their contributions or providing an initial bonus. But one of the most effective ways of getting people into the pension system is simply to make enrolment automatic. Auto-enrolment, as it is known, makes participation in pension schemes the default, with the option to opt out later. Countries that have implemented this, such as Brazil, Germany, New Zealand, Poland, Russia, Turkey and the United Kingdom, have all seen large increases in pension participation. In the United States participation in voluntary company pension plans was made the default option and enrolment doubled. Chile has gone further and made membership of a pension scheme mandatory. With auto-enrolment, most workers stay in the pension scheme (especially if it is also mandatory for employers to contribute), signing up is easy and there are financial incentives to discourage opting out. Programmes that allow workers to regularly increase their contributions or allocate a proportion of any future increase in salary automatically to their pension have also been successful.[10]

Pension systems also need to adapt to the rapid growth in flexible work patterns described in Chapter 5. Most people under-save for retirement, and those who are self-employed, work part-time or are on temporary contracts are particularly vulnerable to this risk. Workers in these categories are often women, the young or old and those on lower incomes. Bringing flexible workers into the pension system not only widens the pool of contributors; by requiring firms that employ flexible workers to make pension contributions on their behalf we can also reduce the incentive for employers to use non-standard contracts simply in order to save on this cost. Yet, in an attempt to make self-employment attractive and thus reduce the temptation to work in the informal economy, many countries do not require self-employed workers to join earnings-based pension schemes (Australia, Denmark, Germany, Japan, Mexico and the Netherlands) or allow them to make lower contributions, resulting in poorer pensions in old age (Canada, France, Italy, Korea, Norway, Poland, Slovenia, Sweden, Switzerland and the United States).[11]

A more inclusive system would automatically enrol flexible workers into voluntary pensions and require the firms that employ them to contribute to their pensions just as they do for the rest of their staff. This is fairly straightforward for part-time and temporary workers, but more complex for the self-employed, who do not have employment contracts and may work for many different employers. One option is to have the worker pay both the employee and employer contribution (although this would make self-employment less attractive); another is to have the state contribute to pensions of those self-employed who are very low earners to encourage them to save for retirement. Over time, it makes sense for pension systems to harmonise coverage, contributions and entitlements between traditional and flexible workers for a host of reasons: it reduces the risks associated with poverty in old age, ensures fairness, pools risks more efficiently and enables greater mobility of workers between types of employment.

Another way to increase the number of workers contributing to pension schemes is simply to bring more people into work. Chapter 2 described how women's participation in the labour force is rising almost everywhere as girls are educated, social norms change and access to childcare is improved. Rapidly ageing countries like Japan are actively encouraging more women to work by increasing childcare provision and changing those aspects of their tax system that disincentivise women from working.[12] Supporting women to stay in work by eliminating discriminatory policies and investing in care provision for children and the elderly will make pension systems more sustainable. Similarly, migrant workers have been important new contributors to pension systems, accounting for 65 per cent of the growth in the workforce in the United States and 92 per cent in the EU.[13] Of course migration has social and political consequences, but it can also be part of the solution by increasing the pool of younger workers contributing to pension systems.

## Share Risks and Make Retirement More Flexible

Most people do not save enough. Surveys across 140 countries show that half of adults in advanced economies and 84 per cent in developing countries did not save for old age.[14] Fortunately, opportunities to save have expanded enormously with digital and mobile banking, new savings products, and robo-advisers providing investment advice at lower costs.

Nudges have also been used effectively to promote savings. In Kenya, for example, an experiment to encourage informal-sector workers to save tried three different interventions to see which worked best: text message reminders written as if from the participant's child, a gold-coloured coin that enabled participants to keep track of their weekly savings and a matching programme that added 10–20 per cent to any money they put aside. Interestingly, the gold coin doubled the average rate of savings and was more effective than a text or financial incentives.[15] In the Philippines an intervention built upon a widely observed aspect of human psychology: the tendency to fear and avoid losses more than to seek and enjoy equivalent gains. Participants made a commitment to save and faced a penalty if they missed their target. This resulted in an 81 per cent increase in savings. Decisions about savings are deeply psychological, and these examples show how behavioural interventions can help.

But many people would simply prefer less responsibility for investment decisions and more certainty about their retirement income. Several countries, including Canada, Denmark and the Netherlands, have developed an alternative to defined contribution schemes that delivers this. Collective defined contribution schemes are based on contributions from both workers and employers, but rather than each individual having their own pension pot, contributions go into a collective pot. The advantage is that the investment risk is spread across a larger group, which reduces volatility and enables lower costs. One study found that a collective scheme would have delivered a steady 28 per cent of salary over the last 50 years, whereas defined contribution schemes delivered between 17 and 61 per cent.[16]

Collective defined contribution schemes may not suit younger workers who prefer a riskier investment portfolio early in their careers. The maximum return on a collective scheme is also lower. On the other hand, very low returns are far less likely. Another advantage is that, unlike defined contribution schemes, in which typically an individual is advised to shift their pension pot away from high-yielding but risky equities and towards safer, though less remunerative, bonds as they get older, this is unnecessary in a collective scheme. Likewise, the risk that a pension will be adversely affected if a contributor happens to retire at a moment when markets are performing poorly is also reduced.

Just as careers have become more like climbing a tree than climbing a ladder, the same should apply to retirement. For many people an abrupt transition from full-time work to retirement is unappealing and not surprisingly comes with a very high risk of death, especially for men. Rather than jump off the career ladder at age 65, better to climb down the tree gradually. Pension schemes should allow people to phase retirement, working flexibly or part-time without adversely affecting their pension arrangements. In Sweden, for example, a person who reaches retirement age can draw all, 75 per cent, 50 per cent, 25 per cent or none of their pension. Whatever is not drawn continues to grow, and if the person continues to work, they can make contributions that add to their income in old age.

Most workers say they would prefer a transition to retirement that involves working part time for some period, but few employers offer this option.[17] Abolishing mandatory retirement ages and introducing flexible work hours and places (including enabling home working) and lifelong learning programmes for older workers as described in Chapter 5 all contribute towards an extension of productive working lives.[18]

Over time, one can imagine older workers earning income from a variety of sources – a minimum state pension, a voluntary employer pension, personal savings and part-time work. Figure 13 shows how the elderly in various countries already have many different sources of income. In France, Italy and Germany the state provides the bulk of income for those over 65. In Turkey pensions provided by employers are most important. In countries like Chile, Korea and Mexico people over 65 get most of their incomes from continuing to work. Such diversification of income in old age should become increasingly common.

**Figure 13. Retirees earn income from a variety of sources**

Income sources of people over 65 years old

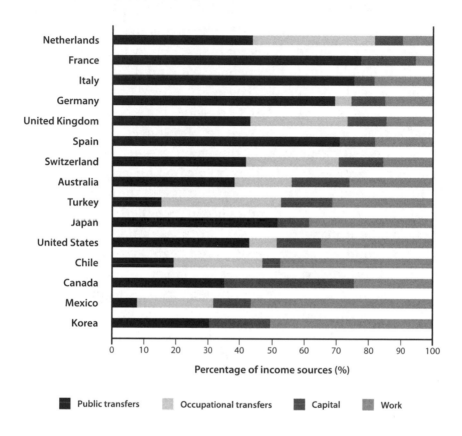

*Who Looks After the Old?*

In Egypt my grandmother presided over a multi-generational household which was the centre of a vast extended family. Lunch was from about 2 p.m. (the time she preferred to eat) until about 6 p.m. as first the grandchildren and great-grandchildren came home from school and later the adults returned from work. Sometimes we were joined by some of her seventeen siblings or their offspring. She did have help, but she was very much in charge of running this complex household including being the chief diplomat for resolving conflicts, the lead spokesperson on family matters and the organiser of all major activities. She loved the company, but it came with a lot of responsibility. As she grew old, she was cared for by the generations she had cared for. This is a family model that still exists in some parts of the world, though it is increasingly being replaced by nuclear families and older people living on their own.

Thus far we have considered ways to provide financially for those who cannot work; now let's consider the second challenge of old age: caring for those who can no longer live independently. As noted at the start of this chapter, older people in all societies have for most of history been cared for predominantly by the women in their families, and this is still the case in most parts of the world. But as families become smaller, more women enter the labour market, the social attitudes of both the elderly and their children change and ageing extends the duration of care, many are struggling to cope. Japan is experimenting with robots that can provide a range of services to the elderly. Many European countries are facilitating the immigration of care workers. New models of cohabitation, community-based care and 'ageing in place' are being tried.

More recently, however, as young people in Europe and the United States find themselves unable to start their own households, the trend towards the Western nuclear family model has reversed. By 2011, 48 per cent of 18- to 34-year-olds in the European Union were living with their parents. Similarly, in the United States, the share of 18–34-year-olds living with their parents rose to a historic high of 36 per cent.[19] This phenomenon is being driven by rising housing costs and the growth of precarious work for young people described in Chapter 5. The proportion of 'boomerang children' has been especially high in countries that went through acute episodes of financial distress, such as Italy and Spain after the 2008 financial crisis, where many young people found themselves unemployed and forced to return to the family home. In many countries, meanwhile, tax and housing policies have encouraged tapping into the value of home equity as a source of pension income, so the old have been acquiring and hoarding housing, while the young cannot afford to buy without help from parents. Hence the monikers 'generation rent' and 'generation landlord'.

Interestingly, families in both advanced and developing countries are facing similar challenges and having to pool income and risks within households to cope with economic uncertainty, precarious work and pensions, rising housing costs and the reversal of policies that encouraged mass home ownership and social housing. Young people increasingly cannot launch independent lives without parental help, while older people with inadequate pensions are sometimes forced to live with their children or become landlords to supplement their incomes. In the face of these pressures, multigenerational households like my grandmother's are proving to be a way for families to maintain their standard of living.

Nonetheless, many elderly people in the coming decades, especially women, will live on their own. The reason is simple: we are living longer.

## Getting Old in the Twenty-First Century

In the twenty-first century living a very long life will be the norm. For men the probability of living to 85 will increase from 50 per cent today to 75 per cent by 2100, and for women from 64 to 83 per cent.[20] In countries like Canada, France, Italy, Japan, the UK and US those born after 2000 (like my children), have a 50 per cent chance of living to their 100th birthday.[21]

The vast majority of the elderly prefer to live independently at home or with their families for as long as they can. Whether the elderly can do so successfully depends on how they age and whether these additional years of life are healthy or not. Research on ageing is increasingly finding that the additional years of life are indeed healthy ones.[22] Nevertheless, many old people need support for daily tasks such as bathing or preparing meals. The least likely to age in good health are people with low incomes who faced deprivation earlier in life; in other words, those most likely to need most help will be those who can least afford to pay for it. And while home care is often more affordable than institutional care (except for those with the most acute needs), even basic support is often unaffordable for the elderly on low incomes.[23]

Most advanced economies provide institutional care for their elderly citizens who cannot afford it; most developing countries place that responsibility on families and communities. The challenge for the future is putting in place a set of policies that support home care for as long as possible. That includes facilitating the provision of care by family members, support for professional carers to make home visits and using technology more creatively. Crucially, it also means better coordination and integration of health care and elderly care, including how they are financed. In most countries the care of the elderly is separate from the health system, resulting in many inefficiencies – most obviously when old people end up in expensive hospital beds when they would be better off at home if they had a bit of support.[24]

These policies are becoming increasingly relevant for developing countries, especially in Asia, where ageing is occurring rapidly and the family support system becomes less robust as people have fewer children, the younger generations are more mobile, and more women are working. China, for example, has introduced support for home carers including training and financial subsidies, and local communities are offering meal services as well as accommodation for their elderly members.[25]

Fundamentally, to make ageing at home viable we must turn unpaid care work into something that is valued and paid for, whether it is provided by a professional or a family member. Some wealthy countries, like the Netherlands and the Nordics, cover the long-term care needs of everyone irrespective of income, but most countries target public support on those who cannot afford it. Broadening that support to pay people to care for their own elderly relatives may seem strange, but it is more humane (to both the elderly and the caregivers), effective and efficient in terms of costs, relative to institutional care. Being cared for by relatives reduces loneliness and the symptoms of depression.[26] A well designed long-term care system has the added advantage of creating more jobs in the care sector while enabling more women to continue to work and thus also contribute towards paying for elderly care through their taxes and pension contributions.

In all countries it is women who benefit most from the provision of support to informal carers.[27] They carry most of the burden of caring for the elderly in the form of lost income and mental health problems, which ironically can contribute to their own impoverishment when they themselves are old.[28] Policies that support informal carers such as cash benefits, pension credits, respite care to give informal carers breaks and flexible working arrangements that enable workers to take time off for caregiving are all beneficial and help women especially. It will come as no surprise that the countries that have the best-funded systems for long-term care (such as the Netherlands, Denmark, Sweden and Switzerland) also have the highest rates of female employment and the lowest gender inequality.

Technology can also help. Chapter 4 described how telemedicine and home-based health monitoring through smart devices and wearable technologies make it possible to treat many conditions remotely, allowing patients to stay at home. Japan is investing heavily in 'carebots' to avoid having to import large numbers of immigrant care workers, as Europe is doing. Carebots can measure vital signs, call the emergency services, remind people to take their medication or to exercise and even engage in basic conversation.[29] They can detect falls and call for help. Voice-activated technologies and autonomous vehicles can help older people operate equipment independently and remain mobile. During the lockdown in response to Covid-19, we saw how technology can help older people in isolation stay in touch with family and friends.

But while technology can replace some of the more physical aspects of caregiving, it must be complemented with human interaction. If we are to enable more old people to live at home independently, it is crucial that we also deal with loneliness. Japan has developed some of the most interesting models: municipalities are responsible for organising 'salons', which provide older people with the opportunity to meet for social events, cultural or educational opportunities or physical exercise. Studies have shown that participating in a salon results in a halving of long-term care needs and a one-third reduction in the incidence of dementia.[30] Experiments with bringing the old and the young together, such as bringing schoolchildren into care homes and older people into classrooms, have proven to benefit both.[31]

## Dignity in Death

One of the worst aspects of the Covid-19 pandemic was that some people died alone in hospitals when they would undoubtedly have preferred to die at home with their families. Dying in a hospital is more likely to be highly medicalised, involving interventions that do not improve our quality of life but simply buy us more time.[32] From the perspective of the social contract, the challenge here is not about reducing costs – high medical spending at the end of life tends to be incurred by people with chronic conditions who generally have shorter life expectancies[33] – but how to provide a good death, which for most people is one free from pain and surrounded by loved ones. Indeed, many countries are moving away from institutionalisation and returning to death at home, supported, if necessary, by hospice care. Among Medicare beneficiaries in the United States between 2000 and 2015 deaths in hospital fell from 33 to 20 per cent, while home or community deaths increased from 30 to 40 per cent.[34]

Knowing clearly and in advance the preferences of those who are dying makes a huge difference to their well-being and that of their families. Advanced directives, or living wills, provide this clarity, reduce the decision-making burden for families and minimise legal disputes and trauma for the bereaved. They are associated with lower rates of hospitalisa tion, better psychological outcomes and greater satisfaction with the quality of care. Despite all these benefits, only a minority of adults have completed one.[35] In many countries there are taboos around talking about death, but nudges, such as making advanced directives mandatory when individuals are hospitalised, could help. However we achieve it, a new social contract in societies that are ageing needs to include clarity about end-of-life care.

## *Affording Old Age*

Projections of the cost of ageing usually rise exponentially and cause considerable alarm. Based on current trends, health-care and pension expenditures are projected to consume 25 per cent of GDP in advanced economies and 16 per cent in developing countries by 2100.[36] The levels of debt and taxation necessary to spend a quarter of national income on ageing are proba bly unsustainable, which is why we need a new social contract around old age. If sensible decisions are taken now, it will be possible to support the older generation humanely and sustain ably. As we have seen, this will be most challenging for advanced economies that already have large elderly populations with well entrenched entitlements. For low- and middle-income countries still building pension and care systems, the major lesson is to embed automaticity and sustainability in them from the begin ning before entitlements get too costly.

Providing financial security in old age will require a combin ation of longer working lives with retirement ages linked to life expectancy, a minimum state-provided safety net pension, mandatory enrolment in employment-based pension systems for all workers (traditional and flexible) and better risk shar ing. Funding the minimum state pension from taxes on income or consumption (such as VAT) would spread the costs more fairly. The alternative – imposing additional payroll taxes on a shrinking working-age population – would create disincentives to create new jobs.

Ageing populations have also been associated with lower interest rates, as a larger proportion of people try to save for retirement when demand for investment in the economy is weak. In the advanced economies, particularly in Japan and Europe, ageing may have reduced interest rates by 0.75–1.5 per cent, and this effect is likely to persist unless changes in policy provide greater incentives for investment.[37] Low interest rates reduce returns on defined contribution schemes and threaten the solvency of defined benefit schemes. On the other hand, lower interest rates also lower the cost of public debt, making it easier for governments to finance public spending, such as greater public investment that can enable higher private investment.

Families will always play an important role in caring for the elderly, but society needs to support them in affording to doing so. When Japan launched its long-term care insurance scheme, its slogan was 'From Care by Family to Care by Society'.[38] Governments spend very different amounts on elderly care – ranging from 2 per cent of GDP in rapidly ageing Japan to about 0.5 per cent in Italy and even less in Australia, countries where care is provided informally by families or paid for by individuals.[39] How should this be paid for? Care costs are highly unpredictable (as my 94-year-old grandfather found) and therefore a prime case for pooling risk through insurance, either via the state or through private markets.[40]

In practice, there are three models. The Nordics have universal tax-funded systems that provide comprehensive coverage of care regardless of income. Other countries have dedicated social insurance schemes that provide either comprehensive (Netherlands or Japan) or partial (Korea and Germany) coverage of care costs. For example, in Japan most people pay only 10 per cent of the costs of home care up to a maximum monthly amount, while those with high incomes pay 20 per cent. The third option is for the state to provide cash benefits to cover care needs, as is done in Italy. The UK and the US use a variation of this model in which cash benefits are highly targeted to help the poorest while the wealthiest are expected to pay their own care costs. In the developing world there is very little pooling of risk at all, and the costs of care are provided through informal arrangements – in other words, by unpaid family members.

As with pensions, the key to the sustainable funding of long-term care is to broaden the base of contributions. In Japan and Germany, for example, everyone is obliged to contribute to publicly funded care insurance – those who are working as well as retirees. Private markets for care insurance do not work particularly well because those who know they are likely to need care are more likely to seek insurance, making it unprofitable for the insurer, and most people are myopic about the long-term costs of care. Germany was the first to make private care insurance compulsory; Japan has followed, making it compulsory for everyone over 40 years old, and Singapore has made enrolment automatic with an option to opt out. More countries that are ageing should be considering mandatory insurance for elderly care.

Old age will be a bigger part of all our lives. The new social contract envisioned in this chapter would ensure those who can work longer do so in exchange for greater security in old age and a system that enables them to live independently at home for as long as possible. The responsibility for caring for those who can no longer live independently would shift from one borne overwhelmingly by women to one shared by everyone in society. And the risks of poverty and insecurity in old age would be replaced by a shared commitment to support the older generation. After all, they raised us and built the infrastructure and institutions that make us productive today – an important factor to bear in mind as we turn our attention to the social contract between the generations.

# 7

# Generations

Consider this: would you rather earn an average income today or have that same income in medieval times, making you the equivalent of a wealthy landlord? Given this choice, most people choose the present over the past. Why? Because even for someone with an average income the many benefits and comforts of modern life – from medicine and social freedoms to indoor plumbing and mobile phones – outweigh whatever rewards might accrue from having land and serfs. This reflects the success of our social contract across the generations: put simply, most people are much better off than their distant ancestors. In fact, when (and where) we are born is probably the biggest determinant of the standard of living we enjoy and the opportunities we have.

Despite that success over time, young people today in many countries are angry about the world they are inheriting and are unconvinced of the inevitability of progress. There are two dimensions to this anger.[1] First, the younger generations in some countries resent decisions made by baby boomers (those born between the end of World War II and the early 1960s) that have left them with unaffordable education and housing and insecure income prospects. In other words, they are dissatisfied with the distribution of resources and opportunities between the generations currently alive. Second, younger people also worry about the impact of decisions taken over the last century that affect the future of the planet. This is about the distribution of resources and opportunities between those who have lived until now and those who will live in the future, including the unborn. Both of these concerns are mediated through the social contract.

Within families, the social contract between the generations is easy to understand. Parents want to give their children the capabilities and means to have a good life; children want their parents to have a comfortable old age. If parents are able to, they may leave some kind of inheritance to provide their offspring with a greater range of possibilities; children, meanwhile, will often care and support their parents in their later years. Certainly, no parent wants to leave their children a legacy of debts. The practice of holding children responsible for the debts of their parents, which existed in places like ancient Mesopotamia and feudal England, has been banned around the world.[2]

At a societal level, the social contract between the generations is more complex. The legacy we leave to future generations has many dimensions: the stock of human knowledge and culture, inventions, infrastructure, institutions and the state of the natural world. Current and future generations owe a great deal to the efforts of their forebears who invested in education, discovered technologies, built institutions and companies that created wealth and sometimes fought wars for national independence and freedom. Most would agree that we also owe something to the future generations we will never meet, and that each generation should leave the next at least as well off and preferably better off than they were.

This chapter will examine how the social contract is faring in terms of living standards, debt and environmental legacy – and what will need to change if we are to heal the rift that is opening between the generations alive today and together honour our obligations to the generations to come.

## *Living Standards: Differences between Generations and Countries*

In emerging markets such as Brazil, China, India and South Africa most people think the next generation will be better off than their parents (Figure 14). In sharp contrast, in richer countries such as France, Germany, Italy, South Korea and the UK, the majority believe the next generation will be worse off.

In developing countries economic growth rates are higher, there is still a lot of technological catching up to be done, and populations are still young and able to benefit from the demographic dividend – the growth that can arise when the majority of the population are working age. These are all good reasons to expect younger people to indeed be better off than their parents. In the advanced economies, however, young people face very different prospects. Baby boomers benefited from decades of sustained economic growth, secure jobs with benefits and major gains in health and social conditions. Generation X (those born 1966–1980) and millennials (born 1981–2000) have faced a world of more flexible and precarious work, as described in Chapter 5, rising house prices and a period of fiscal austerity after the 2008 financial crisis that reduced social spending in many countries. Although only in their twenties, many of them carry large debt burdens from student loans and credit cards which limit their ability to secure a mortgage on a home or start a family. Meanwhile, Generation Z (those born after 2000, or zoomers) are at the forefront of youth protests about climate change. The income gains and the likelihood of security in old age experienced by past generations have stalled and, in some countries, reversed. In advanced economies, the risks of poverty are shifting from the old to the young.[3]

The pessimism about young people's prospects in many advanced economies is based not just on broad economic trends but on day-to-day lived experience. In almost all advanced economies millennials and Generation X have real incomes little or no higher than their predecessors' were at the same age

## Figure 14. Will young people have a better or worse life than their parents?

Responses by country to this question: To what extent do you feel that today's youth will have a better or worse life than their parents or will it be about the same?

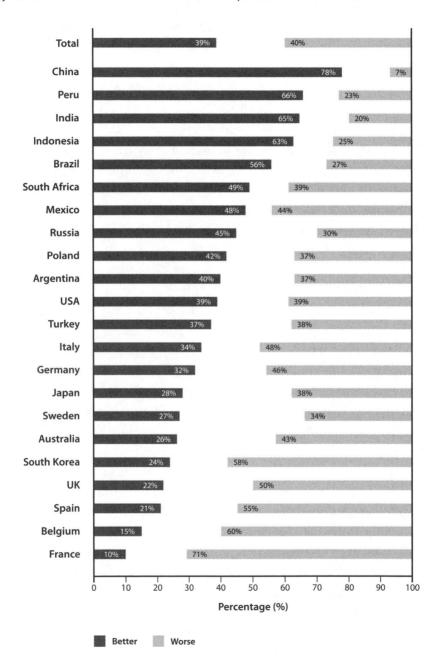

and are more indebted earlier in life than their parents were.[4] This worsening of prospects has been particularly acute in the UK and in countries hard hit by the Eurozone crisis such as Greece, Italy and Spain. The Nordic countries stand out as exceptions, having been able to deliver rising real earnings and improved livelihoods for the next generation.

## *National Debt: The Next Generation's Legacy*

While parents can no longer leave their debts to their children, societies do leave younger generations a legacy of government debt which must be paid back through future taxes.[5] Where that debt has been used to finance new productive capacity (better educated people, new technologies, better infrastructure) the higher incomes that result from these investments should make it easy to repay, but where the debt has been used to finance unsustainable consumption or white elephant projects with low returns, future generations have been saddled with additional burdens.

After the 2008 financial crisis, many advanced economies accumulated considerable debts to cushion the massive recession which occurred. That public debt ranged from about 50 per cent of GDP to 90 per cent, with Japan and Italy the major outliers with debts well above 100 per cent of GDP. In the developing world, meanwhile, many countries took advantage of the very low interest rates to borrow on global financial markets. Investors, keen to generate higher returns in a world of low interest rates, happily lent to many African, Asian and Latin American economies which as a result found they had much greater access to borrowing on more favourable terms than ever before.

However, many were already starting to wonder about the burden on future generations of having to repay this huge debt burden when along came Covid-19. As a result, debt levels in both advanced and developing countries are reaching levels never seen before in human history, even after World War

II. Advanced economies have borrowed heavily to weather the economic consequences of the pandemic. Because interest rates are low, servicing this debt looks affordable for now. Developing countries have not been able to borrow as much, and some low-income countries have benefited from a moratorium on debt payments, but the current picture is sobering (Figure 15). Countries such as Japan, Italy, Greece, Venezuela and Lebanon have government debts twice the size of their economies. Young people in these countries will pay out a significant part of their future incomes for the obligations incurred by their governments.

The obvious question is how will future generations pay this back? In previous episodes of high debt, countries repaid

**Figure 15. Debt levels are high in many countries**

Debt as a share of GDP

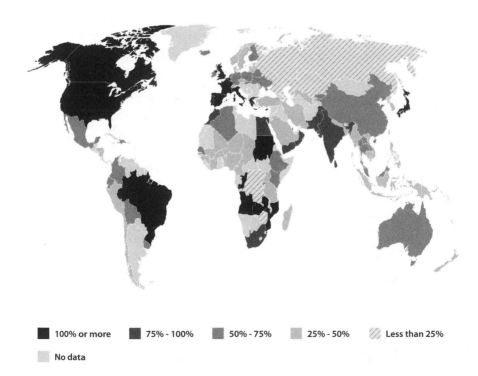

■ 100% or more ■ 75% - 100% ■ 50% - 75% ■ 25% - 50% ⫽ Less than 25%

▨ No data

it through three strategies: faster economic growth; austerity, imposed either through higher taxes or cutting public spending; or keeping interest rates artificially low and allowing higher inflation – what economists call financial repression. The latter strategy punishes savers and the private sector and forces everyone to suffer higher inflation in order to ease the burden on debtors and the government.

Clearly faster growth is the most appealing, but also difficult to orchestrate. When I was at the IMF, we spent a great deal of time evaluating whether countries could repay their debts. We found that even a very small (0.5 per cent) change in the economic growth rate would have a huge impact on debt sustainability, mainly because of the power of compounding. Many of the policies outlined in this book – investing more in education, enabling women to join the labour market, extending working lives – would help raise future growth, increase productivity and thus make it more possible for future generations to shoulder these debts.

The other options – austerity and inflating the debt away – are unappealing. After Covid-19, most governments will be under pressure to spend more, especially on health and addressing the inequities that the pandemic has revealed. And financial repression is harder to orchestrate in a world of globalised financial markets. But the one silver lining is that interest rates are expected to remain low, making the servicing of these debts more affordable. So perhaps we will be able to sustain these higher debt levels for now, but only if we do enough in the meantime to invest wisely and enable future generations to thrive economically, which is the only way they will be able to settle our bills.

## *Environmental Inheritance*

Economists tend to think about the inheritance of each generation in terms of the different types of 'capital' that determine the productive capacity, or wealth, of a country. These are three-fold: human capital (the educated people, the institutions and social structures they create); produced capital (technologies, machines, infrastructure); and natural capital (land, the climate, biodiversity). While changes to human and produced capital are often reversible (people can change their minds and invest more or less over time), changes to natural capital can be irreversible. Once a species is lost or a glacier has melted, it may be impossible to get back, so depleting natural capital should be done with this risk of extinction in mind, including the consequences for highly interdependent ecosystems.

In the case of the climate, we know that we are leaving the next generation with a hotter planet than the one we inherited. Scientists estimate that human activity has already raised the temperature of the world by approximately one degree Celsius above pre-industrial levels.[6] This will persist for centuries. What this means for our planet's future is highly uncertain, and the potentially compounding effects of even higher temperatures are even more so. What we do know is that these effects tend to be felt via the world's water in the form of storms, floods, droughts, desertification, ocean acidification and sea-level rise. All of these have implications for the well-being of nature and humans.

We also know that we are leaving the next generation less biodiversity and that this is being lost faster than at any time in human history. Extinction rates are between 100 and 1000 times higher than the averages seen over the past several million years. On average, there has been a 60 per cent decline in mammals, birds, fish, reptiles, and amphibians over the last 40 years. About one million animal and plant species are threatened with extinction.[7]

What would a purely economic analysis say about how we have managed the intergenerational legacy of capital or wealth? One way to answer this question is to measure how much capital we are giving future generations and how that has evolved over time. An attempt to do so across 140 countries between 1992 and 2014 is shown in Figure 16.[8] It shows that each person in the future will inherit twice as much produced capital, 13 per cent more human capital, but 40 per cent less

**Figure 16. Global inheritance of produced, human and natural capital**

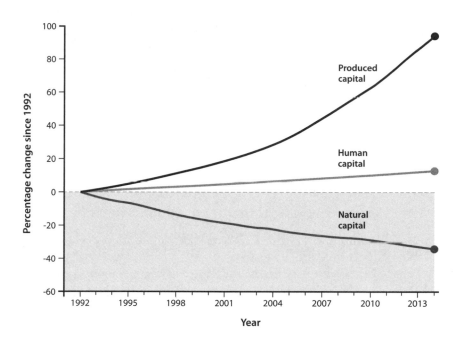

natural capital. Does that pattern of inheritance leave future generations better off?

From the actions of young people across the world, it seems they are not convinced. 'You will die of old age, we will die of climate change,' said the placard carried by one student protester at the climate strike in London on 20 September 2019. In over 150 countries around the world, 2500 protests were held to demand action on the environment. Young people were in the majority, skipping school to attend, some doing so weekly as part of the Fridays for Future movement started by Greta Thunberg of Sweden. This was perhaps the most visible expression of many young people's belief that older generations are stealing their futures, but is this a fair criticism?

A purely economic analysis would frame the question this way: have we given future generations enough human and physical capital to compensate them for the depletion of the natural environment? Or have we overinvested in human and physical capital and underinvested in natural capital? The problem for an economist is that much of the value of the environment is not reflected in market prices. In many places people can pollute rivers, cut down forests or emit carbon at almost zero cost, and so there is a tendency to underinvest in nature since the returns on that investment do not appear in market-based calculations. So how else might we measure the return on natural capital?

The economist Partha Dasgupta, who has done a great deal of work on the environment, has grappled with this question. He has estimated the rate of return on natural capital by using the amount of biomass the planet produces each year relative to the stock.[9] He comes up with a rate of return of about 19 per cent a year, which is far higher than the 5 per cent average return on produced capital such as housing and shares in companies. On these calculations, the world has been overinvesting in produced capital and underinvesting in natural capital, which has a far higher return if the environment's true worth to society is measured properly. He also argues that investing in the environment reduces variability and uncertainty, including on the returns to other investments. For example, having more species of bumble bees diversifies risk and provides a sort of insurance for our ecosystem.

An overall assessment of the social contract between the generations would have to conclude that we have left future generations vast human and physical wealth in the form of knowledge, technology, infrastructure and institutions. But we have also left them a depleted natural environment with serious consequences for the climate and biodiversity. In the advanced economies we are also seeing signs that improvements in living standards have slowed and that future generations may not see the kinds of gains that previous generations experienced. And all countries are accumulating debts – to cope with the coronavirus pandemic as well as with ageing – that will weigh on future generations. What would a more sustainable social contract between the generations look like?

### Defining Sustainability Between the Generations

There are many definitions of a sustainable social contract between current and future generations. In 1987 the Brundtland Commission, established by the United Nations to promote global sustainable development, defined it as 'development that meets the needs of the present without compromising the ability of future generations to meet their own needs'.[10] Four years later the economist Robert Solow wrote, 'sustainability is an injunction not to satisfy ourselves by impoverishing our successors'.[11] Because it is about sharing well-being between present people and future people, sustainability involves weighing up the merits of current consumption versus investing and providing for subsequent generations. The problem is that future generations are not represented in today's market or political system and cannot participate in negotiating to secure their interests in the social contract.

So how should the social contract take into account people who do not yet exist? Moral philosophers tend to argue that we should give the same weight to the well-being of future generations as we do to that of those alive today, otherwise we are simply discriminating based on dates of birth. Economists generally take a different view: when weighing up the costs and benefits of a course of action, they have tended to give less weight to future generations than to current ones. In the language of economics, they discount (reduce the value) of the income of future generations relative to the income of those alive today so that a benefit in the future counts for less than a benefit today.[12]

Proponents of this social discount rate argue that future generations will be wealthier than us and have access to many technologies that we cannot even imagine, which has indeed been the case for the past few thousand years of human history. They also argue that there are many poor people today who should not be asked to make sacrifices for the hypothetical welfare of those who do not even exist. Opponents argue that discounting curtails the options (potentially even the existence) of future generations too much, that some of the losses we impose may be irreplaceable and irreversible, and that there are too many risks and uncertainties which must be taken into account in decisions so far out in the future.

While whether to discount the income of future generations may seem like a tedious and abstruse economic argument, it is the central issue that determines the urgency of acting on climate change.[13] Let me illustrate the debate about discounting with examples using marshmallows, jam and swimming pools.

In a famous experiment conducted at Stanford University in 1972 children were left in a room alone with a marshmallow and told that if they waited fifteen minutes and refrained from eating it, they would get a second marshmallow.[14] The children, who were between three and five years old, fidgeted, covered their eyes and tried to distract themselves to avoid temptation. Later in life, those who had succeeded in delaying the gratification of their desire for marshmallows were found to have higher test scores. We might say that these children, who valued future consumption more than immediate gratification, used a lower discount rate on future benefits than those who gobbled up the marshmallows. The lesson for our purposes is that those who are able to restrain themselves can ultimately make themselves better off, especially if they make investments that generate high returns – such as doubling your marshmallow consumption in just fifteen minutes or education or infrastructure that makes future generations better off.

Now let's turn to jam. In Lewis Carroll's 1871 book *Through the Looking-Glass* the White Queen promises Alice 'jam every other day', but the promise is a hollow one since 'the rule is, jam tomorrow and jam yesterday – but never jam today'.[15] The great twentieth-century economist John Maynard Keynes used this story to illustrate the perils of obsessing about the future: 'The "purposive" man is always trying to secure a spurious and delusive immortality for his acts by pushing his interest in them forward into time. He does not love his cat, but his cat's kittens; nor, in truth, the kittens, but only the kittens' kittens, and so on forward for ever to the end of cat-dom. For him jam is not jam unless it is a case of jam to-morrow and never jam to-day.'[16]

The lesson here is that asking people, especially poor people with immediate needs, to sacrifice something today can be fundamentally at odds with the purpose of our economy, which is to ensure that everyone has enough to live with dignity. Keynes argued that excessive saving can lead to stagnation, and that sometimes consuming more now is the best way to avoid economic catastrophe.

Finally let's turn to swimming pools. When I worked on the first major report the World Bank did on the environment in 1992 we had a debate about whether a swimming pool could be a substitute for a lake. Clearly a swimming pool can offer some of the goods a lake provides – a place for swimming and recreation – but not others, such as an ecosystem for wildlife, a watershed or storage of fresh water. In other words, some goods have easy substitutes: for example, if we use up all the world's copper, there are other materials that have sufficiently similar properties that we can use them instead. But others are not easily replaced, or we may want to preserve them for their intrinsic value, in which case our calculus should be different. The lesson here is that we should aim to leave the next generation not the exact same legacy of resources that we inherited, but instead a comparable set of opportunities.

What conclusions can we draw from these stories of marshmallows, jam and swimming pools? History teaches us that discounting on the basis that future generations are likely to be wealthier is legitimate, even if we think arguing that their well-being is worth less than ours (what economists call pure-time discounting) is not; a fair social contract should not discriminate based on when we are alive. Nonetheless, restraining ourselves in order to make high-return investments in areas such as green technologies make sense because it increases the scope for additional marshmallows tomorrow. At the same time, some jam should be eaten today if people would otherwise go hungry. And while we should seek to equalise opportunities for well-being within and across time, the nature of those opportunities may vary if we believe that goods and services can be substitutes for one another. Put simply, we should eat some jam today, postpone marshmallows for tomorrow and recognise that swimming pools can only do so much.

Of course, the overarching and unavoidable problem is that we do not know what opportunities future generations might aspire to or what technologies they may have access to, so making decisions now for them is fraught with uncertainty. In such a situation it is usually best to make choices that leave options open and are robust in the light of different possible futures. When making decisions over very long time horizons, it is also best to test them against various ethical and practical assumptions.[17] For example, decisions might be tested in the context of different scenarios about future technological progress or the risks around catastrophic events. This precautionary approach makes sense when we do not have all the information we need, we lack full knowledge of future preferences and potential outcomes, and we want to avoid irreversible losses.

Where we choose to draw the line will depend to some extent on our current circumstances. Consider this question, for example. Is it fair to ask current generations to make sacrifices for the future when so many people still live in poverty today? The view in many developing countries is that past environmental destruction has enabled the accumulation of wealth in the advanced economies and therefore rich countries should bear the responsibility for fixing the problem. But while the needs of today's poor are urgent and need to be addressed now, that is no excuse to avoid addressing climate risks as well. The answer is in finding a fair way to share the burden, given different countries' wealth and relative contribution to the degradation of the environment.[18] Fair burden-sharing is at the heart of negotiations about climate change, and many of the more efficient solutions involve transferring resources from rich to poor countries in order to reduce emissions at lower cost.[19]

## Redressing Environmental Damage

Imagine your great-grandparents time-travelling from the past to meet you now. In the vast majority of cases they would surely have a favourable view of the legacy they have left us. We have so much more material wealth than they could have imagined; far fewer of us live with the risks of starvation and poverty; our access to information and education is so much greater than ever before, and most of us have political and social freedoms they would envy. They might regret the lives lost to wars, the forests and species destroyed and the risks around the climate, but by and large they would think they left us a better world than the one they inherited.

What would we say if we travelled into the future to meet our great-grandchildren? In terms of education and physical capital, we have continued to invest, and the gains, particularly in the developing world, have been very large. But we have probably underinvested in natural capital and, especially in the advanced economies, depleted those resources too much all over the world. Some of this can be compensated for by new technologies and skills that will make future generations better off, but some of the loss in natural capital needs to be reversed to ensure the well-being of future generations, especially where we face potential tipping points and irreversible losses. Many young people today clearly share this view and have embraced environmental activism.

The agenda for redressing the environmental damage we have done is clear. First, as the Hippocratic oath says, do no harm – or, in this case, no more harm. At the moment governments around the world provide subsidies that actively encourage the exploitation of the environment for agriculture, water use, fisheries and fossil fuels to the tune of $4–6 trillion annually.[20]

These subsidies mean that it is not just free to deplete the natural world, the taxpayer actually pays people to do it! Second, we must invest more in the conservation and restoration of the biosphere, for example by planting trees.[21] Current public and private spending on conservation is about $91 billion, less than 0.02 per cent of what is spent on subsidies to degrade the environment.[22] Increasing our spending on conservation 50-fold would still leave 99 per cent of the savings to be made from eliminating subsidies available for other uses.

The third step is to measure things properly: where market prices do not convey the true value of environmental services, we must find other ways to factor them into our calculations and decisions. There are now well-developed methodologies for measuring environmental impacts and incorporating them properly into national accounts.[23] If we don't measure and price things properly, the market on its own will incentivise excessive depletion of natural capital. Companies will tend to create technologies that economise on things they have to pay for (such as labour) and overexploit things they do not have to pay for, like air quality, congestion or a diverse habitat. Similarly, we may also go astray if we focus on GDP as the sole measure of success, instead of wider measures such as well-being and the capability of the population.

Measuring things properly includes taking into account all of the services that nature provides. Consider the contribution of whales. They are dramatic animals and clearly play an important role in the marine ecosystem, but whales also capture a huge amount of carbon. If this is taken into account, the IMF estimates that each living whale provides carbon services worth $2 million (and each forest elephant is worth $1.76 million).[24] Restoring the global population of whales would remove as much carbon as planting two billion trees. Nature is the world's best carbon-capture technology, and if we include its services in our calculations, we will make better investments.

Wales (not the animal but the nation) has developed an interesting approach to taking such values into account: it has appointed the world's first 'minister for future generations'.[25] Her job is to monitor government policies in areas such as transport, energy and education to ensure that they take into account the interests of the unborn. For example, a proposed road around Newport was challenged for its potential impact on biodiversity and consequences for public debt. While she cannot reverse decisions, she can act as a voice for the unheard and make sure issues get addressed.

The fourth step towards redressing environmental damage is using fiscal policy – the government's power to tax and spend – in order to change the incentives that shape public behaviour so as to actually reverse environmental damage. Taxing the use of carbon, for example, is one obvious way to reduce greenhouse gases and could substitute for other levies so as not to raise the overall tax burden. Those on low incomes who were adversely affected by this would need to be compensated (neglecting to do this is what got President Macron into trouble with the *gilets jaunes*). Chapter 8 includes more detail on the potential role of carbon taxes.

Fiscal policy could also include subsidies to green technologies. Such subsidies have helped develop many renewable technologies such as solar and wind power that are now commercially successful and are making the transition to greener energy faster and more affordable. The benefit of these investments will also be felt by future generations, providing them with more options to preserve natural capital. But in the near term we still have an opportunity to make a real difference with over $100 trillion of investment in infrastructure set to occur over the next 20 years, mainly in the developing world. As economist Nick Stern of the LSE has said, 'The way investments will be made, in transport, energy, water, buildings and land, will determine whether we can hold global warming to well below 2 centigrade degrees, or whether we are doomed to cities where people can neither move nor breathe, and to ecosystems that will collapse.'[26]

## Towards a New Social Contract Between the Generations

Covid-19 brought many inter-generational tensions to the fore. The old bore the brunt of the disease's impact on health; the young had to sacrifice economically and socially to protect the elderly. The young will also have to repay the huge public debts that are being incurred to combat the pandemic, in most advanced economies doing so with income prospects already poorer than their parents'. Living through a pandemic during the impressionable years of 18–25 will surely have a large and enduring negative impact on young people's confidence in political institutions and their trust in political leaders, especially in democracies where citizens expect governments to be responsive and accountable.[27]

How can we rebalance the social contract between the generations? We must do as much as we can to redress environmental damage and find ways to help reduce the fiscal burden on future generations. To achieve this, today's older people may need to work longer and link retirement ages explicitly to life expectancy, as discussed in Chapter 6. The measures described in Chapter 4 – achieving universal basic health care and managing rising health costs, including through the use of technology – would also help reduce fiscal pressures.

We also need to invest in the next generation to enable them to be productive over what will be very long working lives. Ideally, each young person would start their life with an educational endowment which enabled them to acquire new skills throughout their career, as discussed in Chapter 3. The active labour market policies discussed in Chapter 5 – helping workers to retrain and get into the jobs of the future – would also support productivity. And better early-years education and support for women who work would mean we could tap into all the talent in our societies. The resulting gains in productivity would help pay for the elderly care needs of an ageing population and make debt more sustainable in the future. These are enlightened investments by one generation in the next and provide the basis for a new social contract between the generations.

As we have seen, the politics of such a change are complicated by the fact that old people tend to be more effective at exercising political power than the young. Research has shown that the proportion of old people in the population has a significant impact on the pattern of public spending.[28] Put simply, more old people means more spending on pensions and less on education. Older voters are more averse to policies – such as low interest rates and quantitative easing – intended to increase economic demand and maintain full employment but which lower returns on savings and risk more inflation. Having retired, they also generally care less about unemployment, compared to the average citizen.[29] Political parties in ageing societies, such as Germany or Japan, are increasingly forced to cater to these preferences. Some might argue that the wealthier the elderly are, the more will be passed on to the next generation through inheritance, but the distribution of inherited wealth is highly unequal (a topic that will be discussed in the next chapter), and some things – like the environment – cannot be inherited privately but must be shared.

Instead, the Cambridge political scientist David Runciman has argued (somewhat mischievously) that the voting age should be reduced to six (you read that right, six) to counterbalance the growing ageism of democracies.[30] Otherwise young people's interests will never be adequately reflected in parliaments and elections, while those of the unborn never get considered at all. In a revealing moment during an encounter between Senator Diane Feinstein and a group of impassioned US schoolchildren arguing for a 'green new deal', she countered, 'but you didn't vote for me'.[31] Her point was not that they should have voted for her; they obviously could not have done so. It was that her duty was to represent the interests of those who had voted for her, a group which didn't include them.

While boycotting school and demonstrating for climate action ensure headlines, voting is still the most powerful mechanism to achieve change in democracies. One way or another, we must find a way to give more weight to the voices and interests of younger and future generations. Otherwise the social contract that shapes the future will be designed exclusively by those who will not live to see it, with no input from those who will.

# 8

# A New Social Contract

The 4th of July is the day the United States celebrates its declaration of independence, usually with fireworks and summer barbecues, but for his 4th of July speech in 1962 President John F. Kennedy called for a 'declaration of interdependence'. He wanted to signal that because people and countries depended so much on each other, there were mutually beneficial gains to be had from cooperation. Kennedy was referring in particular to the interdependence between the emerging European Economic Community and the United States, founded some 175 years previously.[1] But his sentiments apply equally to the interdependencies within countries.[2]

Five years later, Martin Luther King, the great American civil rights leader, gave a Christmas sermon that expressed something similar: 'In a real sense all life is inter-related. All men are caught in an inescapable network of mutuality, tied in a single garment of destiny. Whatever affects one directly, affects all indirectly. I can never be what I ought to be until you are what you ought to be, and you can never be what you ought to be until I am what I ought to be.'[3]

The Covid pandemic was in many ways a great revealer, making these interdependencies all the more apparent. The virus circumnavigated the world, affecting everyone, but those with health vulnerabilities the most. All of us depended on millions of people we had never met behaving responsibly and on health systems in faraway places being able to cope. Within countries it was brought home which workers were essential – without nurses, truckers, supermarket employees, sanitation workers our lives would cease to function. It is a great irony that many of these essential workers were among the lowest paid and the most likely to be in precarious work with minimal job security.

This book has argued that the reason we see so much disappointment in many societies is that our social contract has broken under the weight of technological and demographic changes. As a consequence, more risks – caring for their children, maintaining their skills if they become unemployed, taking care of themselves when they get old – are being borne by individuals. We are increasingly living in 'you're on your own' societies, a situation which gets translated into the politics of anger, an epidemic of mental health issues and both young and old fearing for their futures.[4] Yet in many areas bearing risks individually is not just inequitable, it is also far less efficient and productive than sharing them across society.

We need a social contract that delivers a better architecture of both security and opportunity for everyone, a social contract that is less about 'me' and more about 'we', recognises our interdependence and uses it for mutual benefit. We need a social contract that is about pooling and sharing more risks with each other to reduce the worries we all face while optimising the use of talent across our societies and enabling individuals to contribute as much as they can. It also means caring about the well-being not just of our own grandchildren, but of others' too, since they will all occupy the same world in future.

Three broad principles underpin all of the arguments put forward thus far:

1. *Security for all*. Everyone should be guaranteed a minimum for a decent life. The level of this minimum will depend on what a country can afford.
2. *Maximum investment in capability*. Society should invest as much as it can afford in creating opportunities

for its citizens to be productive and to contribute for as long as they can to the common good. Also for the common good, society should provide incentives to reduce things we want less of, such as carbon emissions and obesity.

3. *Efficient, fair sharing of risks.* Too many risks are being borne in the wrong place and could be better managed if allocated differently between individuals, families, employers and the state.

This chapter outlines what a new social contract based on these principles might look like, describes what its economic benefits could be, and suggests how it might be financed and delivered.

## We Owe Each Other More

Drawing together the lessons of the previous chapters, what are the actual ingredients of this new social contract? Let's begin with the foundation: the guaranteed basics for a decent life to which everyone is entitled – a minimum income, an educational entitlement, a basic health-care package and protection from poverty in old age.

There are many ways to provide a floor to people's incomes – minimum wages, tax credits that top up the incomes of low-wage workers and cash transfers targeted to the neediest households. A minimum education entitlement needs to include early-years support and lifelong learning, the latter financed through general taxation, by employers or through loans on generous terms. Minimum health care should include everything that the World Health Organization recommends in its essential health package. There should be a threshold that defines which health interventions are funded publicly that rises with per capita income. Minimum benefits – such as sick leave and unemployment insurance – should be provided to all workers regardless of the type of employment contract they have. And there should be a minimum state pension linked to life expectancy that is publicly funded to prevent poverty in old age.

The key to making such a social contract economically viable is tapping into all of the capabilities in society and thereby increasing productivity. Higher productivity translates into higher incomes, higher tax receipts and greater capacity to pay for the costs of more generous investment in education and social insurance. There is huge untapped talent in the growing pool of educated women, minorities and children born into poor families who are unable to live up to their potential. This is not politically correct equality-speak. Recall the evidence in Chapter 2 that 20–40 per cent of the productivity gains in the United States between 1960 and 2010 could be attributed to breaking the monopoly held by white men on good jobs and utilising the talents of women, black men and ethnic minorities more efficiently.[5] Similarly, if today's 'lost Einsteins' (women, minorities and children from low-income families) were enabled to invent to the same degree as white men from high-income families, the rate of innovation could quadruple.[6] Such opportunity-enhancing policies reduce the need to redistribute income and provide people with more capabilities and the freedom to fulfil their version of a good life.

Creating a labour market that taps into all this talent starts with improved early-years education because interventions before children get to school age are the most effective and economical way to equalise opportunities and increase social mobility. But unlocking talent also requires new policies for the provision of childcare and elderly care because these currently consume a vast quantity of unpaid female labour. Enabling women to be more productive necessitates a fairer division of labour within families and communities.

Labour markets around the world are becoming ever more flexible, but future social contracts need to balance flexibility with greater security.[7] This can be achieved by sharing more risks with employers (through payroll taxes), regulation (mandating minimum wages and benefits for flexible workers), developing collective-bargaining mechanisms for flexible workers, or public insurance and training financed through general taxation. In this way employers would retain the flexibility to adjust their workforces knowing that individuals would be able to sustain a decent standard of living and be given adequate support to find a new job. Employees, meanwhile, would have more certainty about their incomes and be able to plan their lives, including invest in their skills, form a family or buy a home.

Making all this financially sustainable requires everyone to contribute to society for as long as they can. This means retiring later. Pension ages should be linked to life expectancy to maintain the balance between years in work and years in retirement. It also means learning new skills later in life. Better funding of adult learning is the necessary complement to a flexible labour market in which workers will have careers potentially spanning more than 50 years. Reskilling can be funded collectively – through taxes, unions or companies – but is best provided in close collaboration with employers to make it more effective. Enlightened companies will increasingly see environmental sustainability, paying their fair share of taxes and commitment to their employees and communities as central to their strategies. Investors, meanwhile, will increasingly factor such commitments into their valuations of firms' share prices, and financial markets reward firms that manage these risks intelligently. Regulations should make sure that everyone is held to a minimum standard so there is a level playing field for all employers.

A new social contract will also require individuals to take greater responsibility for their health, in particular using technology for better independent self-care. Where health costs are shared, society should use nudges and taxes to encourage individuals to take better care of their health and to provide clarity on their end-of-life preferences. For example, during the Covid pandemic it was perfectly reasonable for society to ask individuals to wear masks to slow the spread of the disease. Similarly, requiring vaccinations, taxing cigarettes and unhealthy foods and incentivising exercise are legitimate interventions in societies where health risks are shared.

Young people today are also calling for a renegotiation of the social contract between the generations. Those alive today need to address the legacy of environmental loss and debt. Taking action on climate change and loss of biodiversity must be a priority, given there is clear evidence that we have drawn too heavily on environmental assets. Encouraging investment in green technologies is another way to give the next generation a wider set of opportunities for a healthy environment but it is not enough. The younger generation will inherit wealth in the form of human and physical capital, but they will have to support the largest generation of elderly ever to have existed. Investing generously in their education is essential if they are to achieve the levels of productivity that will be needed to afford caring for us in the future.

The economics of a new social contract and how we can afford it are the questions we will turn to now. For all countries, implementing a new social contract would require a combination of policies. Three key strategies are required: increased productivity, rethinking fiscal policy and a new contract with business.

## Increasing Productivity

Many of the measures outlined above are designed to increase productivity because in economic terms greater productivity is ultimately how we make everything better: if we grow the pie, there will be more of it to share. For developing countries, there are still unexploited opportunities to match the productivity of advanced economies. These catch-up gains will come from the adoption of better technologies and management practices, investments in education and infrastructure, and encouragement of greater efficiency as a result of competition. Developing countries also have the opportunity to leapfrog by adopting frontier digital technologies, as they did when many countries skipped building a fixed-line phone network and jumped immediately to mobile technology.

When I was a student, I had a summer job in an office in Egypt. When copies of a letter that I had drafted were required, the secretary was asked to type it three times because the cost of her labour was less than the cost of running the photocopying machine in the office. That seemingly irrational decision is what happens in an economy where labour is cheap, and workers are stuck in low-productivity jobs.[8]

Since the financial crisis in 2008, recovery, particularly in the advanced economies, has been characterised by more people in work but doing low-productivity jobs. A good example is the re-emergence of hand car washes in many countries – large numbers of usually immigrant men are employed to clean cars manually by businesses which could use drive-through machines invented decades ago.[9] Since workers are cheap, firms have little incentive to invest in the tools that make them more productive – machinery, computers, mobile technology and better software. In fact, since 2008 the growth of capital per worker has been growing at the slowest rate in post-war history.[10] The state needs to invest in skills and create an environment where higher levels of investment in the tools that make workers productive are encouraged. Transforming the economy to a lower-carbon future provides one important opportunity to promote these higher levels of investment.

The digital revolution provides another huge opportunity to increase the productivity of workers. In the early days of the computer revolution in the 1960s and 70s, economist Robert Solow famously said, 'You can see computers everywhere except in the productivity statistics.' Today we see a similar phenomenon with a massive rise in digital patents and innovation but continuing stagnation in productivity. The policies described in Chapters 3 (Education) and 5 (Work) provide some of the answers to how labour productivity can be increased; Chapter 4 describes some of the ways in which applications of digital technologies might make our health systems more efficient. But we must also tackle another reason for lagging productivity today: the slow and uneven pace of digital innovation across the economy.[11]

One estimate is that Europe overall operates at only 12 per cent of its digital potential, while the United States is at 18 per cent.[12] Some sectors such as information and communications, media, financial services and professional services are digitising rapidly; sectors such as education, health care and construction are not. The Covid pandemic may accelerate digitisation in some of these lagging sectors as areas like telemedicine and online learning are forced to accelerate. Similarly, online retail, which is about twice as efficient as in-store sales, will grow its market share massively in the wake of the pandemic. In Chapters 3 and 4 we saw the various opportunities for more efficient and higher-quality digital services in education and health, though these will need to be balanced with maintaining the important human aspects of the relationships between teachers and students and between carers and patients.

Another important way to increase productivity is to foster competition. There is growing evidence in many countries of what economists call concentration – when a small number of firms dominate a particular market – and growing monopoly power in many industries. Recent data for the US shows a disturbing increase in concentration in banking, aviation, pharmaceuticals, health insurance and technology platforms.[13] This has been made possible by rising corporate spending on political lobbying and resulted in a reduction of the share of national income that goes to workers relative to owners. Restoring competition and thinking about competition policy differently for the digital economy is an important way to raise productivity in countries where such concentration is taking place.[14]

## *Rethinking Fiscal Policy: How Do We Pay for a New Social Contract?*

When I was deputy governor at the Bank of England between 2014 and 2017, we kept interest rates low to encourage borrowing, spending and investment and thus keep the economy running close to capacity. Interest rates are now at historic lows because global savings remain high relative to investment. Global savings are high because people face insecurity and populations are ageing, which is why interest rates are lowest in Japan and Europe, the parts of the world ageing most rapidly. This reduces demand for goods and services and slows rates of economic growth (recall Keynes' warning about delaying the consumption of jam in Chapter 7).

Better social insurance could reduce this tendency towards what economists refer to as secular (meaning long-term) stagnation. For example, Chinese households save over 30 per cent of their incomes in part because until recently they have had little or no unemployment protection, health insurance or pensions. With the introduction of better social insurance in China, this percentage should come down.

On the other side of the equation, investment is low because governments have not created an environment where firms see good opportunities to grow. But many of the elements of a new social contract as described here, such as education and infrastructure to reduce carbon emissions, could increase demand and investment, especially in developing countries, where profitable opportunities exist if risks can be reduced. The problem of economic stagnation is not one that central bankers and monetary policy can solve, but a new social contract could.

But would a new social contract require massive increases in public spending and taxation? It depends. Increasing publicly supported childcare, early-years education and lifelong learning would require more spending, as would achieving universal health care and a minimum state pension. But some of this spending is investment and would generate higher future tax revenues (recall the estimates in Chapter 3 of a rate of return of about 10 per cent on public investments in education) or net benefits if they were measured properly – such as to the environment, as discussed in Chapter 7. These investments can therefore be sensibly financed through borrowing, especially in advanced economies, where interest rates are at historic lows. But some of this spending – on pensions and elements of health care, for example – is recurrent and would need to be financed from tax revenues. Is this feasible?

For most countries, the answer is yes. Most advanced economies collect taxes equivalent to 30–40 per cent of GDP. Here, funding a new social contract would require the combination of measures already discussed to raise productivity (longer working lives, better use of talent) and hence tax revenues, which could be supplemented by some modest tax increases or reallocation of resources. But no country has managed to raise revenues sustainably above 50 per cent of GDP, and so countries with the highest rates of taxation, such as France or Denmark, would not probably be able to raise further revenues and would have to rely on economic growth and reallocation to fund changes to the social contract.

By contrast, most developing countries collect about half as much tax as advanced economies (15–20 per cent of GDP) and therefore have much more scope to mobilise government revenues.[15] The problem is that the official rates of taxation in many developing economies are similar to those in advanced economies, but difficulties with collection and compliance mean that revenues fall short.[16] With a high proportion of workers in the informal sector (so not paying tax), developing countries have to depend more on levies on trade and consumption. The challenge for the developing world, therefore, is getting more workers into formal employment and building the political and administrative capacity to raise revenues, if they are to deliver on citizens' rising expectations for better public services.

How much would a better social contract cost for developing countries? Estimates by the World Bank of a core package that included prenatal care, immunisation, preschool provision and support for early-childhood literacy and numeracy would cost about 2.7 per cent of GDP in low-income countries (LICs) and 1.2 per cent in lower-middle-income countries (LMICs).[17] A more comprehensive package that added access to water and sanitation and higher-quality primary schools would cost 11.5 per cent of GDP for LICs and 2.3 per cent for LMICs. If developing countries wanted to add income support targeted to the poorest adults, this would cost 9.6 per cent of GDP in the poorest countries, 5.1 per cent in LMICs and 3.5 per cent in upper-middle-income countries. While these are large sums, there is scope for boosting revenues in most developing countries through better collection from the growing numbers of formal-sector workers but also better use of existing taxes such as value added tax, taxes on tobacco and alcohol and by reducing energy subsidies.

It is tempting to invoke the Robin Hood solution of taxing the rich and giving the money to the poor in order to fund a new social contract. But most countries find that in practice measures that fundamentally change and equalise the distribution of opportunities are far more powerful than anything the state can do through the retroactive redistribution of incomes.[18] So-called pre-distribution policies, such as equalising access to good education or providing additional investment in deprived communities, are also more empowering to the individuals affected and reduce the risk of chronic dependence on state support. And if we are able to achieve fairer outcomes via the labour market (by helping the poor into better, higher-paid work), this has the added advantage of reducing the need for benefit payments and the taxation that pays for it. With the right regulations, we can shift expectations and ensure that employers provide the enhanced benefits and training needed to generate these opportunities. It should only be if these policies fail that redistribution of income through the welfare state becomes necessary.[19]

When redistribution is necessary, it is more effective when it takes the form of public spending on benefits, services and interventions that support the poor rather than just raising taxes on the wealthy. Having said that, a striking trend since the 1980s has been that most tax systems around the world have tended to tax the wealthy less. Top marginal income tax rates have declined sharply across advanced and developing countries since the Reagan/Thatcher revolution of the 1980s (Figure 17). Corporate tax rates have also been lowered as countries compete to attract foreign investment. By contrast, payroll taxes on labour income have tended to increase in order to cover the rising costs of pensions, health care and unemployment insurance. It is particularly striking that at a time when wages have become more unequal, the tax system has been working even less hard to redress this.[20]

### Figure 17. Top tax rates have fallen everywhere

Top marginal tax rate of income tax (i.e. the maximum rate of taxation applied to the highest part of income)

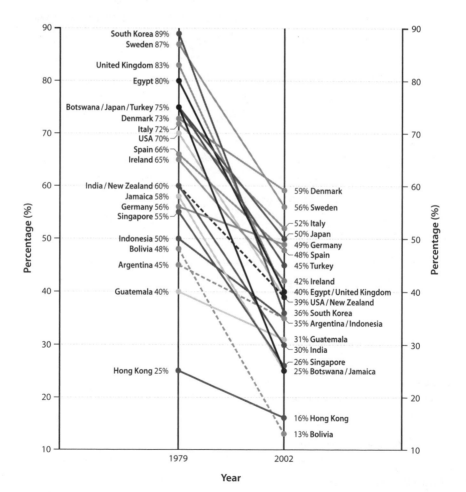

Adjusting tax rates in the opposite direction, to make them more progressive, would not be enough to pay for the social contract, but it would certainly help. The problem, though, is that it is actually very hard to redress income inequality by raising tax rates because the rich and their accountants are good at finding ways to reduce tax bills and, in some cases, are highly mobile and able to locate themselves or their businesses in low-tax jurisdictions.

Recent experience with wealth taxes illustrates the challenges. There are three ways to tax wealth – you can tax it when it is transferred to the next generation through an inheritance charge, you can tax income from wealth such as capital gains or dividends, or you can tax people's stock of wealth each year through measures like property taxes. Many countries tax inheritances and income from wealth; only a few tax the stock of wealth itself (currently only Colombia, Norway, Spain, Switzerland). In response to political pressure and/or implementation challenges, Finland, France, Iceland, Luxembourg, the Netherlands and Sweden have actually abolished the wealth taxes they once had.[21]

Nonetheless, because wealth inequality is far greater than income inequality, many economists have argued that taxing inherited wealth (which is seen as unearned) and redistributing it is key for equalising opportunity in a society. And because of concerns about rising wealth inequality and because governments everywhere are looking for new sources of revenue, there has been a resurgence of interest in wealth taxes. Tony Atkinson of LSE was the first to argue for a progressive inheritance tax that paid for a capital endowment for every young person.[22] More recently, Thomas Piketty has argued that people should only have temporary ownership of their wealth, which should be taxed away over time through inheritance and property taxes to fund a capital endowment for every adult over 25.[23] For France, he has proposed that every young person should receive about €120,000 to ensure that capital circulates throughout society and expands opportunities early in life when they are needed most. Other recent work has also focused on how wealth taxes can help address not just inequality but also improve productivity. A promising strand of research argues that wealth taxes can improve economic efficiency by penalising those holding assets in low-return activities and incentivising those generating higher returns.[24] The implication is that a wealth tax of 2–3 per cent a year would allow governments to increase efficiency, promote economic growth and reduce inequality all at once.

Another way to raise revenue is by taxing what economists call bads (in contrast to goods). These are things we want to see less of, such as pollution, smoking, overconsumption of alcohol and unhealthy foods. In Chapter 4 we saw that trillions of dollars are being lost to unhealthy behaviours each year and that there are significant social and economic benefits to be had from using tax policy to change those behaviours. In Chapter 7 we saw that many countries are paying people to destroy the planet with subsidies for energy or water or land use, and that removing those subsidies would be a critical step towards improving our environmental legacy.

But we need to do more than that if we are to slow climate change to acceptable levels, and there are few solutions more effective than a carbon tax. This would be levied on the amount of carbon in any fuel source. The beauty of such a far-reaching tax is that it would effectively change the price of everything in the economy, in turn affecting what people consume and how they behave. For individuals, taking public transport would suddenly become much cheaper than driving. Buying food produced nearby would automatically be more affordable than food flown across the world. For companies, it would create a huge incentive to invest in greener technologies and to produce in ways that reduce carbon emissions. It wouldn't rely on self-restraint, trying to meet quantitative targets, trading emissions permits or having to do complicated calculations of the carbon footprint of your every action. The market would sort all of that out for you and deliver lower carbon emissions at the lowest cost to the economy, which is why economists tend to favour this policy.

Objections to a carbon tax are that it adds to the tax burden and could adversely affect the poor. The *gilets jaunes* brought France to a standstill because of their opposition to the introduction of higher taxes on diesel fuel. They were angry not about measures to combat climate change but about who paid the costs of adjusting to a low-carbon future. However, it is possible to design a carbon tax that neither raises the tax burden nor hurts the poor. How would such a scheme work? First, the tax rate would initially be set low and increased only gradually to allow everyone to adjust. Second, the proceeds from the tax would be returned to citizens, either in cash or by reducing other taxes. If 100 per cent was returned, the tax would be revenue neutral but still have a big effect on incentives to use carbon in the economy; if less than 100 per cent was returned, it would generate income for the state. Inevitably, some countries would have to take the lead and impose a carbon tax before others, potentially leaving them at a competitive disadvantage. An adjustment in border taxes – imposing increased taxes on imports from other countries that do not have a carbon tax – would help to level the playing field and provide incentives for others to impose such a tax too. Ultimately, the objective would be to raise carbon taxes to a level that reduces the risks of catastrophic climate change.

This approach – returning the income from carbon taxes to citizens – has been called a fee and dividend scheme in the United States and a carbon cheque in Canada and France.[25] And since the rich tend to consume more carbon, it is possible to devise a scheme of this kind that can actually benefit the poor. Estimates for the US, for example, show that a relatively modest carbon tax of $49 per tonne would make the poorest 10 per cent of the population better off and everyone except the highest earners net beneficiaries. A study in France found that a carbon cheque that varied between rural and urban areas could make everyone in the bottom half of income distribution better off.[26] For countries that needed to raise revenue and therefore chose not to reimburse the entire tax, it could generate considerable resources for financing the social contract. For example, one estimate is that a tax rate of $115 per tonne of carbon in the US would generate a substantial 3 per cent of national income.[27]

Finally, philanthropy, faith-based institutions and charities currently play an important complementary role to the state in financing and delivering important aspects of the social contract. Charities have existed across the world since ancient times, reflecting a common view that those who are better off should support the poor, help the sick and contribute to enhancing public life. Recent growth in the assets of foundations and charities has been massive, in part because of the growth in wealth. Global foundation assets exceed $1.5 trillion, with spending primarily focused on education (35 per cent), social welfare (21 per cent) and health (20 per cent).[28] In many countries part of the social contract is delivered by volunteers and individuals giving freely of their time to benefit their communities. This should be encouraged and celebrated as a complement, but not a substitute, for a better social contract.

## A New Social Contract with Business

Many of the policies discussed in previous chapters require different expectations about the respective roles of business and the state. Since the 1980s, much of government policy has been focused on maximising efficiency through the liberalisation of trade, privatisation and relaxing regulations in the labour market. Firms have been able to cut costs, reduce benefits and outsource their supply chains. By and large, consumers have benefited from this, but some workers have seen their incomes stagnate and now face greater insecurity in their lives. In theory, those who have lost out from these reforms – whether individuals or communities – should have been compensated by, and ultimately benefit from, more rapid economic growth. In practice, that has rarely happened and certainly not to the degree required.

More importantly, who wants to be a loser, even if you do get compensation? A new social contract with business should focus instead on creating more winners by investing in education and skills, by bringing better infrastructure to deprived areas and by promoting innovation and productivity, all of which reduce the need for redistribution or compensation. While part of the new social contract will be achieved through public spending and part through regulation, part of it must come about by changing what is expected of the private sector. Figure 18 gives an example of how it could be structured and financed.[29]

**Figure 18. Possible structure for a new deal between employers and workers**

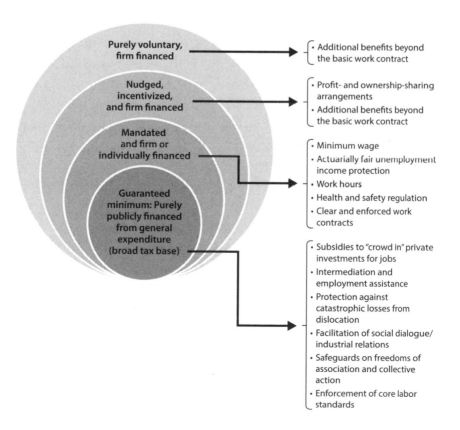

At the core of this new deal are minimum protections against catastrophic losses provided to all and paid for through general taxation. These include public funding to help workers adjust to job losses because of major economic shocks and support for transition to new jobs. Parental leave benefits and support for parents in flexible work could also be covered by governments, which would reap the benefits of equalising labour market opportunities between men and women. The next circle includes those measures achieved through mandatory regulations: minimum wages, limitations on and guarantees of hours of work, giving workers a voice and unemployment insurance. After that come voluntary measures such as enhanced pensions, additional training and profit-sharing schemes – an especially powerful way of incentivising workers to be productive and bringing the interests of owners and their employees into better alignment.

The trend towards more flexible patterns of work means that the burden of taxation also needs to shift to create a more level playing field between capital (those who invest) and workers (those who are employed).[30] Between 2000 and 2015 average corporate tax rates in advanced economies declined from 32 to 25 per cent, benefiting owners and investors.[31] Meanwhile, taxes on labour, which fall on both the employer and the employee and are used to fund unemployment insurance, pensions and sometimes health insurance, have grown. This model originated in the idea that employers would be the providers of social insurance, paid for by them and their employees, but in many countries including Japan and much of Latin America the revenues generated from payroll taxes already do not cover the costs of pension obligations, for example.

The bias in our tax systems favouring capital and penalising labour may also mean that firms are under-investing in training workers and over-investing in automation. This is particularly the case in rapidly ageing countries such as Germany and Korea that are adopting automation technologies more quickly as a way to cope with the fact that a smaller working-age population will need to be highly productive to support the elderly.[32] One estimate for the US shows that the current system taxes labour at a rate of 25.5–33.5 per cent, while the effective tax rate on capital is about 5 per cent – down from 10 per cent in the 2010s and 20 per cent in the 1990s and early 2000s.[33] Bringing the tax rates on labour and capital more closely into alignment would result in better decisions by firms on how much labour they employ. Reducing the taxation of labour relative to capital would also increase overall employment and labour's share of income.

A better model would tax business differently. This is not to suggest that the overall burden of taxation on business need rise. Instead, it may be possible to raise corporate tax rates but also reduce payroll taxes by funding core unemployment benefits, minimum pensions, some training costs and parental leave from general taxation. Australia and New Zealand, for example, have already chosen to shift away from payroll taxes and fund the core of their pension systems from general taxation, and many developing countries – including Bangladesh, Lesotho, Namibia and Sudan – are now adopting the model of a basic social pension for the elderly funded out of general taxation.[34]

Regulations that mandate the provision of benefits for all kinds of employees – full time, part time and self-employed freelancers – would provide security that does not discriminate by type of work or type of worker and reduce the incentive to create jobs under informal working arrangements as a way to avoid paying for social insurance. It is also possible to give extra incentives to firms to train their workers, as many countries do when they want to promote research and innovation.[35] Countries such as Austria provide generous tax credits to firms and to individuals for training costs. Such tax credits can also be targeted at low- and middle-skilled workers or at smaller firms, which find it harder to afford training. In the US, the states of Connecticut, Georgia, Kentucky, Mississippi, Rhode Island and Virginia are experimenting with such an approach.

Alongside better distribution of the burdens between business and government is a need to act on corporate tax avoidance by global companies, which are currently able to account for their profits in low-tax jurisdictions. Every year 40 per cent of the global profits of multinationals are shifted into tax havens. In the UK more than 50 per cent of the subsidiaries of foreign multinational companies currently report no taxable profits.[36] In the US, 91 companies on the Fortune 500 index, including Amazon, Chevron and IBM, paid an effective federal tax rate of zero in 2018.[37]

This situation is unfair to domestic companies, which cannot avoid national taxation, and to the citizens of the countries in which these multinational firms operate, who are deprived of the revenues. The current situation is a relic of the twentieth century, which assessed company tax liabilities according to where the legal entity was physically based. This is outdated in a digital world of globalised supply chains, where companies manage their books to legally base themselves in any number of places to reduce their tax burden. The IMF estimates that $500–600 billion of income from corporate tax is lost every year as a result.[38] Developing countries are especially hard hit in relative terms given their smaller tax bases. Estimates of how much individuals have stashed away in tax havens range from $8.7 trillion to $36 trillion, which translates into about $200 billion in lost income tax revenues each year.[39]

A fairer solution is possible based on proposals developed at the OECD through negotiations between 137 countries. First, governments would be given the right to tax companies based on sales in their territory, regardless of where the legal entity is located. Second, there would be a minimum level of tax that all multinationals would have to pay, thus reducing the scope for countries to compete for their presence by lowering their corporate tax rates. For Europe this would mean a bigger share of profits from US technology giants, for the US a bigger slice of the profits of European products sold in the US.[40] In both cases, shareholders in those companies would probably earn less. Developing countries are likely to be net beneficiaries since they have fewer multinationals able to exploit these loopholes in international taxes. The OECD estimates that the two reforms would raise corporate tax revenues by 4 per cent worldwide, which is worth $100–240 billion annually.[41]

Business leaders increasingly acknowledge that the narrow focus on short-term shareholder value has resulted in inequality, stagnant productivity, poor innovation and environmental degradation.[42] A new social contract with business would have firms paying higher corporate taxes and providing all workers with benefits, while society at large would share more of the risks around minimum incomes, parental leave, pensions and the development of new skills. This would give substance to the growing acceptance by business leaders of the need to think more about the purpose of business and its obligations to wider stakeholders.[43] It would also be good for their businesses. Being able to rely on the availability of skilled workers, high-quality infrastructure and a good safety net would reduce their costs and allow them to innovate flexibly. Already, consumers and a new generation of workers are putting a premium on employers who behave responsibly. But realising a new social contract with business will require more than just rhetoric and some good corporate citizens. It will require us to make concrete changes to taxation, regulation and corporate governance.

### Getting There: The Politics of a New Social Contract

Social contracts are deeply political. They reflect a country's history, its values and circumstances. In the past they evolved as the product of religious traditions and cultural norms governing the obligations of kinship and the roles of the sexes and latterly through industrial relations and negotiations between employers and workers. In most countries today the evolution of social contracts depends on the structure of the political system, the effectiveness of mechanisms that hold the powerful to account, the emergence of political coalitions and the opportunities created by crises.

Some kinds of government are more capable of delivering better social contracts. Democracies per se are not necessarily more capable, but democracies where the executive is constrained by free and fair elections with high participation and a free media tend to be better at delivering longer lives for their citizens and better economic outcomes.[44] Autocracies in which leaders have personal power and few constraints tend to perform poorly. Countries that are not democracies but have an effective 'selectorate' who hold policymakers to account (such as the communist party in China) can also deliver effective outcomes for their citizens.[45]

Constraining the executive and holding it to account are especially important for avoiding those bad decisions that lead to sharp falls in income or, in extremis, civil wars. Amartya Sen once said, 'No famine has ever taken place in the history of the world in a functioning democracy.'[46] This is because democratic governments have to win elections and face public criticism, and therefore have strong incentives to avert catastrophes (or at least appear to be doing so) and deliver improvements in the lives of their citizens. Governments subject to greater accountability from legislatures, the judiciary and the media are more likely to have social contracts focused on the common good rather than serving the private interests of a narrow group.

Politicians in democracies are well aware that good economic performance tends to deliver gains at the ballot box. But too few realise that the well-being of their citizens can deliver about twice as much of an electoral gain than improvements in citizens' incomes. Research on 153 parliamentary elections across Europe since the 1970s found that citizens' subjective satisfaction with their lives was a much better predictor of who they would vote for than conventional economic measures such as GDP growth, unemployment or inflation.[47] The determinants of that subjective well-being are the key elements of the social contract such as good health and meaningful work.

What kind of political systems deliver better social contracts? Countries with more presidential, winner-takes-all political systems tend to have smaller states and less generous social contracts. Majoritarian political systems, such as those in the United States and the UK, create fewer incentives to look after minorities; instead, politicians are incentivised to concentrate benefits on the large numbers in the middle class. Countries governed by proportional representation tend to provide more support to their citizens, probably because of the broad co-alitions needed to achieve political consensus. Authoritarian regimes which face little accountability have fewer pressures to deliver on the social contract and sometimes use the state simply to enrich themselves and their cronies. In fragile states the social contract is thinnest because the government usually has difficulty raising revenue, lacks legal and policy capacities and has limited ability to deliver public services.

In many countries, in fact, the main challenge is not government's willingness but its ability to deliver on citizens' expectations. This is true in large parts of the developing world in Africa, Latin America, the Middle East and south Asia, where the issue is whether the state can raise revenue and deliver the basic public goods like education, health and infrastructure that citizens demand. In those countries that have young populations which possess the power of the ballot box citizens at least have the capacity to choose parties and leaders who are more likely to deliver on their expectations. In countries that are not democracies citizens face the hard task of finding other mechanisms to pressure ruling elites.

In advanced economies the challenge is less that of state capacity and more one of political gridlock among various interest groups. Some cling on to those parts of the social contract that benefit them (such as early retirement ages) while others (like the young or disadvantaged) either cannot or do not vote in order to secure their interests. Voter suppression, manipulation of political boundaries, lobbying and outright corruption can all thwart reform. Perhaps the most critical intervention needed in such places is to make it easier for everyone to vote so that those who are most disadvantaged get a voice in shaping the social contract. Finding secure digital options for voting is surely the next important step for democracies.[48] Throughout history, more inclusive political systems tend to precede more generous social contracts.

Can countries build more generous social contracts in a world of globalisation and mobile capital, or does the need to compete with other nations mean a race to the bottom is unavoidable? The answer is that they can. Among the countries that have successfully navigated globalisation there is a wide range of social contracts, some generous, some not. There does not seem to be any significant relationship between an economy's openness and the degree to which, for example, it has generous redistributive policies.[49] In fact, countries that are more open to trade tend to have higher levels of public spending on worker retraining as a way to cushion any shocks from the world economy.[50] In future, many companies may simplify their supply chains and move production closer to local markets in response to the Covid-19 pandemic, which will give governments even more autonomy in their policy choices.

While the political structure and capability of the state are important, change can also arise because of crises and the new coalitions that emerge as a result of them. In the fourteenth century the bubonic plague wiped out half the population of England. The resulting labour shortages gave workers more power to negotiate higher wages, which was the beginning of the end of feudalism. In eastern Europe the bubonic plague had the opposite effect, as landlords consolidated their power in what became known as the Second Serfdom, with more use of unpaid labour and the creation of more extractive institutions.[51]

Critical junctures can create opportunities for more inclusive economic arrangements as people demand more from society.[52] In the twentieth century the Great Depression spawned the New Deal in the United States. World War II begat the creation of the modern welfare state in the UK and the Marshall Plan across Europe. The current global pandemic is such a moment of opportunity for change. The most vulnerable are suffering, and the tragedy has exposed the weakness of health systems, the inadequacy of safety nets and the paucity of mechanisms for caring for the old. A generation of young people have missed out on major parts of their education and are set to suffer the biggest losses in income.[53] Women have been less affected by the virus itself but are bearing the brunt of its economic and social costs through job losses and rises in unpaid work and domestic violence during lockdowns.[54] Meanwhile, governments have accumulated huge debts that will need to be repaid through future gains in productivity. In many countries people will undoubtedly press for better management of risks and improved social insurance to protect the vulnerable.

Can societies and governments respond to so many huge challenges at the same time? One of the things I have learned after decades of conducting negotiations is that, sometimes, making the problem bigger makes it easier to solve. Including more issues in the discussion allows you to trade off costs and benefits and to build coalitions for change. If I am an employee in my late fifties looking forward to retirement, I might be willing to work longer if I know that my children will get a lifetime educational endowment. Similarly, a young person might be happy to pay more tax if they feel society has invested generously in their education, will continue to support them in learning new skills and provide them with security in old age.

The coalition for a new social contract is potentially large and diverse. Young people have already mobilised in pursuit of action for the environment. They may soon do the same in support of a lifelong educational entitlement to make up for what they have lost. Those in precarious work, especially women, whose careers are often less continuous than men's, will increasingly demand better benefits from flexible working, more investment in education and improved retraining policies. The pandemic has also made the case for universal health care and public health interventions such as mandating the wearing of masks or encouraging the maintenance of a healthy weight.

For the old, a new settlement on minimum pensions and elderly care could compensate for reform of retirement ages.

Achieving a better social contract is ultimately about increasing the accountability of our political systems. How this happens will vary between countries. In democracies the core requirements are participation in elections, media coverage of the issues outlined in this book and the fostering of public discourse and legislative and judicial pressures on those in power to deliver for everyone in society. In those countries that are not democracies frustrated citizens will find other, perhaps less orderly, ways to pressure their leaders for change. But in all cases it is greater accountability that will ensure that collective interests are served fairly, efficiently and effectively.

## *Towards a New Social Contract for the Twenty-First Century*

We owe each other more. A more generous and inclusive social contract would recognise our interdependencies, provide minimum protections to all, share some risks collectively and ask everyone to contribute as much as they can for as long as they can. This is not about increasing the welfare state, but about investing in people and building a new system of risk sharing to increase overall well-being.

Change will come inevitably because the forces of technology, demography and environmental pressures will drive it. The question is whether we prepare for that change or continue to allow our societies to be buffeted by these powerful forces, as we have in recent decades. This book lays out the challenges we face and provides a menu of alternatives for a better social contract around families, education, health, work, old age and between the generations. It is not a blueprint, but it provides a direction of travel that is economically feasible. Nor is it a fixed menu – countries may choose to implement some elements and not others depending on their values and preferences. In practice, most social contracts have been reformed in stages and over decades as a result of continuous pressure from society.

Abraham Lincoln said, 'The best way to predict your future is to create it.' Citizens have shaped the architecture of opportunity in their societies for centuries, and those choices have shaped our lives. We are at a moment in history when new choices need to be made. It is within our gift to shape a social contract that gives us, and those that come after us, a better future. The final passage of the Beveridge Report states, 'Freedom from want cannot be forced on a democracy or given to a democracy. It must be won by them. Winning it needs courage and faith and a sense of national unity: courage to face facts and difficulties and overcome them; faith in our future and in the ideals of fair-play and freedom for which century after century our forefathers were prepared to die; a sense of national unity overriding the interests of any class or section.'[55] We owe it to each other, and to ourselves, to muster that courage and sense of unity.

# Illustration Notes and Credits

Figure 1. 'Low income' refers to families in the bottom 10% of the income distribution. OECD average is based on 24 member countries. Dorothée Rouzet, Aida Caldera Sánchez, Théodore Renault and Oliver Roehn, 'Fiscal Challenges and Inclusive Growth in Ageing Societies', OECD Economic Policy Paper 27, September 2019: https://doi.org/10.1787/c553d8d2-en

Figure 2. Office for Budget Responsibility (OBR), 'Fiscal Sustainability Report', 2018: https://cdn.obr.uk/FSR-July-2018-1.pdf

Figure 3. Income shown is real purchasing power parity. Christoph Lakner and Branko Milanovic, 'Global Income Distribution: From the Fall of the Berlin Wall to the Great Recession', *World Bank Economic Review* 30:2, 2016, pp. 203–32.

Figure 4. Cristian Alonso, Mariya Brussevich, Era Dabla-Norris, Yuko Kinoshita and Kalpana Kochar, 'Reducing and Redistributing Unpaid Work: Stronger Policies to Support Gender Equality', IMF Working Paper, October 2019: https://www.imf.org/~/media/Files/Publications/WP/2019/wpiea2019225-print-pdf.ashx

Figure 5. The horizontal axis shows female employment-population ratios. This measures the proportion of a country's female population aged 15 years and above that is employed. The vertical axis shows public spending on family benefits as a share of GDP. Sandra Tzvetkova and Esteban Ortiz-Ospina, 'Working women: What determines female labor force participation?', 2017: https://ourworldindata.org/women-in-the-labor-force-determinants. Data derived from OECD, *Society at a Glance*, OECD Publishing, 2019: https://data.oecd.org/socialexp/family-benefits-public-spending.htm; International Labour Organization, ILOSTAT database, data retrieved in September 2018; Gapminder, HYDE, 2016, and United Nations Population Division, 2019: https://www.gapminder.org/data/documentation/gd003/

Table 1. The 'high' private return to primary education in high-income countries is due to an outlier 1959 estimate of 65% for Puerto Rico, a country classified as high-income under our current-per-capita income classification system. George Psacharopoulos and Harry Patrinos, 'Returns to Investment in Education: A Decennial Review of the Global Literature', Policy Research Working Paper 8402, World Bank, 2018.

Figure 6. OECD, *Getting Skills Right: Future Ready Adult Learning Systems*, OECD Publishing, 2019: https://doi.org/10.1787/9789264311756-en.

Figure 7. OECD, *Getting Skills Right: Future Ready Adult Learning Systems*, OECD Publishing, 2019: https://doi.org/10.1787/9789264311756-en.

Figure 8. OECD, *Health at a Glance 2015: OECD Indicators*, OECD Publishing, 2015: https://doi.org/10.1787/4dd50c09-en

Figure 9. Irene Papanicolas, Alberto Marino, Luca Lorenzoni and Ashish Jha, 'Comparison of Health Care Spending by Age in 8 High-Income Countries', JAMA Network Open, 2020, e2014688: https://doi:10.1001/jamanetworkopen.2020.14688

Table 2. WEF, *The Future of Jobs Report 2018*, World Economic Forum, 2018.

Figure 10. Truman Packard, Ugo Gentillini, Margaret Grosh, Philip O'Keefe, Robert Palacios, David Robalino and Indhira Santos, *Protecting All: Risk Sharing for a Diverse and Diversifying World of Work*, World Bank, 2019: https://doi: 10.1596/978-1-4648-1427-3. Used under CC BY 3.0 IGO.

Figure 11. OECD, *Health at a Glance 2019: OECD Indicators*, OECD Publishing, 2019: https://doi.org/10.1787/4dd50c09-en

Figure 12. OECD, *Health at a Glance 2019: OECD Indicators*, OECD Publishing, 2019: https://doi.org/10.1787/4dd50c09-en

Figure 13. Dorothée Rouzet, Aida Caldera Sánchez, Théodore Renault and Oliver Roehn, 'Fiscal Challenges and Inclusive Growth in Ageing Societies', OECD Economic Policy Paper 27, September 2019: https://doi.org/10.1787/c553d8d2-en

Figure 14. Base of 18,810 adults aged 16 years and above in 22 countries, fieldwork conducted September–October 2016. Fahmida Rahman and Daniel Tomlinson, *Cross Countries: International Comparisons of Intergeneration Trends*, Intergenerational Commission Report, Resolution Foundation, 2018.

Figure 15. IMF, *Fiscal Monitor: Policies for the Recovery*, International Monetary Fund, October 2020.

Figure 16. Shunsuke Managi, and Pushpam Kumar, *Inclusive Wealth Report 2018*, © 2018 UN Environment, Routledge, 2018. Reproduced by permission of Taylor & Francis Group.

Figure 17. Esteban Ortiz-Ospina, 'Taxation', 2016: https://ourworldindata.org/taxation. Data derived from Alan Reynolds, 'Marginal Tax Rates', *The Concise Encyclopedia of Economics*, Library of Economics and Liberty, 2008, data retrieved September 22, 2016: http://www.econlib.org/library/Enc/MarginalTaxRates.html; Gapminder, HYDE, 2016, and United Nations Population Division, 2019: https://www.gapminder.org/data/documentation/gd003/

Figure 18. Truman Packard, Ugo Gentillini, Margaret Grosh, Philip O'Keefe, Robert Palacios, David Robalino and Indhira Santos, *Protecting All: Risk Sharing for a Diverse and Diversifying World of Work*, World Bank, 2019: https://doi: 10.1596/978-1-4648-1427-3. Used under CC BY 3.0 IGO.

# Notes

## Preface

1   This is based on data from the media database Factiva for the last 30 years. Commentators particularly used 'Things fall apart' in referring to the rise in terrorist violence in France, the Brexit referendum in the UK and the election of Donald Trump in the United States. Fintan O'Toole, 'Yeats Test Criteria Reveal We Are Doomed', *Irish Times*, 28 July 2018.

2   In *Why Nations Fail* Acemoglu and Robinson talk about 'critical junctures', when periods of deep instability create opportunities for sweeping institutional change without any clarity about the outcome. Daran Acemoglu and James A. Robinson, *Why Nations Fail*, Crown Publishing Group, 2012.

3   Milton Friedman famously said, 'Only a crisis – actual or perceived – produces real change. When that crisis occurs, the actions that are taken depend on the ideas that are lying around. That, I believe, is our basic function: to develop alternatives to existing policies, to keep them alive and available until the politically impossible becomes the politically inevitable.' Milton Friedman, *Capitalism and Freedom*, University of Chicago Press, 1962.

4   Carole Seymour-Jones, *Beatrice Webb: Woman of Conflict*, Allison and Busby, 1992.

5   Many post-colonial leaders were influenced by the Fabians, including Jawaharlal Nehru in India, Obafemi Awolowo in Nigeria, Muhammad Ali Jinnah in Pakistan, Lee Kuan Yew in Singapore and Michel Aflaq in the Arab world.

6   There is an interesting anecdote about Margaret Thatcher's only visit to the Conservative Research Department in the summer of 1975. When presented with the case for why the party should opt for a pragmatic 'middle way' to gain more political support, she reached into her briefcase, pulled out a copy of Hayek's *The Constitution of Liberty* and announced, 'This is what we believe,' and banged Hayek's book forcefully on the table. John Ranelagh, *Thatcher's People: An Insider's Account of the Politics, the Power, and the Personalities*, Fontana, 1992. Ronald Reagan acknowledged the impact of Hayek on his own thinking and honoured him at the White House.

7    Anthony Giddens, *The Third Way: The Renewal of Social Democracy*, Polity Press, 1998. See also Julian LeGrand and Saul Estrin, *Market Socialism*, Oxford University Press, 1989.

## Chapter 1: What Is the Social Contract?

1    For a useful exposition of the philosophical underpinnings of the structure of society and its relation to social contract theory, see Leif Wenar's summary of John Rawls's views in Leif Wenar, 'John Rawls', *The Stanford Encyclopedia of Philosophy*, Spring 2017 edition.
2    Steven Pinker, *Enlightenment Now: The Case for Reason, Science, Humanism, and Progress*, Penguin/Viking, 2020; Hans Rosling, Ola Rosling and Anna Rosling Rönnlund, *Factfulness: Why Things Are Better Than You Think*, Sceptre, 2018.
3    Edelman 2019 Trust Barometer Global Report: https://www.edelman.com/sites/g/files/aatuss191/files/201902/2019_Edelman_Trust_Barometer_Global_Report.pdf.
4    For a wonderful history of the role of collecting revenue in state formation, see Margaret Levi, *Of Rule and Revenue*, University of California Press, 1989.
5    The notion of the social contract can be found as early as 400 BC in Plato's *Crito* and *The Republic*, in which he described the legal system as a sort of contract between the individual and the state. Later, medieval writers like Augustine and Thomas Aquinas explored what it means to be a good citizen and how much individual autonomy there should be relative to collective interests.
6    Thomas Hobbes, *Leviathan*, Penguin Classics, 1651/2017.
7    John Locke, *Two Treatises of Government*, J. M. Dent, 1689/1993. Locke's views on when it is legitimate to rebel against the sovereign were highly influential on the founding fathers of the United States and the authors of the US constitution.
8    Jean-Jacques Rousseau, *The Social Contract*, Penguin Classics, 1762/1968.
9    Adam Smith, *The Theory of Moral Sentiments*, Cambridge University Press, 1759/2002. For a modern interpretation, see Jesse Norman, *Adam Smith: Father of Economics*, Penguin, 2018.
10   Howard Glennerster, *Richard Titmus: Forty Years On*, Centre for Analysis of Social Exclusion, LSE, 2014.
11   Or as Michael Sandel says, 'Democracy does not require perfect equality, but it does require that citizens share in common life.' Michael Sandel, *What Money Can't Buy: The Moral Limits of Markets*, Penguin, 2012, p. 203.
12   John Rawls, *A Theory of Justice*, Belknap, 1971.
13   Ibid, p. 73. Rawls had two other principles in his theory of justice: the liberty principle (that we should all have access to the greatest possible set of equal basic liberties such as free speech, freedom of association and conscience, etc.), and the difference principle (that income, wealth and the social basis of self-respect should be distributed to maximum benefit for the most deprived in our societies).
14   Gary Solon, 'What Do We Know So Far About Intergenerational Mobility?' *Economic Journal*, 2018; Michael Amior and Alan Manning, 'The Persistence of Local Joblessness', *American Economic Review*, 2018.
15   Average life expectancy in Bavaria at the time was 37.7 for men and 41.4 for women, largely because of high child mortality. The German retirement age was lowered to 65 in 1916, which today translates into the state paying a pension for about twenty years. Martin Kohl, 'Retirement and the Moral Economy: An

Historical Interpretation of the German Case', *Journal of Ageing Studies* 1:2, 1987, pp. 125–44.

16  For a summary of Beveridge's achievements, see Nicholas Timmins, *The Five Giants: A Biography of the Welfare State*, Harper Collins, 2017.

17  OECD, *OECD Employment Outlook 2018*, OECD Publishing, 2018.

18  World Bank Group, 'Closing the Gap: The State of Social Safety Nets 2017', World Bank, 2017.

19  Francesca Bastagli, Jessica Hagen-Zanker, Luke Harman, Valentina Barca, Georgina Sturge and Tanja Schmidt, with Luca Pellerano, 'Cash transfers: what does the evidence say? A rigorous review of programme impact and of the role of design and implementation features', Overseas Development Institute, July 2016.

20  Ugo Gentilini, Mohamed Bubaker Alsafi Almenfi, Pamela Dale, Ana Veronica Lopez, Canas Mujica, Veronica Ingrid, Rodrigo Cordero, Ernesto Quintana and Usama Zafar, 'Social Protection and Jobs Responses to COVID-19 : A Real-Time Review of Country Measures', World Bank, 12 June 2020.

21  Alberto Alesina and Edward Glaeser, *Fighting Poverty in the U.S. and in Europe: A World of Difference*, Oxford University Press, 2004.

22  Holger Stichnoth and Karine Van der Straeten, 'Ethnic Diversity, Public Spending and Individual Support for the Welfare State: A Review of the Empirical Literature', *Journal of Economic Surveys* 27:2, 2013, pp. 364–89. Stuart Soroka, Richard Johnston, Anthony Kevins, Keith Banting and Will Kymlicka, 'Migration and Welfare Spending', *European Political Science Review* 8:2, 2016, pp. 173–94.

23  Nicholas Barr, *The Economics of the Welfare State*, 5th edition, Oxford University Press, 2012, p. 174.

24  John Hills, *Good Times, Bad Times: The Welfare Myth of Them and Us*, Policy Press, 2014.

25  Barr talks about the welfare state as a device for optimal risk sharing as: (1) insurance at birth against unknowable future outcomes to help relieve poverty; (2) a response to market failures to address technical problems in private insurance, especially around unemployment, medical risks and social care; and (3) a contribution to economic growth to build human capital and encourage risk taking. See Nicholas Barr, 'Shifting Tides: Dramatic Social Changes Mean the Welfare State is More Necessary than Ever', *Finance and Development* 55:4, December 2018, pp. 16–19.

26  Amartya Sen, *Commodities and Capabilities*, North Holland, 1985; Amartya Sen, 'Development as Capability Expansion', *Journal of Development Planning* 19, pp. 41–58, 1989; Amartya Sen, *Development as Freedom*, Oxford University Press, 1999.

27  Margaret Thatcher interviewed in Douglas Keay, 'Aids, education and the year 2000', *Women's Own*, 31 October 1987, pp. 8–10.

28  Franklin Delano Roosevelt, 'Second Inaugural Address', 20 January 1937.

29  Milton Friedman, 'The Social Responsibility of Business is to Increase its Profits', *New York Times Magazine*, 13 September 1970.

30  The conclusion of a research programme on the future of the corporation led by Colin Mayer was that 'the purpose of business is to produce profitable solutions to the problems of people and the planet, and in the process it produces profit'. See Colin Mayer, *Prosperity: Better Business Makes the Greater Good*, Oxford University Press, 2018.

31  Barr, *The Economics*, Box 10.2, p. 274.

32  Globalisation is often blamed for the fall in wages of low-skill workers, but the evidence points to technology being the biggest driver. One estimate shows that trade accounts for 10–20 per cent of the change in wages, immigration for even less, and by far the biggest impact coming from technology shifting labour demand in favour of higher-skill workers. Phillip Swagel and Matthew Slaughter, 'The Effects of Globalisation on Wages in Advanced Economies', IMF Working Paper, 1997.

33  For economic analyses of the impact of globalisation on labour markets in the advanced economies, see Joseph Stiglitz, *Globalization and Its Discontents*, W. W. Norton, 2002; Paul Krugman and Anthony Venables, 'Globalization and the Inequality of Nations', *Quarterly Journal of Economics*, 110:4, 1995, pp. 857–80; Paul Collier, *The Future of Capitalism: Facing the New Anxieties*, Penguin Random House, 2018; Raghuram Rajan, *The Third Pillar: The Revival of Community in a Polarized World*, William Collings, 2019; David Autor and David Dorn, 'The Growth of Low Skill Service Jobs and the Polarization of the U.S. Labor Market', *American Economic Review* 103:5, 2013, pp. 1553–97. Stories like that of Janesville, an industrial town near Detroit that tried to cope with the impact of car-plant closures, are typical; it provides a poignant description of the human costs of economic disruption. Amy Goldstein, *Janesville: An American Story*, Simon and Schuster, 2018. For a contrasting view, Iversen and Soskice argue that capital is chasing highly skilled workers, who are concentrated in major urban centres, and national governments actually have considerable policy autonomy. See Torben Iversen and David Soskice, *Democracy and Prosperity: Re-inventing Capitalism Through a Turbulent Century*, Princeton University Press, 2019.

34  David H. Autor, David Dorn and Gordon H. Hanson, 'The China Shock: Learning from Labor-Market Adjustment to Large Changes in Trade', *Annual Review of Economics* 8, 2016, pp. 205–40; Mark Muro and Joseph Parilla, 'Maladjusted: It's Time to Reimagine Economic Adjustment Programs', Brookings, 10 January 2017.

35  There has been a view in the academic literature that female labour force participation follows a U-shape, with high levels in very poor countries (where women are involved in agriculture) and in very rich countries. Recent data show more heterogenous patterns. Stephan Klasen, 'What Explains Uneven Female Labour Force Participation Levels and Trends in Developing Countries?' *World Bank Research Observer* 34:2, August 2019, pp. 161–97.

36  Naila Kabir, Ashwini Deshpande and Ragui Assaad, 'Women's Access to Market Opportunities in South Asia and the Middle East and North Africa', Working Paper, Department of International Development, London School of Economics in collaboration with Ahoka University and the Economic Research Forum, 2020.

37  Esteban Ortiz-Ospina and Sandra Tzvetkova 'Working Women: Key Facts and Trends in Female Labour Force Participation', *Our World in Data*, Oxford University Press, 2017.

38  Jonathan Ostry, Jorge Alvarez, Raphael Espinoza and Chris Papgeorgiou, 'Economic Gains from Gender Inclusion: New Mechanisms, New Evidence', IMF Staff Discussion Paper, 2018.

39  Daniel Susskind and Richard Susskind, *The Future of the Professions*, Oxford University Press, 2015.

40  Andrew McAfee and Erik Brynjolfsson, *The Second Machine Age*, W. W. Norton, 2014.

41  IPCC, *Special Report Global Warming of 1.5 degrees*, Intergovernmental Panel on Climate Change, 2018.

42  Rattan Lal and B. A. Stewart (editors), *Soil Degradation*, Volume 11 of *Advances in Soil Science*, Springer-Verlag, 1990; Sara J. Scherr, 'Soil degradation: a threat to developing country food security by 2020?' International Food Policy Research Institute, 1999.

43  Gerardo Ceballos, Anne H. Ehrlich and Paul R. Ehrlich, *The Annihilation of Nature: Human Extinction of Birds and Mammals*, Johns Hopkins University Press, 2015, p. 135.

44  FAO, *The State of World Fisheries and Aquaculture 2018 – Meeting the Sustainable Development Goals*, United Nations Food and Agriculture Organization, 2018.

# Chapter 2: Children

1   Adalbert Evers and Birgit Riedel, *Changing Family Structures and Social Policy: Child Care Services in Europe and Social Cohesion*, University of Gießen, 2002, p.11.

2   The principle of subsidiarity was enshrined first in the Weimar Republic's 1922 Youth Welfare Law and has been reaffirmed in subsequent amendments to that law. Margitta Mätzke, 'Comparative Perspectives on Childcare Expansion in Germany: Explaining the Persistent East-West Divide', *Journal of Comparative Policy Analysis: Research and Practice* 21:1, 2019, pp. 47–64; Juliane F. Stahl and Pia S. Schober, 'Convergence or Divergence? Educational Discrepancies in Work-Care Arrangements of Mothers with Young Children in Germany', *Work, Employment and Society* 32:4, 2018, pp. 629–49.

3   The convergence in the occupational distribution between 1960 and 2010 in the United States explains between 20 and 40 per cent of growth in aggregate output per person through the improved allocation of talent. See Chang-Tai Hsieh, Erik Hurst, Charles I. Jones and Peter J. Klenow, 'The Allocation of Talent and U.S. Economic Growth', *Econometrica* 87:5, September 2019, pp. 1439–74.

4   This phenomenon of talented women replacing mediocre men also occurs in the political sphere. See Timothy Besley, Olle Folke, Torsten Persson and Johanna Rickne, 'Gender Quotas and the Crisis of the Mediocre Man: Theory and Evidence from Sweden', *American Economic Review* 107:8, 2017, pp. 2204–42.

5   Columbia Law School, 'A Brief Biography of Justice Ginsburg', Columbia Law School web archive. Her contemporary on the Supreme Court, Justice Sandra Day O'Connor, despite being ranked third in her class at Stanford Law School, could only find a job as a legal secretary in 1952.

6   Rhea E. Steinpreis, Katie A. Anders and Dawn Ritzke, 'The Impact of Gender on the Review of the Curriculum Vitae of Job Applicants and Tenure Candidates: A National Empirical Study', *Sex Roles* 41, 1999, pp. 509–28; Shelley J. Correll, Stephen Benard and In Paik, 'Getting a Job: Is there a Motherhood Penalty?' *American Journal of Sociology* 112:5, March 2007, pp. 1297–1338; Kathleen Feugen, Monica Biernat, Elizabeth Haines and Kay Deaux, 'Mothers and Fathers in the Workplace: How Gender and Parental Status Influence Judgements of Job-Related Competence,' *Journal of Social Issues* 60:4, December 2004, pp. 737–54.

7   Arlie Russell Hochschild and Anne Machung, *The Second Shift: Working Parents and the Revolution at Home*, Viking, 1989.

8   Cristian Alonso, Mariya Brussevich, Era Dabla-Norris, Yuko Kinoshita and Kalpana Kochar, 'Reducing and Redistributing Unpaid Work: Stronger Policies to Support Gender Equality', IMF Working Paper, October 2019: https://www.imf.org/~/media/Files/Publications/WP/2019/wpiea2019225-print-pdf.ashx.

9   Alonso et al., *Reducing and Redistributing Unpaid Work*, p. 13.

10  Emma Samman, Elizabeth Presler-Marshall and Nicola Jones with Tanvi Bhaktal, Claire Melamed, Maria Stavropoulou and John Wallace, *Women's Work: Mothers, Children and the Global Childcare Crisis*, Overseas Development Institute, March 2016.

11  In a recent article Melinda Gates observed, 'In the United States, seventy-five per cent of mothers have passed up work opportunities, switched jobs, or left the workforce because of childcare responsibilities. Mothers are three times as likely as fathers to quit their jobs to take care of children or other family members. Over 60 per cent of unemployed women cite family responsibilities as the reason they're not working. One-third of Baby Boomer women care for an elderly parent, and 11 per cent of them have left the workforce to provide full-time care.' See Melinda Gates, 'Gender Equality Is Within Our Reach', *Harvard Business Review*, October 2019.

12  For evidence from the UK, see Monica Costa Rias, Robert Joyce and Francesca Parodi, 'The Gender Pay Gap in the UK: Children and Experience in Work', Institute for Fiscal Studies, February 2018.

13  Jonathan D. Ostrey, Jorge Alvarez, Rafael A. Espinosa and Chris Papageorgiou, 'Economic Gains from Gender Inclusion: New Mechanisms, New Evidence', IMF Staff Discussion Note, October 2018.

14  For more on the debate between familialisation and defamiliasation models, see Ruth Lister, '"She has other duties": Women, citizenship and social security', in Sally Baldwin and Jane Falkingham (editors), *Social Security and Social Change: New Challenges*, Harvester Wheatsheaf, 1994; Gøsta Esping-Andersen, *Social Foundations of Post-industrial Economies*, Oxford University Press, 1999; Roger Goodman and Ito Peng, 'The East Asian welfare states: peripatetic learning, adaptive change, and nation-building', in Gøsta Esping-Andersen (editor), *Welfare States in Transition: National Adaptations in Global Economies*, Sage, 1996, pp. 192–224; Huck-Ju Kwon, 'Beyond European Welfare Regimes: Comparative Perspectives on East Asian Welfare Systems', *Journal of Social Policy* 26:4, October 1997, pp. 467–84; Ito Peng and Joseph Wong, 'East Asia', in Francis G. Castles, Stephan Leibfried, Jane Lewis, Herbert Obinger and Christopher Pierson (editors), *The Oxford Handbook of the Welfare State*, Oxford University Press, 2010; Mi Young An and Ito Peng, 'Diverging Paths? A Comparative Look at Childcare Policies in Japan, South Korea and Taiwan', *Social Policy and Administration* 50:5, September 2016, pp. 540–55.

15  Emma Samman, Elizabeth Presler-Marshall and Nicola Jones with Tanvi Bhatkal, Claire Melamed, Maria Stavropoulou and John Wallace, 'Women's Work: Mothers, Children and the Global Childcare Crisis', Overseas Development Institute, March 2016, p. 34.

16  Ibid., p. 34.

17  In China female labour force participation fell in urban areas because government provision of childcare fell and reliance on grandmothers increased. But if grandmothers delay retirement, their ability to provide free childcare will fall, and government may need to reinstate public options in future. See Yunrong Li, 'The effects of formal and informal childcare on the Mother's labor supply – Evidence from Urban China', *China Economic Review* 44, July 2017, pp. 227–40.

18  Daniela Del Boca, Daniela Piazzalunga and Chiara Pronzato, 'The role of grandparenting in early childcare and child outcomes', *Review of Economics of the Household* 16, 2018, pp. 477–512.

19  OECD average education expenditure in 2016 was 5.0 per cent (https://data. worldbank.org/indicator/SE.XPD.TOTL.GD.ZS). OECD average health expenditure in 2017 was 12.55 per cent (https://data.worldbank.org/indicator/SH.XPD. CHEX.GD.ZS).

20  Chris M. Herbst, 'The Rising Cost of Child Care in the United States: A Reassessment of the Evidence', IZA Discussion Paper 9072, 2015, cited in Samman et al., *Women's Work*, p. 33.

21  Daniela Del Boca, Silvia Pasqua and Chiara Pronzato, 'Motherhood and market work decisions in institutional context: a European perspective', *Oxford Economic Papers* 61, April 2009, pp. 1147–1171; Joya Misra, Michelle J. Budig and Stephanie Moller, 'Reconciliation policies and the effects of motherhood on employment, earnings and poverty', *Journal of Comparative Policy Analysis: Research and Practice* 9:2, 2007, pp. 135–55.

22  Gøsta Esping-Andersen, *Why We Need a New Welfare State*, Oxford University Press, 2002; Olivier Thévenon, 'Family Policies in OECD Countries: A Comparative Analysis', *Population and Development Review* 37:1, March 2011, pp. 57–87; Paolo Barbieri and Rossella Bozzon, 'Welfare labour market deregulation and households' poverty risks: An analysis of the risk of entering poverty at childbirth in different European welfare clusters', *Journal of European Social Policy* 26:2, 2016, pp. 99–123.

23  Giulia Maria Dotti Sani, 'The Economic Crisis and Changes in Work–Family Arrangements in Six European Countries', *Journal of European Social Policy* 28:2, 2018, pp. 177–93; Anne Gauthier, 'Family Policies in Industrialized Countries: Is there Convergence?' *Population* 57:3, 2002, pp. 447–74; Misra et al., 'Reconciliation policies'; Joya Misra, Stephanie Moller, Eiko Strader and Elizabeth Wemlinger, 'Family Policies, Employment and Poverty among Partnered and Single Mothers', *Research in Social Stratification and Mobility* 30:1, 2012, pp. 113–28; Thévenon, 'Family Policies'.

24  ILO, *Maternity and paternity at work: law and practice across the world*, International Labour Organisation, 2014, cited in Samman et al., *Women's Work*, p. 47.

25  Analysis using firm-level data for a sample of 33,302 firms in 53 developing countries shows that women's employment among private firms is significantly higher in countries that mandate paternity leave versus those that do not. A conservative estimate suggests an increase of 6.8 percentage points in the proportion of women workers associated with mandating paternity leave. See Mohammad Amin, Asif Islam and Alena Sakhonchik, 'Does paternity leave matter for female employment in developing economies? Evidence from firm-level data', *Applied Economics Letters* 23:16, 2016, pp. 1145–48.

26  ODI, *Women's Work: Mothers, Children and the Global Childcare Crisis*, Overseas Development Institute, 2016.

27  An important part of the literature focuses on the relationship between the cost of childcare and female labour force participation. The hypothesis being tested is that the more affordable the service, the more it is used, and the more likely it is that those women will participate in the labour market. Both Anderson and Levine and Blau and Currie provide a detailed review of estimates for the elasticity of female labour supply with respect to the cost of childcare in the US. Most of the findings suggest that, as the price of childcare falls, maternal labour force participation increases. There is however a large variation in the magnitude of the estimates. Patricia Anderson and Philip Levine, 'Child Care and Mother's Employment Decisions', in David Card and Rebecca Blank (editors),

*Finding Jobs: Work and Welfare Reform*, Russell Sage, 2000; David Blau and Janet Currie, 'Pre-School, Day Care, and After-School Care: Who's Minding the Kids?' *Handbook of the Economics of Education* 2, 2006, pp. 1163–1278; Mercedes Mateo Diaz and Lourdes Rodriguez-Chamussy, 'Childcare and Women's Labor Participation: Evidence for Latin America and the Caribbean', Technical Note IDB-TN-586, Inter-American Development Bank, 2013.

28  Based on household surveys with almost 130,000 women in 21 developing countries, the child penalty in the developing world is estimated to be about 22 per cent and falls to 7 per cent when taking into account factors such as age, education and marital status. The penalty declines as children get older and actually reverses for those women who have older daughters who can share responsibility for household tasks, thereby enabling their mothers to earn more, and declines as children grow older. Jorge M. Agüeroa, Mindy Marksb and Neha Raykarc, 'The Wage Penalty for Motherhood in Developing Countries', Working Paper, University of California Riverside, May 2012.

29  Henrik Kleven, Camille Landais, Johanna Posch, Andreas Steinhauer and Josef Zweimuller, 'Child Penalties across Countries: Evidence and Explanations', *American Economic Association Papers and Proceedings* 2019. There is also no evidence that child penalties are a result of a biological comparative advantage of women caring for children. See Henrik Kleven, Camille Landais and Jakob Egholt Sogaard, 'Does Biology Drive Child Penalties? Evidence from Biological and Adoptive Families', Working Paper, London School of Economics, May 2020.

30  All three countries increased their financial support for childcare during the first decade of the 2000s. That said, in Japan much of the increase has taken the form of financial support for the family to care for their children, Korea has strengthened policy to support the family's use of care services, and Taiwan has provided financial support primarily in the form of leave provisions.

31  Takeru Miyajima and Hiroyuki Yamaguchi, 'I Want to, but I Won't: Pluralistic Ignorance', *Frontiers in Psychology* 20, September 2017: doi:10.3389/fpsyg.2017.01508.

32  Ingólfur V. Gíslason, 'Parental Leave in Iceland Gives Dad a Strong Position', *Nordic Labour Journal*, April 2019.

33  Rachel G. Lucas-Thompson, Wendy Goldberg and JoAnn Prause, 'Maternal work early in the lives of children and its distal associations with achievement and behavior problems: a meta-analysis', *Psychological Bulletin* 136:6, 2010, pp. 915–42.

34  Charles L. Baum, 'Does early maternal employment harm child development? An analysis of the potential benefits of leave taking', *Journal of Labor Economics* 21:2, 2003, pp. 409–448; David Blau and Adam Grossberg, 'Maternal Labor Supply and Children's Cognitive Development', *Review of Economics and Statistics* 74:3, August 1992, pp. 474–81.

35  Committee on Family and Work Policies, *Working Families and Growing Kids: Caring for Children and Adolescents*, National Academies Press, 2003.

36  Jane Waldfogel, Wen-Jui Han and Jeanne Brooks-Gunn, 'The effects of early maternal employment on child cognitive development', *Demography* 39:2, May 2002, pp. 369–92.

37  Lucas-Thompson et al., 'Maternal work early in the lives of children', pp. 915–42.

38  Ellen S. Peisner-Feinberg, Margaret R. Burchinal, Richard M. Clifford, Mary L. Culkin, Carollee Howes, Sharon Lynn Kagan and Noreen Yazejian, 'The relation of preschool child-care quality to children's cognitive and social developmental trajectories through second grade', *Child Development* 72:5, 2001, pp. 1534–53.

39  Eric Bettinger, Torbjørn Hægeland and Mari Rege, 'Home with mom: the effects of stay-at-home parents on children's long-run educational outcomes', *Journal of Labor Economics* 32:3, July 2014, pp. 443–67.

40  Michael Baker and Kevin Milligan, 'Maternal employment, breastfeeding, and health: Evidence from maternity leave mandates', *Journal of Labor Economics* 26, 2008, pp. 655–92; Michael Baker and Kevin Milligan, 'Evidence from maternity leave expansions of the impact of maternal care on early child development', *Journal of Human Resources* 45:1, 2010, pp. 1–32; Astrid Würtz-Rasmussen, 'Increasing the length of parents' birth-related leave: The effect on children's long-term educational outcomes', *Labour Economics* 17:1, 2010, pp. 91–100; Christopher J. Ruhm, 'Are Recessions Good for Your Health?' *Quarterly Journal of Economics* 115:2, May 2000, pp. 617–50; Sakiko Tanaka, 'Parental leave and child health across OECD countries', *Economic Journal* 115:501, February 2005, F7–F28.

41  Maya Rossin, 'The effects of maternity leave on children's birth and infant health outcomes in the United States', *Journal of Health Economics* 30:2, March 2011, pp. 221–39.

42  Lucas-Thompson et al., 'Maternal work early in the lives of children'.

43  Kathleen McGinn, Mayra Ruiz Castro and Elizabeth Long Lingo, 'Learning from Mum: Cross-National Evidence Linking Maternal Employment and Adult Children's Outcomes', *Work, Employment and Society* 33:3, 2019, pp. 374–400.

44  Susan Kromelow, Carol Harding and Margot Touris, 'The role of the father in the development of stranger sociability in the second year', *American Journal of Orthopsychiatry* 60:4, October 1990, pp. 521–30.

45  Vaheshta Sethna, Emily Perry, Jill Domoney, Jane Iles, Lamprini Psychogiou, Natasha Rowbotham, Alan Stein, Lynne Murray and Paul Ramchandani, 'Father–Child Interactions at 3 months and 24 Months: Contributions to Child Cognitive Development at 24 Months', *Infant Mental Health Journal* 38:3, 2017, pp. 378–90.

46  J. Kevin Nugent, 'Cultural and psychological influences on the father's role in infant development', *Journal of Marriage and the Family* 53:2, 1991, pp. 475–85.

47  Alonso et al., *Reducing and Redistributing*, p. 21.

## Chapter 3: Education

1  Max Roser and Esteban Ortiz-Ospina, 'Primary and Secondary Education', *Our World in Data*, 2020.

2  World Bank, 'World Bank Development Report 2018: Learning to Realize Education's Promise', World Bank Group, 2018, p. 4.

3  World Bank, 'World Bank Education Overview: Higher Education (English)', World Bank Group, 2018.

4  The returns to education are also 2 per cent higher for girls than boys. See George Psacharopoulos and Harry Patrinos, 'Returns to Investment in Education: A Decennial Review of the Global Literature', Policy Research Working Paper 8402, World Bank, 2018.

5  Jack B. Maverick, 'What is the Average Annual Return on the S&P 500?' *Investopedia*, May 2019.

6  UK Government, 'Future of Skills and Lifelong Learning', Foresight Report, UK Government Office for Science, 2017.

7  Richard Layard and George Psacharopoulos, 'The Screening Hypothesis and the Returns to Education', *Journal of Political Economy* 82:5, September–October

1974, pp. 985–98; David Card and Alan B. Krueger, 'Does School Quality Matter? Returns to Education and the Characteristics of Public Schools in the United States', *Journal of Political Economy* 100:1, February 1992, pp. 1–40; Damon Clark and Paco Martorell, 'The signalling value of a high school diploma', *Journal of Political Economy* 122:2, April 2014, pp. 282–318.

8   Daron Acemoglu, 'Technical Change, Inequality, and the Labor Market', *Journal of Economic Literature* 40:1, March 2002, pp. 7–22.

9   Claudia Goldin and Lawrence F. Katz, *The Race between Education and Technology*, Harvard University Press, 2008.

10   World Bank, 'World Bank Development Report: The Changing Nature of Work', World Bank Group, 2019, p. 71.

11   A one-standard-deviation increase in complex problem-solving skills is associated with a 10–20 per cent wage premium. See Peer Ederer, Ljubica Nedelkoska, Alexander Patt and Sylvia Castellazzi, 'How much do employers pay for employees' complex problem solving skills?' *International Journal of Lifelong Learning* 34:4, 2015, pp. 430–47.

12   Lynda Gratton and Andrew Scott, *The 100 Year Life: Living and Working in an Age of Longevity*, Bloomsbury, 2016.

13   Ibid., p. 110.

14   OECD, *OECD Employment Outlook 2019: The Future of Work*, Organisation for Economic Co-operation and Development, 2019, Chapter 3.

15   William Johnson (*later* Cory), king's scholar 1832–41, master 1845–72, in his *Eton Reform II*, as adapted by George Lyttelton in writing to Rupert Hart-Davis.

16   J. Fraser Mustard, 'Early Brain Development and Human Development', in R. E. Tremblay, M. Boivin and R. De V. Peters (editors), *Encyclopedia on Early Childhood Development*, 2010: http://www.child-encyclopedia.com/importance-early-childhood-development/according-experts/early-brain-development-and-human.

17   Arthur J. Reynolds, Judy A. Temple, Suh-Ruu Ou, Irma A. Arteaga and Barry A. B. White, 'School-Based Early Childhood Education and Age-28 Well-Being: Effects by Timing, Dosage, and Subgroups', *Science* 333, 15 July 2011, pp. 360–64.

18   Rebecca Sayre, Amanda E. Devercelli, Michelle J. Neuman and Quentin Wodon, 'Investing in Early Childhood Development: Review of the World Bank's Recent Experience', World Bank Group, 2014.

19   Paul Glewwe, Hanan G. Jacoby and Elizabeth M. King, 'Early childhood nutrition and academic achievement: A longitudinal analysis', *Journal of Public Economics* 81:3, 2001, pp. 345–68; Emiliana Vegas and Lucrecia Santibáñez, 'The Promise of Early Childhood Development in Latin America and the Caribbean', Latin American Development Forum, World Bank, 2010.

20   In addition to vast country-level evidence, they developed a simulation showing a benefit of $10·6 billion for increasing preschool enrolment to 25 per cent in all countries, and $33·7 billion for increasing to 50 per cent, with a benefit-to-cost ratio as large as 17·6 to 1. See Patrice L. Engle, Maureen M. Black, Jere R. Behrman, Meena Cabral de Mello, Paul J. Gertler, Lydia Kapiriri, Reynaldo Martorell, Mary Eming Young and the International Child Development Steering Group, 'Child development in developing countries 3: Strategies to avoid the loss of developmental potential in more than 200 million children in the developing world', *Lancet* 369, January 2007, p. 229–42; Patrice Engle, Lia Fernald, Harold Alderman, Jere Behrman, Chloe O'Gara, Aisha Yousafzai, Meena Cabral de Mello, Melissa Hidrobo, Nurper Ulkuer, Ilgi Ertem and Selim Iltus, 'Strategies

for Reducing Inequalities and Improving Developmental Outcomes for Young Children in Low and Middle Income Countries', *Lancet* 378, November 2011, pp. 1339–53.

21  Engle et al., 'Child development'.

22  Paul Gertler, James Heckman, Rodrigo Pinto, Arianna Zanolini, Christel Vermeersch, Susan Walker, Susan M. Chang and Sally Grantham-McGregor, 'Labor market returns to an early childhood stimulation intervention in Jamaica', *Science* 344, 30 May 2014, pp. 998–1001.

23  The body of accumulated evidence shows that participation in a variety of preschool programmes not only enhances children's school readiness and early school performance (Lynn A. Karoly, Peter W. Greenwood, Susan S. Everingham, Jill Houbé, M. Rebecca Kilburn, C. Peter Rydell, Matthew Sanders and James Chiesa, 'Investing in Our Children: What We Know and Don't Know About the Costs and Benefits of Early Childhood Interventions', RAND Corporation, 1998; Crag T. Ramey and Sharon Landesman Ramey, 'Early intervention and early experience', *American Psychologist* 53:2, 1998, pp. 109–20; Karl R. White, 'Efficacy of Early Intervention', *The Journal of Special Education* 19: 4 (1985), pp. 401–16) but is associated, many years later, with reduced incidence of remedial education (W. Steven Barnett, 'Long-Term Effects of Early Childhood Programs on Cognitive and School Outcomes', *The Future of Children* 5:3, 1995, pp. 25–50; Karoly et al., 'Investing'; Jack P. Shonkoff and Deborah A. Phillips (editors), *From neurons to neighborhoods: The science of early childhood development*, National Academy Press, 2000), delinquent behaviour (Eliana Garces, Duncan Thomas and Janet Currie, 'Longer-Term Effects of Head Start', *American Economic Review* 92:4, 2002, pp. 999–1012; Arthur J. Reynolds, Judy A. Temple, Dylan L. Robertson and Emily A. Mann, 'Long-term Effects of an Early Childhood Intervention on Educational Achievement and Juvenile Arrest: A 15-Year Follow-up of Low-Income Children in Public Schools', *Journal of the American Medical Association* 285:18, 2001, pp. 2339–46; L. J. Schweinhart, H. V. Barnes and D. P. Weikart, 'Significant Benefits: The High/Scope Perry Preschool Study through Age 27', Monographs of the High/Scope Educational Research Foundation 10, High/Scope Press, 1993; Karoly et al., 'Investing') and higher levels of educational attainment (Frances A. Campbell, Craig T. Ramey, Elizabeth Pungello, Joseph Sparling and Shari Miller-Johnson, 'Early Childhood Education: Young Adult Outcomes From the Abecedarian Project', *Applied Developmental Science* 6:1, 2002, pp. 42–57; Consortium for Longitudinal Studies (Ed.), *As the twig is bent: Lasting effects of preschool programs*, Erlbaum, 1983; Reynolds et al, 'Long-term Effects'; Schweinhart et al., 'Significant Benefits'; Ramey and Ramey, 'Early Intervention'; Barnett, 'Long-Term Effects'; Shonkoff and Phillips, *From neurons to neighborhoods*; Garces, Thomas and Currie, 'Longer-Term Effects'; Reynolds et al., 'Long-term Effects'; Schweinhart et al., 'Significant Benefits'; Campbell et al., 'Early Childhood Education'.

24  Reynolds et al., 'School-Based Early Childhood Education', pp. 360–64. Interestingly, in other studies early-childhood education has been found to benefit girls more than boys. For example in North Carolina research has found that boys' baseline conditions tended to be better with fathers more likely to be present and more financial resources available, see Jorge Luis Garcia, James J. Heckman and Anna L. Ziff, 'Gender differences in the benefits of an influential early childhood program', *European Economic Review* 109, 2018, p. 9–22.

25  World Bank, 'World Bank Development Report 2019', p. 75.

26  Ibid.

27  OECD, 'OECD Family database', Organisation for Economic Co-operation and Development, 2019: http://www.oecd.org/els/family/database.htm.

28  World Bank, 'World Bank Development Report 2019', pp. 74–75.

29  Joseph Fishkin, *Bottlenecks: A New Theory of Equal Opportunity*, Oxford University Press, 2014.

30  Canadian Literacy and Learning Network, 'Seven Principles of Adult Learning', 2014: website, Office of Literacy and Essential Skills, Government of Canada.

31  Malcolm S. Knowles, Elwood F. Holton III and Richard A. Swanson, *The adult learner: The definitive classic in adult education and human resource development*, Elsevier, 2005.

32  World Bank, 'World Bank Development Report 2019'.

33  A. D. Ho, J. Reich, S. Nesterko, D. T. Seaton, T. Mullane, J. Waldo and I. Chuang, 'HarvardX and MITx: The first year of open online courses, Fall 2012–Summer 2013', 2014.

34  David Card, Jochen Kluve and Andrea Weber, 'What Works? A Meta-Analysis of Recent Active Labor Market Program Evaluations', *Journal of the European Economic Association* 16:3, June 2018, pp. 894–93.

35  OECD, *Getting Skills Right: Future Ready Adult Learning Systems*, OECD Publishing, 2019.

36  Ibid.

37  For examples of how different countries divide the costs of adult learning, see ibid.

38  Ibid., p. 96.

39  A good example of building the capacity of small and medium-sized enterprises to develop their staff is a programme in Korea through which such employers can access a set of complementary subsidies including financial support to hire external consultants to analyse the company's training needs, build the capacity of the CEO and managers, and accompany the process of becoming a learning organisation. Further subsidies are available for setting up learning groups and to fund staff responsible for managing these groups. Funds can be also used to provide training to CEOs and staff responsible for learning activities. The final set of subsidies allows companies to take part in peer-learning activities and share their experience of building a learning organisation. See OECD, *Getting Skills Right: Engaging low-skilled adults in learning*', OECD Publishing, 2019, p. 20.

40  Archie Hall, 'Shares in Students: Nifty Finance or Indentured Servitude?' *Financial Times*, 12 November 2019.

41  Thomas Piketty, *Capital and Ideology*, Harvard University Press, 2020.

42  To manage the risk of the recipient defaulting on the loan and to accommodate administration costs, an additional charge could be added. But for the scheme to be attractive enough to work, repayment of the loan would only start once a certain income threshold had been achieved.

## Chapter 4: Health

1   Daniel R. Hogan, Gretchen A. Stevens, Ahmad Reza Hosseinpoor and Ties Boerma, 'Monitoring universal health coverage within the Sustainable Development Goals: development and baseline data for an index of essential health services', *Lancet Global Health* 6, 2018, pp. e152–68.

2   Other estimates suggest a minimum of 5 per cent of GDP plus a minimum of $86 per person to deliver basic primary care in all low-income countries. See Di Mcintyre, Filip Meheus and John-Arne Røttingen, 'What Level of Domestic Government Health Expenditure Should We Aspire to for Universal Health Coverage', *Health Econ Policy Law* 12:2, 2017, pp. 125–37.

3   WHO, *Global Spending on Health: A World in Transition*, World Health Organization, 2019.

4   ILO, 'World Social Protection Report 2014/15: Building economic recovery, inclusive development and social justice', International Labour Organisation, 2014.

5   The World Health Assembly adopted by consensus the WHO Global Code of Practice on the International Recruitment of Health Personnel, but the first report on the code's implementation was not positive. See Allyn L. Taylor and Ibadat S. Dhillon, 'The WHO Global Code of Practice on the International Recruitment of Health Personnel: The Evolution of Global Health Diplomacy', *Global Health Governance* V:1, Fall 2011; Amani Siyam, Pascal Zurn, Otto Christian Rø, Gulin Gedik, Kenneth Ronquillo, Christine Joan Co, Catherine Vaillancourt-Laflamme, Jennifer dela Rosa, Galina Perfilieva and Mario Roberto Dal Poz, 'Monitoring the implementation of the WHO Global Code of Practice on the International Recruitment of Health Personnel', *Bulletin of World Health Organization* 91:11, 2013, pp. 816–23.

6   Kenneth Arrow, 'Uncertainty and the Welfare Economics of Medical Care', *American Economic Review* 53:5, 1963, pp. 941–73.

7   Ruud Ter Meulen and Hans Maarse, 'Increasing Individual Responsibility in Dutch Health Care: Is Solidarity Losing Ground?' *Journal of Medicine and Philosophy: A Forum for Bioethics and Philosophy of Medicine* 33:3, June 2008, pp. 262–79.

8   Five criteria are often cited to justify public health interventions: (1) effectiveness, (2) proportionality, (3) necessity, (4) least infringement and (5) public justification. James F. Childress, Ruth R. Faden, Ruth D. Gaare, Lawrence O. Gostin, Jeffrey Kahn, Richard J. Bonnie, Nancy E. Kass, Anna C. Mastroianni, Jonathan D. Moreno and Phillip Nieburg, 'Public health ethics: mapping the terrain', *Journal of Law Medical Ethics* 30:2, June 2002, pp. 170–78.

9   Ruben Durante, Luigi Guiso and Giorgio Gulino, 'Asocial capital: Culture and Social Distancing during Covid-19', Centre for Economic Policy Research Discussion Paper DP14820, June 2020; John Barrios, Efraim Benmelech, Yael V. Hochberg, Paola Sapienza and Luigi Zingales, 'Civic Capital and Social Distancing during the Covid-19 Pandemic', National Bureau of Economic Research Working Paper 27320, June 2020; Francesca Borgonovi and Elodie Andrieu, 'The Role of Social Capital in Promoting Social Distancing During the Covid-19 Pandemic in the US', *Vox*, June 2020.

10  Maloney and Taskin used Google mobility data and found significant declines in restaurant reservations in the US even before the imposition of government lockdowns. William Maloney and Temel Taskin, 'Determinants of Social Distancing and Economic Activity During Covid-19: A Global View', World Bank Policy Research Working Paper 9242, World Bank, May 2020. For the UK, Surico et al. (2020) found that the bulk of the consumption decline occurred before the nationwide lockdown was implemented. Paolo Surico, Diego Kanzig and Sinem Hacioglu, 'Consumption in the Time of Covid-19: Evidence from UK Transaction Data', Centre for Economic Policy Research Discussion Paper DP14733, May

2020. Born et al. (2020) found mobility in Sweden fell to a similar degree with countries that had a lockdown. Benjamin Born, Alexander Dietrich and Gernot Muller, 'The Lockdown Effect: A Counterfactual for Sweden'. Centre for Economic Policy Research Discussion Paper DP 14744, July 2020.

11  There is a vast literature on how health systems are organised. Some argue that it is less important whether a system is public or private than whether there is some choice and competition in the provision of health services. See Julian LeGrand, *The Other Invisible Hand: Delivering Public Services Through Choice and Competition,* Princeton University Press, 2007.

12  Viroj Tangcharoensathien, Anne Mills and Toomas Palu, 'Accelerating health equity: the key role of universal health coverage in the Sustainable Development Goals', *BMC Medicine,* 2015, pp. 1–5.

13  Marc J. Epstein and Eric G. Bing, 'Delivering Health Care to the Global Poor: Solving the Accessibility Problem', *Innovations: Technology, Governance, Globalization* 6:2, 2011.

14  Reuters, 'Ant Financial Amasses 50 Million Users, Mostly Low Income, in New Health Plan', *Reuters: Technology News,* 12 April 2019. I am indebted to Roger Mountfort for bringing this example to my attention.

15  The OECD points out that in the United States 'life expectancy is now more than a year below the OECD average of 80.1, compared to one year above the average in 1970'. See OECD, 'Life expectancy in the US rising slower than elsewhere, says OECD', Organisation for Economic Co-operation and Development, 2013, p.1. On declining life expectancy in the US, see Ann Case and Angus Deaton, *Deaths of Despair and the Future of Capitalism,* Princeton University Press, 2020.

16  Luca Lorenzoni, Alberto Marino, David Morgan and Chris James, 'Health Spending Projections to 2030: New results based on a revised OECD methodology', OECD Health Working Paper 110, 23 May 2019.

17  Aaron Reeves, Yannis Gourtsoyannis, Sanjay Basu, David McCoy, Martin McKee and David Suckler, 'Financing universal health coverage: effects of alternative tax structures on public health systems: cross-national modelling in 89 low-income and middle-income countries', *Lancet* 386:9990, July 2015, pp. 274–80.

18  Claudine de Meijer, Bram Wouterse, Johan Polder and Marc Koopmanschap, 'The effect of population aging on health expenditure growth: a critical review', *European Journal of Ageing* 10:4, 2013, pp. 353–61.

19  Irene Papanicolas, Alberto Marino, Luca Lorenzoni and Ashish Jha, 'Comparison of Health Care Spending by Age in 8 High-Income Countries', JAMA Network Open, 2020.

20  Nghiem and Connelly find that despite common perceptions, the bulk of health expenditure growth is not due to population ageing per se, but the growth in demand for new medical technologies. A 1 per cent increase in GDP per capita is associated with a 0.9 per cent increase in health expenditure per capita. The main driver for increasing health expenditure is technological progress, which accounts for 4 per cent per year and accelerated faster after each decade in the study period. See Son Hong Nghiem and Luke Brian Connelly, 'Convergence and determinants of health expenditures in OECD countries', *Health Economics Review* 7:1, 2017, p. 29. For an assessment of the impact of rising incomes and insurance relative to technology, see Sheila Smith, Joseph P. Newhouse and Mark S. Freeland, 'Income, Insurance, and Technology: Why Does Health Spending Outpace Economic Growth?' *Health Affairs* 28:5, 2009, pp. 1276–84.

21  Lorenzoni et al., 'Health Spending Projections to 2020'.

22 This only works if generic drugs deliver equivalent health gains. There has been some controversy around the quality of generic drugs as a result of poor regulation. See Karen Eban, *Bottle of Lies: The Inside Story of the Generic Drug Boom*, Ecco Press, 2020.

23 For a thorough analysis of how price setting impacts the effectiveness of the health system, see Sarah L. Barber, Luca Lorenzoni and Paul Ong, 'Price setting and price regulation in health care: lessons for advancing Universal Health Coverage', World Health Organization and the Organisation for Economic Co-operation and Development, 2019.

24 Alex Voorhoeve, Trygve Ottersen and Ole F. Norheim, 'Making fair choices on the path to universal health coverage: a précis', *Health Economics, Policy and Law*, 2016.

25 McKinsey, *The Social Contract in the 21st Century*, McKinsey Global Institute, 2020.

26 For advanced economies, see V. G. Paris, G. De Lagasnarie, R. Fujisawa et al., 'How do OECD countries define the basket of goods and services financed collectively', OECD Unpublished Document, 2014. For examples of the use of health technology assessments in developing countries, see Corinna Sorenson, 'The role of HTA in coverage and pricing decisions', *Euro Observer* 11:1, 2009, pp. 1–4; Leon Bijlmakers, Debjani Mueller, Rabia Kahveci, Yingyao Chen and Gert Jan van der Wilt, 'Integrate HTA – A low and middle income perspective', *International Journal of Technology Assessment in Health Care* 33:5, 2017, pp. 599–604.

27 For a framework for assessing individual responsibility for some health care costs, see Gustav Tinghog, Per Carlsson and Carl Lyttkens, 'Individual responsibility for what? – A conceptual framework for exploring the suitability of private financing in a publicly funded health-care system', *Health Economics Policy and Law Journal* 5:2, 2010, pp. 201–23.

28 For a thoughtful summary of the pros and cons of QALYs, see Emily Jackson, *Medical Law*, Oxford University Press, 2019.

29 Melanie Bertram, Jeremy Lauer, Kees De Joncheere, Tessa Edejer, Raymond Hutubessy, Marie-Paule Kieny and Suzanne Hill, 'Cost–Effectiveness Thresholds: Pros and Cons', *Bulletin of the World Health Organization*, 2016.

30 For example, in the UK the National Institute for Clinical Excellence uses £20,000 per QALY to assess affordability. Treatments that cost between £20,000 and £30,000 per QALY are considered under special circumstances, such as the needs of the patient group. Treatments costing over £30,000 per QALY are supposed to be unacceptable, although in practice £40,000 is the threshold at which there is a greater than 50 per cent chance of rejection. See Jackson, *Medical Law*.

31 Karl Claxton quoted in Robin McKie, 'David Cameron's Flagship Cancer Drugs Fund is a Waste of NHS Cash', *Guardian*, 10 January 2015.

32 John Harris, *The Value of Life*, Routledge, 1985, p. 93; Alan Williams, 'Intergenerational Equity: An Exploration of the "Fair Innings' Argument"', *Health Economics* 6:2, March 1997, pp. 117–32.

33 Norman Daniels, *Just Health Care*, Cambridge University Press, 1985; Ronald Dworkin, *Sovereign Virtue: The Theory and Practice of Equality*, Harvard University Press, 2002.

34 Gwyn Bevan and Lawrence D. Brown, 'The political economy of rationing health care in England and the US: the "accidental logics" of political settlements', *Health Economics, Policy and Law* 9:3, 2014, pp. 273–94.

35 Henry J. Aaron and William B. Schwartz, *The Painful Prescription*, Brookings Institution, 1984.

36  Nina Bernstein, 'With Medicaid, Long-Term Care of Elderly Looms as Rising Cost', *New York Times*, 7 September 2012.

37  Marc Mitchell and Lena Kan, 'Digital Technology and the Future of Health Systems', *Health Systems and Reform* 5:2, pp. 112–20.

38  R. L. Cutler, F. Fernandez-Llimos, M. Frommer et al., 'Economic impact of medication non-adherence by disease groups: a systematic review', *British Medical Journal Open*, 2018.

39  For example, a collaboration between Google Deep Mind and the Royal Free NHS Foundation Trust to test a system for diagnosis and detection of acute kidney injury was found to have inadequate controls for informing patients that their data would be used as part of the test. Information Commissioner's Office, 'Royal Free-Google Deep Mind Trial Failed to Comply with Data Protection Law', UK Government Information Commissioner, 3 July 2017.

40  For example, the 'Contract for the Web' was created by experts and citizens from across the world to make sure the digital world is safe, empowering and genuinely accessible to all. Led by Tim Berners-Lee, it sets out principles for governments, companies, civil society organisations and individuals to commit to upholding data privacy. See contractfortheweb.org.

41  Rebecca Masters, Elspeth Anwar, Brendan Collins, Richard Cookson and Simon Capewell, 'Return on investment of public health interventions: a systematic review', *Journal of Epidemiology and Community Health, British Medical Journals*, 2017.

42  David J. Hunter, *Desperately Seeking Solutions: Rationing Health Care*, Longman, 1997.

43  M. Ezzati, S. Vander Hoorn, C. M. M. Lawes, R. Leach, W. P. T. James, A. D. Lopez et al., 'Rethinking the "Diseases of Affluence" Paradigm: Global Patterns of Nutritional Risks in Relation to Economic Development', *PLoS Medicine*, 2005.

44  P. H. M. van Baal, J. J. Polder, G. A. de Wit, R. T. Hoogenveen, T. L. Feenstra, H. C. Boshuizen et al., 'Lifetime Medical Costs of Obesity: Prevention No Cure for Increasing Health Expenditure', *PLoS Medicine*, 2008.

45  Mark Goodchild, Nigar Nargis and Tursan d'Espaignet, 'Global economic cost of smoking-attributable diseases', *Tobacco Control* 27:1, 2018, pp. 58–64.

46  Lord Darzi, 'Better health and care for all: A 10 Point Plan for the 2020s: Final Report of the Lord Darzi Review of Health and Care', Institute for Public Policy Research, 2018.

47  A. W. Cappelen and O. F. Norheim, 'Responsibility in health care: a liberal egalitarian approach', *Journal of Medical Ethics*, 2005.

48  For a very thoughtful analysis of paternalism and public health, see L. O. Gostin and K. G. Gostin, 'A broader liberty: J. S. Mill, paternalism and the public's health', *Public Health*, 2009.

49  John Stuart Mill, *On Liberty*, Cambridge University Press, 1859.

50  John Rawls, *A Theory of Justice*, Harvard University Press, 1971; Sen, *Development as Freedom*.

51  David Buchanan, 'Autonomy, Paternalism, and Justice: Ethical Priorities in Public Health', *American Journal of Public Health*, January 2008.

52  U.S. National Cancer Institute and World Health Organization, *The Economics of Tobacco and Tobacco Control*, National Cancer Institute Tobacco Control Monograph 21, NIH Publication 16–CA-8029A., U.S. Department of Health and Human Services, National Institutes of Health, National Cancer Institute and World Health Organization, 2016.

53 Bundit Sornpaisarn, Kevin Shield, Joanna Cohen, Robert Schwartz and Jürgen Rehm, 'Elasticity of alcohol consumption, alcohol-related harms, and drinking initiation in low- and middle-income countries: A systematic review and meta-analysis', *International Journal of Drug and Alcohol Research* 2:1, 2013, pp. 45–58.

54 L. M. Powell, J. F. Chriqui, T. Khan, R. Wada and F. J. Chaloupka, 'Assessing the potential effectiveness of food and beverage taxes and subsidies for improving public health: a systematic review of prices, demand, and body weight outcomes', *Obesity Reviews* 14:2, 2013, pp.110–28.

55 Michael W. Long, Steven L. Gortmaker, Zachary J. Ward, Stephen C. Resch, Marj L. Moodie, Gary Sacks, Boyd A. Swinburn, Rob C. Carter and Y. Claire Wang, 'Cost-effectiveness of a sugar-sweetened beverage excise tax in the U.S.', *American Journal of Preventive Medicine* 49:1, pp. 112–23.

56 Luz Maria Sánchez-Romero, Joanne Penko, Pamela G. Coxson, Alicia Fernández, Antoinette Mason, Andrew E. Moran, Leticia Ávila-Burgos, Michelle Odden, Simón Barquera and Kirsten Bibbins-Domingo, 'Projected Impact of Mexico's Sugar-Sweetened Beverage Tax Policy on Diabetes and Cardiovascular Disease: A Modeling Study', *PLoS Medicine* 13:11, e.1002158; Adam D. M. Briggs, Oliver T. Mytton, Ariane Kehlbacher, Richard Tiffin, Ahmed Elhussein, Mike Rayner, Susan A. Jebb, Tony Blakely and Peter Scarborough, 'Health impact assessment of the UK soft drinks industry levy: a comparative risk assessment modelling study', *Lancet Public Health* 2:1, e.15–22; Ashkan Afshin, Renata Micha, Michael Webb, Simon Capewell, Laurie Whitsel, Adolfo Rubinstein, Dorairaj Prabhakaran, Marc Suhrcke and Dariush Mozaffarian, 'Effectiveness of Dietary Policies to Reduce Noncommunicable Diseases', in Dorairaj Prabhakaran, Shuchi Anand, Thomas A Gaziano, Jean-Claude Mbanya, Yangfeng Wu and Rachel Nugent (editors), *Disease Control Priorities*, 3rd edition, World Bank, 2017.

57 The $20 trillion in additional revenues is calculated in present discounted-value terms. The Task Force on Fiscal Policy for Health, *Health Taxes to Save Lives: Employing Effective Excise Taxes on Tobacco, Alcohol and Sugary Beverages*, Bloomberg Philanthropies, April 2019.

58 Dawn Wilson, Kate Lorig, William M. P. Klein, William Riley, Allison Sweeney and Alan Christensen, 'Efficacy and Cost-Effectiveness of Behavioral Interventions in Nonclinical Settings for Improving Health Outcomes', *Health Psychology* 38:8, 2019, pp. 689–700.

59 Emma Beard, Robert West, Fabiana Lorencatto, Ben Gardner, Susan Michie, Lesley Owens and Lion Shahab, 'What do cost effective health behaviour-change interventions contain? A comparison of six domains', *PLoS One*, 14:4, 2019.

60 The term comes from the influential book *Nudge*, which is based on a non-paternalistic approach to changing behaviours. For example, rather than regulating the sugar content of foods, a nudge would rely on placing healthy foods where shoppers are most likely to choose them and putting sweets in inaccessible locations. As Sunstein and Thaler put it, 'To count as a mere nudge, the intervention must be easy and cheap to avoid. Nudges are not mandates. Putting the fruit at eye level counts as a nudge. Banning junk food does not.' See Richard Thaler and Cass Sunstein, *Nudge*, Yale University Press, 2008.

61 Chris Perry, Krishna Chhatralia, Dom Damesick, Sylvie Hobden and Leanora Volpe, 'Behavioral Insights in Health Care: Nudging to Reduce Inefficiency and Waste', The Health Fund, December 2015.

62 Michael Marmot and Richardson G. Wilkinson, *Social Determinants of Health*, Oxford University Press, 1999; Richardson G. Wilkinson, *The Impact of Inequality: How to Make Sick Societies Healthier*, W. W. Norton, 2005.

63  Michael Marmot and Jessica Allen, 'Social Determinants of Health Equity', *American Journal of Public Health*, September 2014.

## Chapter 5: Work

1   For a thoughtful description of what happens to a community that has less success with creating opportunities after a factory closes, see Goldstein, *Janesville*.

2   Paul Collier, *The Future of Capitalism: Facing the New Anxieties*, Allen Lane, 2018. It is possible the growth of remote working in the wake of the coronavirus pandemic may change the geography of work and make it possible for jobs to be done from anywhere. This may reduce regional disparities in some countries, although it is too early to tell.

3   In sub-Saharan Africa informal employment exceeds 70 per cent of the labour market; it is 60 per cent in south Asia and 50 per cent in Latin America. See World Bank, 'World Development Report: The Changing Nature of Work'.

4   Part-time paid work was the primary driver of the increase in overall employment between 2000 and 2018. Its share rose in 18 out of 21 countries by an average of 4.1 percentage points, equivalent to 29 million jobs, while that of full-time employment declined by 1.4 percentage points. See McKinsey, *The Social Contract*.

5   Since 2006, across the OECD average job stability (as measured by the length of time spent in the current job) has increased in a number of countries. This is, however, a compositional effect due to an increase in the proportion of older workers, who tend to have longer job tenure. Once this change in the composition of the workforce is taken into account, job tenure actually declined in most countries. See OECD, *OECD Employment Outlook: The Future of Work*.

6   Franz Eiffe, Agnès Parent-Thirion and Isabella Biletta, *Working Conditions: Does employment status matter for job quality?* Eurofound, Publications Office of the European Union, 2018.

7   Vinny Kuntz, 'Germany's two-tier labour market,' *Handelsblatt Today*, 9 December 2016; Nathan Hudson-Sharp and Johnny Runge, *International trends in insecure work: A report for the Trades Union Congress*, National Institute of Economic and Social Research, May 2017.

8   Nikhil Datta, Giulia Giupponi and Stephen Machin, 'Zero Hours Contracts', *Economic Policy*, July 2019.

9   Lawrence F. Katz and Alan B. Krueger, 'The rise and nature of alternative work arrangements in the United States, 1995–2015', *ILR Review* 72:2, March 2019, pp. 382–416.

10  Tito Boeri, Giulia Giupponi, Alan B. Krueger, and Stephen Machin, 'Solo Self-Employment and Alternative Work Arrangements: A Cross-Country Perspective on the Changing Composition of Jobs', *Journal of Economic Perspectives* 34:1, Winter 2020.

11  Jelle Visser, 'Can Unions Revitalise Themselves?' *International Journal of Labour Research* 9:1–2, 2019, pp. 17–48.

12  International Labour Organization, 'Industrial relations data', *ILOSTAT database*, 2020, https://ilostat.ilo.org/data.

13  Truman Packard, Ugo Gentilini, Margaret Grosh, Philip O'Keefe, Robert Palacios, David Robalino and Indhira Santos, *Protecting All: Risk Sharing for a Diverse and Diversifying World of Work*, Human Development Perspectives, World Bank, p. 143.

14 A study by Columbia University found that employees who were laid off during the 1982 recession in Germany earned 10 to 15 per cent less fifteen years
later than their counterparts who had not been laid off. In the United States the
magnitude was 15 to 20 per cent. A study by the State University of New York
found that laid-off employees have an 83 per cent higher chance of developing
a new health condition in the year after their termination than workers who
were not laid off, while other studies have found that life expectancy declines
among those who have lost their jobs. University of Manchester research found
that workers in Britain who had been laid off were 4.5 per cent less likely to
trust other people than those who had not been laid off, an effect that persisted
ten years later. These studies are cited in McKinsey, *The Social Contract*, p. 59.

15 A study by the University of Wisconsin-Madison and the University of South
Carolina found that lay-offs affecting 1 per cent of employees resulted in a 31
per cent increase in voluntary turnover on average after the initial downsizing.
Stockholm University and University of Canterbury researchers found that lay-
off survivors experienced a 41 per cent decline in job satisfaction, a 36 per cent
decline in job commitment, and a 20 per cent decline in job performance. See
McKinsey, *The Social Contract*, p. 59; Johannes F. Schmieder, Till von Wachter
and Stefan Bender, *The long-term impact of job displacement in Germany
during the 1982 recession on earnings, income, and employment*, Columbia
University Department of Economics Discussion Paper 0910–07, 2010; Kate W.
Strully, 'Job loss and health in the US labor market', *Demography* 46:2, May
2009, pp. 221–46; James Lawrence, '(Dis)placing trust: The long-term effects of
job displacement on generalized trust over the adult life course', *Social Science
Research* 50, March 2015, pp. 46–59; Jena McGregor, 'Getting laid off can make
people less trusting for years', *Washington Post*, 19 March 2015; Charlie O.
Trevor and Anthony J. Nyberg, 'Keeping your headcount when all about you are
losing theirs: Downsizing, voluntary turnover rates, and the moderating role of
HR practices', *Academy of Management Journal* 51:2, April 2008, pp. 259–76;
Sandra J. Sucher and Shalene Gupta, 'Layoffs that don't break your company',
*Harvard Business Review*, May–June 2018.

16 McKinsey, *The Social Contract*.

17 European Commission, 'Study on employment and working conditions of aircrews
in the European internal aviation market', European Commission, 2019.

18 Richard Susskind and Daniel Susskind, *The Future of the Professions: How
Technology Will Transform the World of Human Experts*, Oxford University
Press, 2015.

19 Herbert Simon, 'Automation', *New York Review of Books*, 26 May 1966.

20 Martin Sandbu, *The Economics of Belonging*, Princeton University Press, 2020.

21 More than 90 per cent of countries that are members of the International Labour
Organization have one or more minimum wages set by law or through negotia-
tions with unions. See ILO, *Minimum Wage Policy Guide*, International Labour
Organization, 2016.

22 Frank Pega, Sze Yan Liu, Stefan Walter, Roman Pabayo, Ruhi Saith and Stefan K
Lhachimi, 'Unconditional cash transfers for reducing poverty and vulnerabilities:
effect on use of health services and health outcomes in low- and middle-income
countries', *Cochrane Database of Systematic Reviews* 11, 2017; Independent
Commission for Aid Impact, *The Effects of DFID's Cash Transfer Programmes
on Poverty and Vulnerability: An Impact Revew*, Independent Commission for
Aid Impact, 2017; Francesca Bastagli, Jessica Hagen-Zanker, Luke Harman,
Valentina Barca, Georgina Sturge and Tanja Schmidt, with Luca Pellerano, 'Cash

transfers: what does the evidence say? A rigorous review of programme impact and of the role of design and implementation features', Overseas Development Institute, July 2016.

23  Guy Standing, *Basic Income: And How We Can Make it Happen*, Pelican Books, 2017.

24  Anna Coote and Edanur Yazici, *Universal Basic Income: A Union Perspective*, Public Services International and the New Economics Foundation, April 2019.

25  Sigal Samuel, 'Everywhere Basic Income has been Tried in One Map: Which Countries Have Experimented with Basic Income and What were the results?' *Vox*, 19 February 2020.

26  The IMF estimates the costs at 3–6 per cent of GDP in selected countries. See IMF, *Fiscal Monitor: Tackling Inequality*, International Monetary Fund, October 2017.

27  Dominique Guillaume, Roman Zytek and Mohammad Reza Farzin, 'Iran—The Chronicles of the Subsidy Reform', Working Paper, IMF Middle East and Central Asia Department, July 2011.

28  Thomas Piketty, *Capital and Ideology*, Harvard University Press, 2020. In the US Ackerman and Alstott argued for a capital grant of $80,000 at the age of 21, see Bruce Ackermann and Anne Alstott, *The Stakeholder Society*, Yale University Press, 1999.

29  O. Bandiera, R. Burgess, N. Das, S. Gulesci, I. Rasul and M Sulaiman, 'Labor Markets and Poverty in Village Economies', *Quarterly Journal of Economics* 132:2, 2017, pp. 811–70.

30  Mosely B. Ingham, 'The Fundamental Cure for Poverty is Not Money But Knowledge: Lewis's Legacy', in *Sir Arthur Lewis*, Great Thinkers in Economics Series, Macmillan, 2013.

31  Brian Bell, Mihai Codreanu and Stephen Machin, 'What can previous recessions tell us about the Covid-19 downturn?' Paper 007, Centre for Economic Performance, London School of Economics, August 2020.Shania Bhalotia, Swati Dhingra and Fjolla Kondirolli, 'City of Dreams no More: The Impact of Covid-19 on Urban Workers in India', Centre for Economic Performance, London School of Economics, September 2020. Jack Blundell and Stephen Machin, 'Self-employment in the Covid-19 crisis', Centre for Economic Performance, London School of Economics, May 2020.

32  'Why so Many Dutch People World Part-time', *The Economist*, 11 May 2015.

33  Matthew Taylor, Greg Marsh, Diane Nicol and Paul Broadbent, *Good Work: The Taylor Review of Modern Working Practices*, Department for Business, Energy and Industrial Strategy, 2018, p. 72.

34  McKinsey, *The Social Contract*.

35  Nikhil Datta, Giulia Giupponi and Stephen Machin, 'Zero Hours Contracts and Labour Market Policy', *Economic Policy* 34:99, July 2019, pp. 369–427.

36  Tito Boeri, Giulia Giupponi, Alan B. Krueger and Stephen Machin, 'Solo Self-Employment and Alternative Work Arrangements: A Cross-Country Perspective on the Changing Composition of Jobs', *Journal of Economic Perspectives*, Winter 2020.

37  Taylor et al., *Good Work*.

38  Larry Fink, 'Profit & Purpose: Larry Fink's 2019 Letter to CEOs', *BlackRock*, 2019; Colin Mayer, *Principles for Purposeful Business*, British Academy, 2019.

39  Dani Rodrik and Charles Sabel, 'Building a Good Jobs Economy', HKS Working Paper RWP20–001, November 2019; Paul Osterman, 'In Search of the High Road: Meaning and Evidence', *International Labour Review* 71:1, 2018, pp. 3–34.

40  Kurt Vandaele, 'Will trade unions survive in the platform economy? Emerging patterns of platform workers' collective voice and representation in Europe', ETUI Working Paper 2018/5, European Trade Union Institute, 2018.

41  David Card, Jochen Kluve and Andrea Weber, 'What Works? A Meta-Analysis of Recent Active Labor Market Program Evaluations', *Journal of the European Economic Association* 16:3, June 2018, pp. 894–931; John P. Martin, 'Activation and active labour market policies in OECD countries: stylised facts and evidence on their effectiveness', IZA Policy Paper 84, June 2014; Gordon Betcherman, Karina Olivas and Amit Dar, 'Impacts of Active Labour Market Programs: New Evidence from Evaluations', Social Protection Discussion Paper 0402, World Bank, 2004; Amit Dar and Zafiris Tsannatos, 'Active Labour Market Programmes: A Review of the Evidence from Evaluations', Social Protection Discussion Paper 9901, World Bank, 1999.

42  Verónica Escudero, 'Are active labour market policies effective in activating and integrating low-skilled individuals? An international comparison', *IZA Journal of Labour Policy* 7:4, 2018.

43  Thomas Kochan and William Kimball, 'Unions, Worker Voice, and Management Practices: Implications for a High-Productivity, High-Wage Economy', *RSF: The Russell Sage Foundation Journal of the Social Sciences* 5:5, December 2019.

44  OECD, 'Back to Work: Sweden: Improving the Re-employment Prospects of Displaced Workers', Organisation for Economic Co-operation and Development, 2015. Another example of a successful programme is Project QUEST (Quality Employment through Skills Training), founded in San Antonio, Texas in 1992. In the late 1980s San Antonio was hit by a wave of plant closures, an early portent of broader dislocations to come. The displaced workers lacked the skills for the new jobs being created in health care, IT and other sectors, and the service-sector jobs for which they were qualified paid too little to support a middle-class family. Two faith-based organisations worked with the region's largely Hispanic population, local community colleges and employers using a programme of intensive counselling, training and financial support enabled by strong management information systems. Evaluations nine years later show that participants earned about 10 per cent more than the control group, and benefits were greatest for the groups that were the most at risk. See Anne Roder and Mark Elliott, *Nine Year Gains: Project QUEST's Continuing Impact*, Economic Mobility Corporation, 2019; Dani Rodrik and Charles Sabel, 'Building a Good Jobs Economy'; Ida Rademacher, Marshall Bear and Maureen Conway, 'Project QUEST: a case study of a sectoral employment development approach', Sectoral Employment Development Learning Project Case Studies Series, Economic Opportunities Program, Aspen Institute, 2001.

45  OECD, 'Getting Skills Right: Engaging low skilled adults in learning', Organisation for Economic Co-operation and Development, 2019; OECD, 'Back to Work: Sweden'; Eurofound, *Working Conditions: Does employment status matter for job quality?*

46  Danish Government, *Prepared for the future of work: Follow-up on the Danish Disruption Council*, Danish Government, February 2019.

47  OECD, Back to Work: Improving the Reemployment Prospects of Displaced Workers, OECD, 2016.

48  Erik Brynjolfsson and Paul Milgrom, 'Complementarity in Organizations', in Robert Gibbons and John Roberts (editors), *The Handbook of Organizational Economics*, Princeton University Press, 2012.

49  Lorin Hitt and Prasanna Tambe, 'Health Care Information Technology, Work Organisation and Nursing Home Performance,' *ILR Review* 69:4, March 2016, pp. 834–59.

50   WEF, *Towards a Reskilling Revolution: A Future of Jobs for All*, World Economic
     Forum, 2019.

## Chapter 6: Old Age

1    Without policy changes, ageing pressures could increase the public debt burden
     by an average of 180 per cent of GDP in G20 advanced economies and 130 per
     cent of GDP in G20 emerging economies over the next three decades. Alternatively,
     tax revenue would need to increase by between 4.5 and 11.5 percentage points
     of GDP by 2060 in G20 countries to stabilise public debt-to-GDP ratios at their
     current levels. See Dorothée Rouzet, Aida Caldera Sánchez, Théodore Renault
     and Oliver Roehn, 'Fiscal Challenges and Inclusive Growth in Ageing Societies',
     OECD Economic Policy Paper 27, September 2019.
2    Countries such as Chile in 1981 and Mexico in 1997 replaced their public
     pay-as-you-go defined benefit schemes by privately funded mandatory defined
     contribution schemes. More recently, as a complement to their public pen-
     sion schemes, Estonia, Hungary, Poland, the Slovak Republic and Sweden have
     introduced mandatory privately funded defined contribution schemes or raised
     the contribution rates that fund them. In the Netherlands consecutive adjust-
     ments of pension rules have made the funded defined benefit scheme more of
     a hybrid system. In other countries like the United States the share of defined
     benefit plans among occupational pensions has slowly declined in favour of more
     defined contribution plans. OECD, *Pensions at a Glance 2019: OECD and G20
     Indicators*, Organisation for Economic Co-operation and Development, 2019.
3    For example, reforms have included raising contribution rates (Canada, UK),
     cutting benefits or limiting the indexation of pensions to inflation (Argentina,
     Greece), indexing pensions to life expectancy (Japan), raising retirement ages
     (Indonesia, Russia, UK) and reducing options for early retirement. For many
     examples, see Rouzet et al., 'Fiscal Challenges'.
4    Friedrich Breyer and Ben Craig, 'Voting on Social Security: Evidence from OECD
     Countries,' *European Journal of Political Economy* 13:4, 1997, pp. 705–24.
5    See Box 2 in Rouzet et al., 'Fiscal Challenges', p. 29.
6    Rouzet et al., 'Fiscal Challenges'.
7    The OECD estimates that if retirement ages were increased by three years between
     2015 and 2060 – when life expectancy at 65 years is projected to increase by
     4.2 years on average – the total pension benefits of low-educated retirees relative
     to those of the highly educated groups would be reduced by 2.2 per cent. See
     OECD, *Preventing Ageing Unequally*, Organisation for Economic Co-operation
     and Development, 2017, p.41.
8    The OECD notes, 'Pension policy measures to take account of socio-economic
     differences in life expectancy could target the benefit formula (granting higher
     accrual rates for low earnings, as applied in Portugal), the level of contribution
     rates (increasing with income such as in Brazil) or through a higher wage ceil-
     ing for contributions than for pension entitlements. In DC schemes, the annuity
     factors for conversion of assets into a pension benefit could be set in ways that
     increase pensions for people with low pensionable income (who die earlier on
     average) while people with high pensionable income (who die later on average)
     would receive lower benefits. The United Kingdom introduced a rare example
     of this through private "enhanced annuities": higher annuities are paid for the
     same accumulated pension assets to people with certain health or behavioural
     factors which are associated with lower life expectancy, such as smoking, obesity

or cardiovascular disease, and which are more prevalent in lower socio-economic groups. The OECD calls for more accurate mortality data by socio-economic groups so that higher benefits could be offered to people with higher health risks. Schemes "rewarding" risky behaviours should be designed carefully though.' See OECD, *Preventing Ageing Unequally*, p. 59.

9  Nicholas Barr, 'Gender and Family: Conceptual Overview,' World Bank Discussion Paper 1916, April 2019.

10  Richard H. Thaler and Shlomo Benartzi, 'Save More Tomorrow™: Using Behavioral Economics to Increase Employee Saving', *Journal of Political Economy* 112:S1, 2004, S164–S187.

11  For a detailed review of these issues, see OECD *Preventing Ageing Unequally*.

12  Japan has a spousal deduction in the income tax system that creates disincentives for women to work. See Randall S. Jones and Haruki Seitani, 'Labour Market Reform in Japan to Cope with a Shrinking and Ageing Population', Economics Department Working Paper 1568, Organisation for Economic Co-operation and Development, 2019; 'Japan: Selected Issues', IMF Country Report 17/243, IMF Asia Pacific Department, 2017, IMF International Monetary Fund, Organisation for Economic Co-operation and Development.

13  Rouzet et al., 'Fiscal Challenges'.

14  Asli Demirguc-Kunt, Leora Klapper, Dorothe Singer, Saniya Ansar and Richard Jake Hess, *The Global Findex Database 2017: Measuring Financial Inclusion and the Fintech Revolution*, World Bank Group, 2018.

15  Merve Akbas, Dan Ariely, David A. Robalino and Michael Weber, 'How to Help the Poor to Save a Bit: Evidence from a Field Experiment in Kenya', IZA Discussion Paper 10024, IZA, 2016.

16  Kevin Wesbroom, David Hardern, Matthew Arends and Andy Harding, 'The Case for Collective DC: A new opportunity for UK pensions', White Paper, Aon Hewitt, November 2013.

17  Only about 40 per cent of employers offer flexible time schedules in the United States, while in Europe nearly 80 per cent of people over 55 cite the lack of opportunities to retire gradually by reducing their hours as an important reason to stop working altogether. See, Rouzet et al., 'Fiscal Challenges', p. 49.

18  For example, Germany provides subsidies for wages and training costs to encourage firms to train the low skilled and workers over 45. Australia is scaling up skills assessment and guidance for workers over 50. Korea provides vouchers to buy approved training courses for workers over 40, non-regular workers and small and medium-sized enterprises willing to undertake training on their own initiative. Rouzet et al., 'Fiscal Challenges', p. 42.

19  Lindsay Flynn and Herman Mark Schwartz, 'No Exit: Social Reproduction in an Era of Rising Income Inequality,' *Politics & Society* 45:4, 2017, pp. 471–503.

20  OECD, *Preventing Ageing Unequally*.

21  Kaare Christensen, Gabriele Doblhammer, Roland Rau and James W Vaupel, 'Ageing Populations: The Challenges Ahead,' *Lancet* 374:9696, 2009, pp. 1196–208.

22  The dynamic equilibrium hypothesis is associated with Manton and posits that life-expectancy increases are equalled by additional years without disability or poor health. See Kenneth G. Manton, 'Changing Concepts of Morbidity and Mortality in the Elderly Population', *Milbank Memorial Fund Quarterly, Health and Society* 60:2, 1982, pp. 183–244. A review by Lindren found that experience in high income countries has tended to support the hypothesis of healthy ageing. See Bjorn Lindgren, 'The Rise in Life Expectancy, Health Trends among the Elderly, and the Demand for Care – A Selected Literature Review', NBER Working Papers 22521, National Bureau of Economic Research, 2016.

23  Providing care, even for people with lower-level needs, can be costly relative to a pensioner's disposable income. In the 13 OECD countries for which data are available, 6.5 hours of professional care per week costs on average half of the median disposable income of a person over aged 65. Those with greater needs – equivalent to over 40 hours of care per week – would require on average three times the median disposable income of an older person. In such cases of acute needs institutional care may be cheaper, but even that still costs more than twice an elderly person's median disposable income. Only the most well-off older people can cover costs for moderate needs from their incomes. The cost of home care for 22.5 hours per week of professional care is equal to 96 per cent of the disposable income for someone in the 80th percentile of the income distribution but more than twice the disposable income of someone in the 20th. See OECD, *Preventing Ageing Unequally*, p. 239.

24  For an account of the inefficiencies of separating social care from health care in the UK, see Ruth Thorlby, Anna Starling, Catherine Broadbent and Toby Watt, 'What's the Problem with Social Care and Why Do We Need to Do Better?'Health Foundation, Institute for Fiscal Studies, King's Fund and Nuffield Trust, 2018.

25  Du Peng, 'Long-term Care of Older Persons in China', SDD-SPPS Project Working Paper Series, United Nations Economic and Social Commission for Asia and the Pacific, 2015.

26  Tineke Fokkema, Jenny De Jong Gierveld and Peal A. Dykstra, 'Cross-national Differences in Older Adult Loneliness,' *Journal of Psychology* 146:1–2, 2012, pp. 201–28.

27  Women aged 50 and over in countries with low-level social protection (those where public spending on long-term care is less than 1 per cent of GDP) were 41 per cent more likely to provide daily informal care than their male counterparts in 2013. In countries with high levels of social protection (where public spending on long-term care exceeds 2 per cent of GDP) the rate was only 23 per cent. See OECD, *Preventing Ageing Unequally*, p. 246.

28  Informal carers have 20 per cent more mental health problems than other people and are more likely to stop working or reduce their hours. See OECD, *Help Wanted? Providing and Paying for Long-Term Care*, OECD Publishing, 2011. These costs are borne disproportionately by women, who make up between 55 and 70 per cent of informal carers in OECD countries. See OECD, *Health at a Glance 2015: OECD Indicators*, OECD Publishing, 2015.

29  Duncan Jeffries, 'Are Carebots the solution to the Elderly Care Crisis?' *Hack and Craft*, 13 February 2019.

30  Junko Saito, Maho Haseda, Airi Amemiya, Daisuke Takagi, Katsunori Kondo and Naoki Kondo, 'Community-based care for healthy ageing: lessons from Japan', *Bulletin of the World Health Organization* 97:8, 2019, pp. 570–74.

31  Claire McNeil and Jack Hunter, *The Generation Strain: Collective Solutions to Care in an Ageing Society*, Institute for Public Policy Research, April 2014.

32  For a thoughtful discussion of these issues, see Atul Gawande, *Being Mortal: Illness, Medicine and What Matters in the End*, Profile Books, 2015.

33  Eric B. French, Jeremy McCauley, Maria Aragon, Pieter Bakx, Martin Chalkley, Stacey H. Chen, Bent J. Christensen, Hongwei Chuang, Aurelie Côté-Sergent, Mariacristina De Nardi, Elliott Fan, Damien Échevin, Pierre-Yves Geoffard, Christelle Gastaldi-Ménager, Mette Gørtz, Yoko Ibuka, John B. Jones, Malene Kallestrup-Lamb, Martin Karlsson, Tobias J. Klein, Grégoire de Lagasnerie, Pierre-Carl Michaud, Owen O'Donnell, Nigel Rice, Jonathan S. Skinner, Eddy van Doorslaer, Nicolas R. Ziebarth and Elaine Kelly, 'End-Of-Life Medical

Spending In Last Twelve Months Of Life Is Lower Than Previously Reported', *Health Affairs* 36:7, 2017, pp. 1211–21.

34 Deborah Carr and Elizabeth A. Luth, 'Well-Being at the End of Life', *Annual Review of Sociology* 45, 2019, pp. 515–34.

35 A review of 150 studies based on nearly 800,000 subjects published between 2011 and 2016 reported that just 37 per cent of US adults had completed an advance directive. See Kuldeep N. Yadav, Nicole B. Gabler, Elizabeth Cooney, Saida Kent, Jennifer Kim, Nicole Herbst, Adjoa Mante, Scott D. Halpern and Katherine R. Courtright, 'Approximately One in Three US Adults Completes Any Type of Advance Directive For End-Of-Life-Care', *Health Affairs (Milwood)* 36:7, 2017, pp. 1244–51. However, rates are as high as 70 per cent among adults aged 65 and older, those with terminal illness and recent decedents. See Deborah Carr and Sara M. Moorman, 'End-of-Life Treatment Preferences Among Older Adults: An Assessment of Psychosocial Influences', *Sociological Forum* 24:4, December 2009, pp. 754–78; Maria J. Silveira, Scott Y. H. Kim and Kenneth M. Langa, 'Advance Directives and Outcomes of Surrogate Decision Making before Death', *New England Journal of Medicine* 362, 2010, pp. 1211–18.

36 Benedict Clements, Kamil Dybczak, Vitor Gaspar, Sanjeev Gupta and Mauricio Soto, 'The Fiscal Consequences of Shrinking Populations', IMF Staff Discussion Note, October 2015.

37 Noëmie Lisack, Rana Sajedi and Gregory Thwaites, 'Demographic trends and the real interest rate', Staff Working Paper 701, Bank of England, December 2017; Carlos Carvalho, Andrea Ferrero and Fernanda Nechio, 'Demographics and real interest rates: Inspecting the mechanism', *European Economic Review* 88, September 2016, pp. 208–26.

38 Takako Tsutsi and Naoko Muramatsu, 'Care-Needs Certification in the Long-Term Care Insurance System of Japan', *Journal of American Geriatrics Society* 53:3, 2005, pp. 522–27.

39 OECD, *Preventing Ageing Unequally*.

40 For a good exposition of the issues, see Andrew Dilnot, 'Final Report on the Commission on Funding of Care and Support', UK Government, 2010.

## Chapter 7: *The Social Contract Between the Generations*

1 There is another aspect to the intergenerational social contract around what we owe to previous generations because of past wrongs and the need to make amends to their descendants. Debates about compensation for slavery or restitution of objects obtained under colonialism or war are examples of this issue. Although beyond the scope of this book, there is growing agreement that transparency and openness about these issues are an important part of the response.

2 The Code of Hammurabi in ancient Mesopotamia permits a debtor to pledge a family member to work for up to three years to settle a debt and the Magna Carta suggests that parental debt could be inherited by children in feudal England. Although illegal, bonded child labour to settle debts is still practised in parts of south Asia.

3 On average across OECD countries the incomes of older people aged 60–64 have grown by a cumulative 13 per cent more than that of the 30–34 age group. Poverty risks have shifted from older to younger groups in most OECD countries since the mid-1980s. Pensioners have been relatively protected, except in the countries hardest hit by the 2008 financial crisis. Nevertheless, those over 75 are still the most vulnerable to poverty. OECD, *Preventing Ageing Unequally*.

4   Fahmida Rahman and Daniel Tomlinson, *Cross Countries: International Comparisons of Intergeneration Trends*, Intergenerational Commission Report, Resolution Foundation, 2018. For a wider discussion of intergenerational issues in the UK, see David Willets, *The Pinch: How the Baby Boomers Took Their Children's Future – And Why They Should Give It Back*, Atlantic Books, 2010.

5   I will focus on government debt since that is shared by society and must be repaid through future taxes. Household, corporate and financial-sector debt are borne by private individuals and corporations and (in theory at least) are their responsibility. Of course, when public bailouts occur, those private debts can become a burden to society.

6   Intergovernmental Panel on Climate Change, *Special Report: Global Warming of 1.5°C*, United Nations, 2018.

7   Partha Dasgupta, *The Dasgupta Review: Independent Review of the Economics of Biodiversity*, Interim Report, Her Majesty's Treasury, UK Government, April 2020.

8   Shunsuke Managi and Pushpam Kumar, *Inclusive Wealth Report 2018: Measuring Progress Towards Sustainability*, Routledge, 2018.

9   Dasgupta, *The Dasgupta Review*, Box 2A.

10  World Commission on Environment and Development, *Our Common Future*, Oxford University Press, 1987.

11  Robert M. Solow, 'Sustainability: An Economist's Perspective', J. Seward Johnson Lecture, Woods Hole Oceanographic Institution, 1991.

12  For a helpful summary of these debates, see Chapter 6 in Nicholas Stern, *Why are We Waiting? The Logic, Urgency, and Promise of Tackling Climate Change*, MIT Press, 2015. Also see Axel Gosseries, 'Theories of intergenerational justice: a synopsis', *Surveys and Perspectives Integrating Environment and Society* 1:1, May 2008.

13  For a sense of how contentious this debate can be, see William D. Nordhaus, 'A Review of the Stern Review on the Economics of Climate Change', *Journal of Economic Literature* 45:3, September 2007, pp. 686–702; Graciela Chichilnisky, Peter J. Hammond and Nicholas Stern, 'Fundamental utilitarianism and inter-generational equity with extinction discounting', *Social Choice and Welfare* 54, 2020, pp. 397–427. There is consensus on the need to have some positive rate of time preference to take extinction risk into account.

14  Walter Mischel and Ebbe B. Ebbesen, 'Attention In Delay Of Gratification', *Journal of Personality and Social Psychology* 16:2, 1970, pp. 329–37. There was a great deal of subsequent debate about whether there were other factors, such as family income, that determined the differences in behaviour among the children.

15  Lewis Carroll, *Through the Looking Glass*, Macmillan, 1871.

16  J. M. Keynes, 'Economic Possibilities for Our Grandchildren', in J. M. Keynes, *Essays in Persuasion*, Palgrave Macmillan, 2010.

17  Tjalling Koopmans, 'Stationary Ordinary Utility and Impatience,' *Econometrica* 28:7, 1960, pp. 287–309; Tjalling Koopmans, 'On the Concept of Optimal Economic Growth', *Pontificiae Academiae Scientiarum Scipta Varia* 28, reprinted in Tjalling Koopmans, *The Econometric Approach to Development Planning*, North Holland, 1966; Tjalling Koopmans, 'Objectives, Constraints, and Outcomes in Optimal Growth Models', *Econometrica* 35:1, 1967, pp. 1–15; Tjalling Koopmans, 'Representation of Preference Orderings over Time', in C. B. McGuire and R. Radner (editors), *Decision and Organization*, North Holland, 1972.

18  For a comprehensive discussion of how a global climate deal could be orches-trated, see Nicholas Stern, *Why are We Waiting?* MIT Press, 2015.

19 Ishac Diwan and Nemat Shafik, 'Investment, Technology and the Global Environment: Towards International Agreement in a World of Disparities', in Patrick Low (editor), *International Trade and the Environment*, World Bank, 1992.

20 OECD, 'Reforming agricultural subsidies to support biodiversity in Switzerland', OECD Environment Policy Paper 9, OECD Publishing, 2017; Andres A. Luis, Michael Thibert, Camilo Lombana Cordoba, Alexander V. Danilenko, George Joseph and Christian Borga-Vega, 'Doing More with Less: Smarter Subsidies for Water Supply and Sanitation', World Bank, 2019; David Coady, Ian Parry, Nghia-Piort Le and Baoping Shang, 'Global fossil fuel subsidies remain large. An update based on country-level estimates', IMF Working Paper 19:89, International Monetary Fund, 2019.

21 Raffael Jovine, *Light to Life: How Photosynthesis Made and Can Save the World*, Octopus Publishing Group, 2021.

22 This estimate is based on combining domestic public finance for biodiversity-related activities ($67.8 billion per year on average between 2015 and 2017) and estimates of wider finance flows to biodiversity (for example, from economic instruments, philanthropy and impact investing) of between $10.2 billion and $23.2 billion per year. See OECD, 'A Comprehensive Overview of Global Biodiversity Finance', OECD Publishing, 2020.

23 Peter Kareiva, Heather Tallis, Taylor H. Ricketts, Gretchen C. Daily and Stephen Polaski, *Natural Capital: The Theory and Practice of Mapping Ecosystem Services*, Oxford University Press, 2011.

24 Ralph Chami, Thomas Cosimano, Connel Fullenkamp and Sena Oztosun, 'Nature's Solution to Climate Change', *Finance and Development*, 56:4, December 2019, pp. 34–38.

25 Oliver Balch, 'Meet the world's first "minister for future generations"', *Guardian*, 2 March 2019, available at: https://www.theguardian.com/world/2019/mar/02/meet-the-worlds-first-future-generations-commissioner.

26 'Nicholas Stern urges world leaders to invest in sustainable infrastructure during signing ceremony for Paris Agreement on climate change', Press Release, Grantham Research Institute, 22 April 2016.

27 Cevat Giray Aksoy, Barry Eichengreen and Orkun Saka, 'The Political Scar of Epidemics', *Vox*, 15 June 2020.

28 Achim Goerres, 'Why are older people more likely to vote? The impact of ageing on electoral turnout in Europe', *British Journal of Politics and International Relations* 9:1, 2007, pp. 90–121; Julia Lynch and Mikko Myrskylä, 'Always the third rail? Pension income and policy preferences in European democracies', *Comparative Political Studies* 42:8, 2009, pp. 1068–109; Clara Sabbagh and Pieter Vanhuysse, 'Exploring attitudes towards the welfare state: Students' views in eight democracies', *Journal of Social Policy* 35:4, October 2006, pp. 607–28; Vincenzo Galasso and Paola Profeta, 'How does ageing affect the welfare state?' *European Journal of Political Economy* 23:2, June 2007, pp. 554–63; Deborah Fletcher and Lawrence W. Kenny, 'The influence of the elderly on school spending in a median voter framework', *Education Finance and Policy* 3:3, 2008, pp. 283–315.

29 Tim Vlandas, 'Grey power and the Economy: Aging and Inflation Across Advanced Economies', *Comparative Political Studies* 51:4, 2018, pp. 514–52.

30 I am indebted to Daniel Pick for making me aware of this argument. Matthew Weaver, 'Lower voting age to six to tackle bias against the young', *Guardian*, 6 December 2018.

31 YouTube, 'Dianne Feinstein rebuffs young climate activists' call for Green New Deal', 23 February 2019.

## Chapter 8: A New Social Contract

1   John F. Kennedy, Address at Independence Hall, Philadelphia, 4 July 1962. Excerpt available from John F. Kennedy Presidential Library and Museum: https://www.jfklibrary.org/learn/about-jfk/historic-speeches/address-at-independence-hall.

2   More recently, a World Interdependence Summit engaged one million people from one hundred countries online in September 2020 to come together to discuss solving common challenges. See www.oneshared.world.

3   Martin Luther King Junior, 'A Christmas Sermon on Peace', Massey Lecture Series, Canadian Broadcast Corporation, 1967. Martin Luther King went on to make it tangible: 'Did you ever stop to think that you can't leave for your job in the morning without being dependent on most of the world? You get up in the morning and go to the bathroom and reach over for the sponge, and that's handed to you by a Pacific islander. You reach for a bar of soap, and that's given to you at the hands of a Frenchman. And then you go into the kitchen to drink your coffee for the morning, and that's poured into your cup by a South American. And maybe you want tea: that's poured into your cup by a Chinese. Or maybe you're desirous of having cocoa for breakfast, and that's poured into your cup by a West African. And then you reach over for your toast, and that's given to you at the hands of an English-speaking farmer, not to mention the baker. And before you finish eating breakfast in the morning, you've depended on more than half of the world. This is the way our universe is structured; this is its interrelated quality. We aren't going to have peace on earth until we recognise this basic fact of the interrelated structure of all reality.'

4   Eric Lonergan and Mark Blyth, *Angrynomics*, Agenda Publishing, 2020; Anne Case and Angus Deaton, *Deaths of Despair and the Future of Capitalism*, Princeton University Press, 2020.

5   Convergence in the occupational distribution between 1960 and 2010 in the United States explains between 20 per cent and 40 per cent of growth in aggregate output per person through the improved allocation of talent. See Chang-Tai Hsieh, Erik Hurst, Charles I. Jones and Peter J. Klenow, 'The Allocation of Talent and U.S. Economic Growth', *Econometrica* 87:5, September 2019, pp. 1439–74.

6   Alex Bell, Raj Chetty, Xavier Jaravel, Neviana Petkova and John Van Reenen 'Who Becomes an Inventor in America? The Importance of Exposure to Innovation', CEP Discussion Paper 1519, London School of Economics, 2017.

7   One example is the International Labour Organization's Global Commission on the Future of Work, which called on governments to commit to a set of measures in order to address the challenges caused by unprecedented change in the world of work. Among the ten recommendations are: (1) a universal labour guarantee that protects fundamental workers' rights, an adequate living wage, limits on hours of work and safe and healthy workplaces; (2) guaranteed social protection from birth to old age that supports people's needs over the life cycle, (3) a universal entitlement to lifelong learning that enables people to skill, reskill and upskill; (4) managing technological change to boost decent work, including an international governance system for digital labour platforms; (5) greater investments in the care, green and rural economies; (6) a transformative and measurable agenda for gender equality; and (7) reshaping business incentives to encourage long-term investments. ILO, *Work for a Brighter Future: Global Commission on the Future of Work*, International Labour Organization, 2019.

8   For an anthropological view on this phenomenon see David Graeber, *Bullshit Jobs: A Theory*, Allen Lane, 2018.

9  Martin Sandbhu, *The Economics of Belonging*, Princeton University Press, 2020, p. 96.

10  Jaana Remes, James Manyika, Jacques Bughin, Jonathan Woetzel, Jan Mischke and Mekala Krishnan, *Solving the Productivity Puzzle: The role of demand and the promise of digitization*, McKinsey Global Institute, 2018.

11  Robert Gordon, 'US data: Why Has Economic Growth Slowed When Innovation Appears to Be Accelerating?' NBER Working Paper 24554, National Bureau of Economic Research, April 2018.

12  Remes et al., *Solving the Productivity Puzzle*.

13  Jonathan Tepper with Denise Hearn, *The Myth of Capitalism: Monopolies and the Death of Competition*, Wiley, 2018.

14  Thomas Philippon, *The Great Reversal: How America Gave Up on Free Markets*, Belknap Press, 2019.

15  Esteban Ortiz-Ospina, 'Taxation', published online at OurWorldInData.org, 2016.

16  Timothy Besley and Torsten Persson, 'Why Do Developing Countries Tax So Little?' *Journal of Economic Perspectives*, 28:4, 2014, pp. 99–120.

17  World Bank, 'World Development Report: The Changing Nature of Work', pp. 130–36.

18  Countries strike different balances between regulatory tools and spending. McKinsey found three broad groups: (1) countries where regulatory intervention in the market is high and public spending is also high, such as Austria, Belgium, France and Scandinavian countries; (2) countries where intervention is high and public spending middling, such as Germany and the Netherlands; and (3) countries where market intervention is lower and public spending is also relatively low. This latter set includes Japan, South Korea, Switzerland, the UK and the US. Over time, the tendency was towards less regulatory intervention with workers operating in more-flexible labour markets with less-generous retirement benefits, as described in Chapter 5, McKinsey, *The Social Contract*.

19  There is a vast literature on how that redistribution is best organised, as universal or targeted benefits. For a summary, see D. Gugushvili and T. Laenen, 'Twenty years after Korpi and Palme's "paradox of redistribution": What have we learned so far, and where should we take it from here?' SPSW Working Paper 5, Centre for Sociological Research, KU Leuven, 2019.

20  Top income tax rates have fallen most in those countries such as the US where the top 1 per cent of earners capture 20 per cent of pre-tax income compared to 10 per cent in 1970. Europe and Japan have seen less concentration of income at the top 1 per cent of earners. Piketty, Saez and Stantcheva argue that the top tax rate could be over 80 per cent and that there is no evidence that low taxes on the rich raise productivity and growth. Thomas Piketty, Emmanuel Saez and Stefanie Stantcheva, 'Taxing the 1 per cent: Why the Top Tax Rate May be Over 80 per cent', *Vox*/Centre for Economic Policy Research, 8 December 2011.

21  Arun Advani, Emma Chamberlain and Andy Summers, 'Is it Time for a UK Wealth Tax?' Institute for International Inequality, London School of Economics, and Centre for Competitive Advantage in the Global Economy, Warwick University, 2020.

22  Anthony Atkinson, *Inequality*, Harvard University Press, 2015. In fact, Tony Blair's government built on this idea when they created the Child Trust Fund in 2005, although the government's contribution of £250 per child was more modest than envisioned in the original proposal.

23  Piketty, *Capital and Ideology*.

24  Fatih Guvenen, Gueorgui Kambourov, Burhanettin Kuruscu, Sergio Ocampo-Diaz and Daphne Chen, 'Use It or Lose It: Efficiency Gains from Wealth Taxation',

NBER Working Paper 26284, National Bureau of Economic Research, 2019. They argue, 'Under wealth taxation, on the other hand, entrepreneurs who have similar wealth levels pay similar taxes regardless of their productivity, which expands the tax base and shifts the tax burden towards unproductive entrepreneurs. Furthermore, wealth taxes reduce the after-tax returns of high-productivity entrepreneurs less than low-productivity ones, which creates a behavioral savings response, which further shifts the wealth distribution towards the productive ones. Finally, the general equilibrium response of prices to wealth taxes can dampen the aggregate savings incentives, but its effect on reallocation is still in the same direction as the first two effects. The resulting reallocation increases aggregate productivity and output.'

25 James Hansen, 'Environment and Development Challenges: The Imperative of a Carbon Fee and Dividend', in *Oxford Handbook of the Macroeconomics of Global Warming*, Lucas Bernard and Willi Semmler (editors), Oxford University Press, 2015.

26 Sandbhu, *The Economics of Belonging*, p. 186.

27 Hansen, 'Environment and Development Challenges'.

28 Hauser Institute for Civil Society, *The global philanthropy report: Perspectives on the global foundation sector*, Harvard University and UBS, 2014.

29 Truman Packard, Ugo Gentillini, Margaret Grosh, Philip O'Keefe, Robert Palacios, David Robalino and Indhira Santos, *Protecting All: Risk Sharing for a Diverse and Diversifying World of Work*, World Bank, 2019, pp. 180–82.

30 Andrew Summers, 'Taxing wealth: an overview', in *Let's Talk about Tax*, Jonathan Bradshaw (editor), Institute for Fiscal Studies, 2020.

31 OECD, 'Tax Policy Reforms in the OECD', OECD, 2016.

32 Daron Acemoglu and Pascual Restrepo, 'Secular Stagnation? The Effect of Aging on Economic Growth in the Age of Automation', *American Economic Review*, 107, no.5, May 2017, pp. 174–79; Ana Lucia Abeliansky and Klaus Prettner, 'Automation and Demographic Change', GLO Discussion Paper, no. 518, Global Labor Organization, 2020.

33 Daron Acemoglu, Andrea Manera and Pascual Restrepo, 'Does the US Tax Code Favor Automation?' prepared for the Brookings Institution Spring Conference of 2020, 6 April 2020.

34 Packard et al., *Protecting All*, pp. 209–10.

35 Rui Costa, Nikhil Datta, Stephen Machin and Sandra McNally, 'Investing in People: The Case for Human Capital Tax Credits', CEP Industrial Strategy Working Paper, London School of Economics, February 2018.

36 Katarzyna Bilicka, 'Comparing UK Tax Returns of Foreign Multinationals to Matched Domestic Firms', *American Economic Review*, August 2019.

37 Tabby Kinder and Emma Agyemang, 'It is a matter of fairness: Squeezing more tax from multinationals', *Financial Times*, 8 July 2020.

38 Ernesto Crivelli, Ruud A. de Mooij and Michael Keen, 'Base Erosion, Profit Shifting and Developing Countries', IMF Working Paper 15/118, International Monetary Fund, 2015.

39 The $8.7 trillion estimate comes from Zucman, while the $36 trillion estimate is from Gabriel Zucman, 'How Corporations and the Wealthy Evade Taxes', *New York Times*, 10 November 2017; James S. Henry, 'Taxing Tax Havens', *Foreign Affairs*, 12 April 2016.

40 Estimates of the potential gains are huge. Corporate tax revenues could go up by 18–28 per cent in the largest European countries and by 14 per cent in the US (about 0.5 per cent of GDP). Thomas R. Tørsløv, Ludvig S. Wier and Gabriel

Zucman, 'The Missing Profits of Nations', NBER Working Paper 24701, National Bureau of Economic Research, August 2018.

41 OECD, 'OECD Presents outputs of OECD/G20 BEPS Project for discussion at G20 Finance Ministers meeting', OECD, 2015: www.oecd.org/tax/beps-2015–final-reports.htm.

42 See for example the statement on corporate governance from the Business Roundtable, a group of CEOs of major US companies, in August 2019.

43 Colin Mayer, *Prosperity: Better Business Makes the Greater Good*, Oxford University Press, 2019.

44 There is a vast literature on the relative performance of democratic versus authoritarian states. Acemoglu et al. survey performance on a range of redistributive policies (Daron Acemoglu, Georgy Egorov and Konstantin Sonin, 'Political Economy in a Changing World', *Journal of Political Economy*, 123:5, July 2015). Harding and Stasavage look at delivery of a range of public services across Africa (Robin Harding and David Stasavage, 'What Democracy Does (and Doesn't Do) for Basic Services: School Fees, School Inputs, and African Elections', *Journal of Politics* 76:1, January 2014). Besley and Kudamatsu find a strong correlation between life expectancy, infant mortality and democracy (Timothy J. Besley and Masayuki Kudamatsu, 'Making Democracy Work', CEPR Discussion Paper DP6371, 2008). This literature is well summarised in Tim Besley, 'State Capacity, Reciprocity and the Social Contract', *Econometrica* 88:4, July 2020.

45 Besley and Kudamatsu, 'Making Democracy Work'.

46 Amartya Sen, *Development as Freedom*.

47 Analysis by George Ward demonstrates that subjective well-being is a robust predictor of election results even controlling for macroeconomic indicators, various demographic and partisan determinants of individuals' life satisfaction, and using a number of alternative specifications. The magnitude of the relationship is sizable: a one standard deviation change in self-reported well-being is associated with around an 8.5 percentage point swing in the vote share enjoyed by the governing coalition. This contrasts with the impact of income gains where a one standard deviation change in the election-year economic growth rate is associated with a 4.5 percentage point change in government vote share, whilst a one standard deviation change in the unemployment rate over time is predictive of a swing of around 3.5 percentage points. George Ward, 'Is Happiness a Predictor of Election Results?', London School of Economics Centre for Economic Performance Discussion Paper 1343, April 2015.

48 Estonia has been using internet voting since 2005 and has seen a steady increase in voter turnout and the share choosing to vote online. There are of course many debates about the risks of fraud and manipulation, but the system is improving over time. See European Commission, 'Estonian Internet Voting: https://ec.europa.eu/cefdigital/wiki/display/CEFDIGITAL/2019/07/29/Estonian+Internet+voting, 29 July 2019. For a critical view, see Travis Finkenauer, Zakir Durumeric, Jason Kitcat, Harri Hursti, Margaret MacAlpine and J. Alex Halderman, 'Security Analysis of the Estonian Internet Voting System', University of Michigan and Open Rights Group, November 2014.

49 Torben Iversen and David Soskice, 'Democratic limits to redistribution Inclusionary versus Exclusionary Coalitions in the Knowledge Economy', *World Politics* 67:2, April 2015, pp. 185–225.

50 Luis Catao and Maurice Obstfeld (editors), *Meeting Globalization's Challenges: Policies to Make Trade Work for All*, Princeton University Press, 2019, p. 21. Also see their interesting discussion of political ideologies and trade policy on pp. 30–34.

51  Acemoglu and Robinson, *Why Nations Fail*, pp. 96–101.

52  Ibid., pp. 96–123.

53  Michèle Belot, Syngjoo Choi, Egon Tripodi, Eline van den Broek Altenburg, Julian C. Jamison and Nicholas W. Papageorge, 'Unequal consequences of Covid-19 across age and income: Representative evidence from six countries', *Covid Economics* 38, 16 July 2020, pp. 196–217.

54  Alison Andrew, Sarah Cattan, Monica Costa Dias, Christine Farquharson, Lucy Kraftman, Sonya Krutikova, Angus Phimister and Almudena Sevilla, 'The gendered division of paid and domestic work under lockdown', *Covid Economics* 39, 23 July 2020, pp. 109–38.

55  William Beveridge, *Social Insurance and Allied Services*, His Majesty's Stationary Office, 1942.

# Index